Under the Sun:

Myth and Realism in Western American Literature

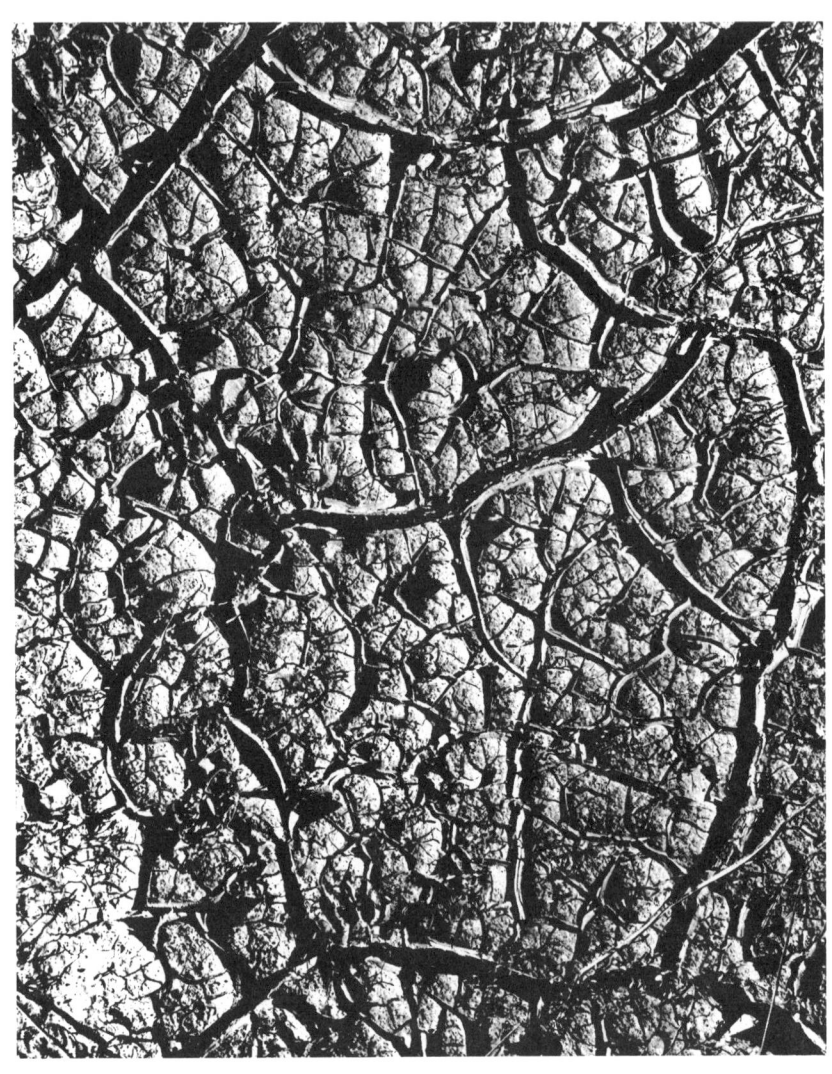

". . . God's country is still a fiction inhabited by people with a love for the facts."

--Wright Morris
God's Country and My People
New York: Harper & Row, 1968.

Under the Sun:

Myth and Realism in Western American Literature

by

Barbara Howard Meldrum
University of Idaho

The Whitston Publishing Company
Troy, New York
1985

Copyright 1985
Barbara Howard Meldrum

Library of Congress Catalog Card Number 85-050609

ISBN 0-87875-303-6

Printed in the United States of America

Pages v-vi constitute an extension of this copyright page.

ACKNOWLEDGMENTS

Grateful acknowledgment is made to the following for permission to use copyrighted material:

Doubleday & Company for quotation from *Angle of Repose* by Wallace Stegner. Copyright, 1971, by Wallace Stegner. Reprinted by permission of Doubleday & Company, Inc.

Thomas Hornsby Ferril, for quotations from the *Rocky Mountain Herald,* February 19, 1927.

Harcourt Brace Jovanovich, Inc., for a quotation from *The Sacred and the Profane* by Mircea Eliade (copyright 1959).

Harper & Row, Publisher, Inc., for lines quoted from *New and Selected Poems* by Thomas Hornsby Ferril. Copyright 1952, 1980 by Thomas Hornsby Ferril. Reprinted by permission of the publisher.

Harper & Row, Publishers, Inc., for quotations from *Giants in the Earth* by O.E. Rølvaag. Copyright, 1927, by Harper & Row, Publishers, Inc. Renewed, 1955, by Jennie Marie Berdahl Rolvaag. Reprinted by permission of the publisher.

Harper & Row, Publishers, Inc. and **Bantam Books** for quotations from *Winter in the Blood* by James Welch. Copyright, 1974, by James Welch. Reprinted by permission of Elaine Markson Literary Agency, Inc.

Madelon Heatherington and **The Georgia Review**, for reprinting of "Romance Without Women: The Sterile Fiction of the American West," copyright 1979.

Houghton Mifflin Company for quotations from *O Pi-*

oneers! by Willa Cather. Copyright, 1913 and 1941, by Willa Sibert Cather. Reprinted by permission of Houghton Mifflin Company.

The Huntington Library for quotations from *A Victorian Gentlewoman in the Far West,* edited by Rodman W. Paul. Reprinted with the permission of the Huntington Library, Art Collections, and Botanical Gardens.

Wright Morris, for photographs from *Structures and Artifacts: Photographs 1933 1954* (University of Nebraska Press, 1975) and *God's Country and My People* (Harper & Row, 1968); also for quotations from *The Man Who Was There* (1945), *The World in the Attic* (1949), *The Field of Vision* (1956), *The Territory Ahead* (1957), *Ceremony in Lone Tree* (1960), *The Inhabitants,* second edition (1972), and *God's Country and My People* (1968).

William Morrow & Company, Inc., for lines quoted from *Words for Denver,* by Thomas Hornsby Ferril (copyright 1966).

Time-Life Books Inc., for quotation from Introduction to *The Ox-Bow Incident,* by Walter Van Tilburg Clark, Time Reading Program Special Edition (copyright 1962), courtesy Time-Life Books, Inc.

University of Nebraska Press, for reprinting of "Classical Myth versus Realism in Crane's 'The Bride Comes to Yellow Sky,'" from *The Anger of Stephen Crane* by Chester L. Wolford. Copyright 1983 by the University of Nebraska Press. Reprinted by permission of the University of Nebraska Press.

Viking Penguin, Inc., for quotation from *The Poetics of Space* by Gaston Bachelard, translated by Maria Jolas. Copyright 1958 by Presses Universitaires de France. Translation copyright 1964 by Orion Press, Inc. Reprinted by permission of Viking Penguin Inc.

Special thanks to **Christopher J. Duers** of Storrs, Connecticut, for the illustrations.

TABLE OF CONTENTS

Acknowledgments.....................................v

Introduction
    Barbara Howard Meldrum........................1

I
REALITY, MYTH, AND THE WEST

Myth, Reality, and the American Frontier
    Max Westbrook...............................10
The West as Archetype
    Harold P. Simonson..........................20

II
WRITING ABOUT THE WEST: HISTORY, REALISM, AND MYTH

Historical Realism and the American West:
The Example of Charles Neider's *The Authentic Death of Hendry Jones*
    Stephen Tatum...............................30
Men, Women, and Madness: Pioneer Plains Literature
    June O. Underwood 50
Western Myth, Mormon Society
    L. L. Lee...................................64
Romance Without Women: The Sterile Fiction of the American West
    Madelon Heatherington.......................74

III
MYTHOLOGIZING IN THE WEST

Mythic Reality: Structure and Theme in Cather's
O Pioneers!
    Ann Moseley 92
Alien Myth and Natural Myth in the Poetry of
Thomas Hornsby Ferril
    James R. Saucerman 106
Classical Myth versus Realism in Crane's "The
Bride Comes to Yellow Sky"
    Chester L. Wolford 128
Realism and Romance in the Western Stories
of Stephen Crane
    Michael J. Collins 138
The Illustrator as Writer: Mary Hallock Foote
and the Myth of the West
    Shelley Armitage 150
Images and Icons: The Fiction and Photography
of Wright Morris
    Joseph J. Wydeven 176

IV
BEYOND MYTH

Beyond Myth: Welch's *Winter in the Blood*
    Jack Brenner 206

Introduction

Barbara Howard Meldrum
University of Idaho

> . . . but the loveliest myth of all America was the far West . . . a lost impossible province . . . where men were not dwarfs and where adventure truly was. For a brief season, consider, the myth so generously begotten became fact. For a few years Odysseus Jed Smith and Siegfried Carson and the wingshod Fitzpatrick actually drew breath in this province of fable. Then suddenly it was all myth again. Wagons were moving down the trails, and nowhere remained any trace of the demigods who had passed this way.
> —Bernard DeVoto

> The myths and symbols with which I deal . . . [are] collective representations rather than the work of a single mind. I do not mean to raise the question whether such products of the imagination accurately reflect empirical fact. They exist on a different plane.
> —Henry Nash Smith

If there is one topic which has consistently attracted the attention of critics working with western American literature, it is the role of myth and realism. Important in any literary studies, myth and realism have special relevance to western literature because the realistic status of the myth is so persistently and provocatively before us. Was the myth once real, but now enveloped in history, as DeVoto asserts? Or did "the myth" never exist in fact, but rather emerge from popular fantasies fed partially by seemingly corroborative facts and primarily by the demands of an eastern audience? Does it matter whether or not myth "accurately reflects empirical fact"? Is a writer who works with western subjects hindered or aided by considerations of authenticity? Can myth emerge from a realistic approach to subject matter? Such questions lie behind these essays.

Definition of terms is not simple where myth and realism are concerned. Max Westbrook opens this collection with some pertinent considerations about terminology, and Harold Simonson follows with a discussion of western primitivism. I wish here simply to add a few considerations of my own. I referred above to "the myth" as though there were one single myth about the West. This of course is not so; nonetheless, critics, including several in this volume, often use the phrase "myth of the West." Typically, we associate the term with acts of conquest (of the land, of Indians, of the forces of evil) and a cluster of values: freedom, courage, honor, daring, manliness. It is linked to the West both temporally and spatially. Temporally, the myth refers to the historical process we call the frontier or westward movement (the frontier itself—the meeting point between civilization and the wilderness—moved westward from the Puritan era to the 1890s). Spatially, the myth refers to a West which did not become geographically fixed until the end of the frontier era; that West is generally distinguished by an arid climate and a landscape of immense proportions. As the historian R. W. Sellars has noted, the size, aridity, and topography of the West constituted special challenges to those who sought to subdue it; yet that vast area was rapidly settled. Moreover, the burgeoning population of the West coincided with movement into a geographically more vast and powerful terrain. "The frontier myths remain strongest [today] where the landscape is biggest—in the West."[1] This bigness has led to what the poet Thomas Hornsby Ferril calls "ancestor worship." From thence come the Odysseus Jed Smiths, the Siegfried Carsons and wingshod Fitzpatricks. Thence, too, come wooden, stereotyped superman heroes who fail as they try to match the bigness of their western setting (both historical and geographic). And paradoxically, that same big West impresses us with human limitations—the brevity of our lives, the insignificance of our fate. O. E. Rølvaag's *Giants in the Earth* exemplifies the dwarfing effect of nature as well as its capacity to exalt human character. David B. Davis, in analyzing the cowboy-hero, notes that the "immensity of the Western environment . . . brings out the best in heroes and the worst in villains."[2]

The myth of the West is, then, a weighty legacy for the western writer. Although the material of that myth would seem to provide endless possibilities for fiction, the expectations of readers and publishers (perhaps even of the writers themselves) may constitute a damming of the stream. Stephen Tatum discusses the problems faced by the writer who seeks to probe the psychological and philosophical dimensions of the mythic material of western history and legend. I am reminded of Walter Van Tilburg Clark's comments on what he sought to do through his writing of *The Ox-Bow Incident*:

> I decided to make war . . . [on a] difficulty which had been blocking me, and blocking every other writer who wanted to write about or out of the West at that time. That difficulty was the limitation imposed—in part directly, but probably even more because of what I sensed to be an almost impenetrable reader expectation—by the popular or formula western story. That kind of story, it seemed to me, had diminished almost beyond usability the people, places, circumstances and meanings of what had been a very real world. And that world, I felt, had to be given back some measure of its reality and dignity before I could even use the later West as I wanted to.
>
> So I set to work . . . to find my way into a typical western story situation, with all the typical western story people, and see if I couldn't make the people come to life and the situation say something that could still be heard.[3]

He gauged his success by the fact that western readers soon wrote him about their presumed discovery of the "real incident" upon which he had based his story (though Clark claims he worked with no specific incident). The authenticity was "like history" but was fiction; the reality was mythic, not simply the myth of the West but universal or primordial truth of human character and destiny.

For Clark, it was possible to use the material of western myth and to discover in it a fictional vitality that was not doomed to cliché. He worked with "what had been a very real world." The fact that it *was* a "real world" seemed somehow to be important—and it seems to be important to most western writers and critics. This is not to say that western fiction may not deviate from fact; but the facts do seem to matter. June Underwood challenges the invalid stereotypes that have too often characterized fiction of the Great Plains region and compares fictional approaches with accounts by diarists and correspondents. Perhaps novelists have overplayed the influence of geography on the psychology of their characters; or perhaps they have discerned a meaning in psychological events that is only hinted at darkly by nonfictional accounts. In another type of comparison, that of fictional and nonfictional accounts of the lives of the mountain men, it could be argued that the novelists have generally made their characters and events more credible than did the early historians, who relied on oral accounts which surely were as much tall tale as fact. Does it make any essential difference whether a writer creates a fictional world that corresponds closely to the "real world"? To Madelon Heathington it does, though the reason takes us back to myth: if western writers were to create "real" women, then the myth of renewal (rebirth, return, a la Northrop Frye) would work in their fiction. To L. L. Lee, fiction about the Mormon experience in the West has been hampered by the very facts of its history; only as Mormon life changes to Utah life does it promise better fiction. The facts do matter; the "real world" must be reckoned with. But in the creation of fiction, as Wright Morris has said, facts are processed by the imagination so that we possess them; they then become a part of the mythic past. The world is "processed into reality."[4]

Western writers do indeed mythologize as they write about their region. This transforming process of fiction is the common subject of the group of essays on "Mythologizing in the West." In some instances, western writers adapt old myths to their regional setting; or, they create new myths; or, they play one myth against another. Ann Moseley describes "mythic realism" in Willa Cather's *O Pioneers!* as a blend of realistic subject matter with mythic patterns drawn from classical Greek and Native American sources; this blend effectively renders the characters' struggles for self-fulfillment in ways that suggest Jungean archetypes (another mythic level)—the reality of universal consciousness. If Cather is successful in incorporating classical mythological motifs, Thomas Hornsby Ferril is not so fortunate in his poetry, claims James Saucerman, who argues that Ferril is more successful when he uses the realistic events, personages, and artifacts of the West to form new myths. Surely there seems to be a strong urge in western writers to create a literature which achieves for its own American setting what ancient writers achieved for Greece. Perhaps this desire is one reason for the frequent echoes of classical myths. One has only to think of Frederick Manfred's many uses of mythological motifs: the blantantly direct Oedipal echoes of *King of Spades,* the far more sublimated Homeric strains of *The Manly-Hearted Woman.* Usually, writers are more successful when the classical motifs do not seem to be imposed upon the subject, but emerge as integral to the work itself.

An exception is parody, which may call for more obvious resonances. Chester Wolford shows how Stephen Crane achieved a mock-epic rendering of the western showdown through a realistic, non-heroic narration of incidents which we would ordinarily expect to be portrayed heroically because of their overtones of western and classical myth. With a somewhat different emphasis, Michael Collins demonstrates that Crane's focus on inward (psychological) experience rather than external events results in a parodic version of the western romance—what Frye calls "ironic myth." Crane's uses of irony suggest the genre we now call the anti-Western. Crane not only helped create the modern Western, but criticized it as well; as Frank Bergon has observed, he wrote anti-Westerns before the formula of the Western had solidified.[5] Demythologizing goes hand-in-hand with mythologizing about the West. Perhaps it could be said that the "honest West" (as Crane calls it) which inspired the Western romances was an ideal but therefore unreal West which never truly existed; whereas the West, or the romances of the West, which inspire the ironies of the anti-Western bring us to the "real" world in which we live—but that "real" world is the "false East" Crane speaks of. His is an eastern view that simultaneously generates and deflates the western myth.

Another facet of mythologizing about the West is working with "the thing itself" (to use the phrase as Wright Morris does): the "raw material" of the West, especially visually perceived subjects. Shelley Armitage and Joseph Wydeven examine the work of two artists who have developed both visual and verbal images of the West: Mary Hallock Foote and Wright Morris. Both critics draw upon the fiction and nonfiction written by their subjects, but focus upon these artists' visual conceptions of the West and the connections between their visual and verbal constructs. Armitage points out how Foote's work benefited from the techniques of illustration she learned in the East. These techniques called for a recording of life in its concrete forms; when applied to western scenes and characters, such an approach led to a reportorial treatment which captured her personal version of western myth. Wydeven examines Morris's phototexts in the light of his prose statements and shows how the photographs reveal objects in the de-particularized manner of myth (general or archetypal rather than particular or individual). At times the objects become icons with ritual uses. Or, objects are shown in the process of decay as they are reclaimed by nature; culture resists but capitulates; history becomes myth through the archetypal dialectic of nature and culture. Although the works of Foote and Morris are clearly dissimilar, these artists are perhaps alike in that their concentration on "the thing itself" leads to more than a rendition of objects; the landscape is metaphysical, the mode is mythic.

The essays I have reviewed thus far deal in various ways with the problems and possibilities posed to the western writer by subject matter which is both realistic and mythic. The final essay of this collection focuses on a novel about the plight of the contemporary dispossessed Indian, but in the process Jack Brenner highlights many of the issues raised by the other essayists. Quite rightly, he objects to a superficial criticism that would begin with categories based on the western myth: Indian story, cowboy tale, or whatever. One must go beyond the myth if the essence of the work is to reveal itself. But, as the other writers of this volume demonstrate, the myths of the West are relevant in ways that can liberate as well as hinder, can feed the imagination as well as stifle it. A collection of stories by contemporary western writers begins with the editorial observation that the "writers of the new west" are "free of the need to write either out of the mythology or against it."[6] This is true, and welcome knowledge; but the case is not one of either-or. A studied avoidance of western mythology is probably as deadening as a naive acceptance. Wright Morris states that the territory ahead is in one sense the territory behind, the mythic past. If that past simply dominates the writer, he or she languishes in a world of dead cliches; but this need not be so. In contrasting D. H. Lawrence to T. S. Eliot, Morris borrows an image from Picasso and says that Lawrence "has a sun in his belly. The sun in the belly of Mr. Eliot is a mythic sun. It is a clinker to manipulate: the fire has gone out it."[7] The writer with a sun in his belly does not ignore the mythic past, but is not bound by it; the task is to "displace an old god with a new one—but the new one will bear an astonishing resemblance to the one it displaced . . . what is dead in tradition, the heavy hand of it, he destroys. In this act of destruction he achieves his freedom as an artist, and what is vital in his art is the tradition that he sustains."[8]

The past does not (or should not) exist apart from the present; connections are important. Brenner shows how James Welch's protagonist must make connections between his own personal past and the ritualistic past of his people. Detachment is a living death, a winter in the blood; without these connections, he cannot "live" in the present, under the sun. Neither can western literature live apart from the warming, life-giving sun of real experience. But that life is not simply transferred to the page; it is transformed through the imagination, "processed into reality." Life thus becomes myth.

The essays in this volume explore many of the facets of that complex topic, the interrelationships of myth and realism in western American literature. For all the variety of their specific subjects and individual approaches, their findings seem to point to one overriding consideration. Western writers need not accurately reflect empirical fact; such authenticity is irrelevant to the creative processes of the imagination. The myths of western literature ring true when they are grounded in empirical fact and transformed into the realities only the imagination can provide. Myth and realism are ultimately one.

NOTES

[1] Richard West Sellars, "The Interrelationship of Literature, History, and Geography in Western Writing," *Western Historical Quarterly,* 4 (1973), 179.

[2] David B. Davis, "Ten-Gallon Hero," *American Quarterly,* 6 (1954), 115-116.

[3] Walter Van Tilburg Clark, *The Ox-Bow Incident,* Time Reading Program Special Edition (1940; rpt. New York: Time Incorporated, 1962), pp. xv-xvi.

[4] Wright Morris, *The Territory Ahead* (1957; rpt. Lincoln: University

of Nebraska Press, 1978), pp. 5-6.

[5] Frank Bergon, ed., *The Western Writings of Stephen Crane* (New York: New American Library, 1979), p. 2.

[6] William Kittredge and Steven M. Krauzer, "Writers of the New West," *TriQuarterly 48* (Spring 1980), 13.

[7] Morris, p. 227.

[8] Morris, p. 230.

PART ONE:

REALITY, MYTH, AND THE WEST

Tackling head-on the problem of definition of terms, **Max Westbrook** examines the meaning ascribed to "reality" and "myth" in literary criticism, points out the pitfalls, and suggests fruitful areas of inquiry for the critic of western American literature. Does "reality" simply mean "authentic realism," or does it implicitly claim metaphysical authenticity, or truth, as well? Can one determine the worth of western literature by a measured assessment of a work's authentic depiction of cultural myths? Might not some western writers reveal in their works a transition from myth-as-truth to myth-as-illusion? Always a provocative critic, Westbrook raises these and other questions, and suggests answers that point toward a more enlightened critical approach to western literature.

Max Westbrook, Professor of English at the University of Texas at Austin, is the editor of *The Modern American Novel: Essays in Criticism,* co-editor of *Twentieth Century Criticism: The Major Statements,* and author of *Walter Van Tilburg Clark.* A past president of the Western Literature Association, he is the author of numerous reviews and essays in the field of American realism and naturalism, cultural studies, and the American West. Having completed a book of poems (*Country Boy,* Thorp Springs Press), he is now at work on a book in which he hopes to unite formalist criticism and archetypal criticism.

Myth, Reality, and the American Frontier

Max Westbrook

Scholars and literary artists who study the American frontier will confront a variety of myths. The religions of native Americans, for example, are usually classified as mythology. There is the pioneer myth, the myth of the American cowboy, even a Hollywood myth, and these and more are actually plural with variations and subdivisions that range from studies in idle and innocent entertainment to the alarming but convincing theory that Lyndon Johnson's Vietnam policy was influenced by his nostalgic worship of frontier heroes who never backed down.

Important to the birth of America, however, was the analysis and rejection of a political myth known as the divine right of kings; and the psychological inheritance of that experience constitutes a national bias. The prejudicial assumption that facts and reason exposed monarchy and birthed democracy and therefore constitute truth, the only truth, is a widespread and long-running characteristic of the American mind.

One result is that a history of or a serious novel about the American West may be an attack on the myth of what we think happened and a presentation of the reality of what—supposedly—did happen. Thus scholars and literary artists who do not assume that *myth* means "false" are, though large in number, a minority; and they are writing for a majority who do make that assumption.

My subject, however, is not vocabulary, word choice. Definitions of *myth* and its relation to *reality*—usually assumed and not stated—range from "false" to "the truth," suggest insights into the fundamental beliefs of the writer, and cause substantive breakdowns in communication and understanding. How many of us, I wonder, would stop to contemplate the conjunction in the commonly offered choice of myth *or* reality. Yet the rhetorical invitation is to conclude that the American West is one of the two, not both, and not a combination. Since it is clear that myths varying from Indian religions to John Wayne movies cannot be stuffed into one of two categories—true or false—it is equally clear that the scores of excellent and thoughtful studies of myth *and* reality in the American West have not been sufficient to our understanding and that more work is needed. The purpose of further study, of course, is not to close the topic but to open it up.

We need, first, to examine *reality,* a favorite word for most of us, regardless of ideological allegiance. The word *reality* turns out to be insideous, for it is philosophically corrupt in a way that allows us to avoid a dilemma. Does *reality* mean "the truth"? If it does, the user is in trouble. Not many would dare make pronouncements about the truth of the American West or know where to find enough footnotes to support such pronouncements. Does *reality,* then, mean "the facts"? If it does, then our use of the word, most of the time, is not quite honest. There are essays which report merely, and a novelist may dream of factual accuracy with the authentic speaking for itself. But even if we put aside the difficulty of determining what the facts are and of having to make non-factual judgments about omitting this or including that and in what order, there would be precious little glory for anyone who achieved the dubious goal of writing about the West—or about any complex subject—while restricted to facts alone.

And that is why we like the word *reality*: it blurs the needed but unnerving distinction between *the real* (the truth) and *the actual* (the facts). It takes on the honor Americans pay to facts, that is, the common but philosophically indefensible association of the facts with the truth; and yet it avoids any obligation to the treacherous responsibilities associated with the words *truth* and *theory.* A scholar or critic who just comes flat-out with it and openly uses a metaphysical vocabulary—*the real* or *the truth*—is immediately on the grill, politically as well as philosophically; thus it is comforting to claim we essay merely to discuss some facts, while planning all along to reach some very unfactual conclusions without obligating ourselves to explain the theoretical basis of those conclusions.

This very common slippage is accurately recorded in *The Oxford English Dictionary.* The first definition of *reality* is "The quality of being real or having an actual existence." In dictionaries, in philosophy, and in standard usage, however, *the real* is that which is permanent, the truth, or what someone thinks is true; and *the actual* is that which changes, information available to the five senses, the facts. *The Oxford English Dictionary,* therefore, has dutifully reported the common usage: *fact* and *truth* are the same, *fact* and *meaning of fact* are the same. All you have to do is invoke the magic word, *reality.*

In subsequent definitions, this pleasantly irresponsible union continues. One, for example, would be quite satisfactory as a definition of the word *metaphysics:* "Real existence; what is real; the aggregate of real things or existences; that which underlies and is the truth of appearances or phenomena." Further definitions of *reality* emphasize the factual but continue the assumption that percepts and concepts are both acts of perception: "In reality, really, actually, in fact"; "a real thing, fact, or state of things"; the "real nature or constitution of something"; that "which constitutes the actual thing, as distinguished from what is merely apparent or external." And these definitions, I repeat, are accurate to our common usage.

The word *myth* is even more difficult to map since its definitions also blur the metaphysical range from fact to truth and include the extremes of prefabrication, nostalgia, propaganda, superstition, romanticized truth, symbolical truth, and just plain truth.

According to Mircea Eliade, writing for the *Encyclopedia Britannica,* "In the language current during the 19th century, 'myth' meant anything that was opposed to 'reality'." Eliade calls this one of the "clichés of Positivism," while other commentators emphasize the nineteenth century's romantic affinity for myths and mythmaking.[1]

Eliade has stated the first and most common of three definitions of *myth*: illusion, the totally or merely imaginary. In *The Oxford Companion to American Literature,* for example, the Paul Bunyan stories are said to have had a possible connection with an actual person but to have become, eventually, "pure mythology," that is, imaginary stories having no connection with the actual world. The word *legend* is often distinguished from *myth* on the grounds that a legend has a basis in history (the legend of Jessie James, for example) while myth does not, with the major difference being formal or stylistic, since neither is obligated to any standard of accuracy or objectivity.

Use of the word *myth* to mean illusion varies, of course. Generally, the variety may be described in terms of the subject matter (a political myth, a social myth) and in terms of the intent (basically, to amuse or to control). Thus *myth* as illusion may be seen as a type of entertainment (overlapping with the word *fable*), a way of making lessons in morality more palatable (overlapping with the word *parable*), a device for maintaining economic and political control ("A Message to Garcia," for example, which glorifies the total and unquestioning devotion of labor to capital), an instrument of racism or sexism (Hollywood's "Woman of the Year," which says that a brilliant and extraordinarily capable career woman should give it all up and learn how to cook for her man and be docile), a more or less innocent or insideous rewriting of regional or national history to promote pride or to lie by making heroes out of villains such as George Armstrong Custer and J. Edgar Hoover. Throughout such variety there is consistent prefabrication, the creation of make-believe stories or revisionist history to entertain, to inspire, or to control.

By the second definition, *myths* are organizing stories which explain a human enterprise, stories which shape the history and values of a given people. The function of such stories is both psychological and practical, for they express a sense of unity, purpose. More than a superior propaganda, *myth* in this sense is alive, on-going, changing; and it may include religions, culture, morality, history, literature, and even practical matters such as agriculture, medicine, hunting, clothing, housing, and politics.

To state the second definition, however, is not to solve the problem, since different readers make different assumptions. Those sympathetic to mythology can read Harvey Fergusson's *Grant of Kingdom* and Conrad Richter's *The Sea of Grass* as accurate if fictive treatments of chapters in the history of the American West. Those unsympathetic to mythology, however, would be inclined to read those two novels as examples of nostalgia for the old West.

Underlying problems in understanding all definitions of *myth* is our characteristic faith in reason and science. The mythology of ancient Athens is considered interesting and important, like the mythology of American Indians, but Olympian gods and the Great Spirit, of course, have nothing to do with truth. Such fancies have been out-dated by science, reason, and the movement from savagery to civilization to the age of nuclear power.

According to the second definition of *mythology,* however, Greek mythology and Catholicism are both myths. Belief in the divine right of kings and in the supremacy of the southern Confederacy are both myths. To put the matter in perspective, imagine a history of twentieth century America written in the twenty-second century. Obviously, there will be a chapter on the Myth of Chemistry, that curious and naïve faith, back in the twentieth century, which led people to a foolish and continuing trust in chemical solutions to all problems long after chemistry had poisoned their food, water, earth, air, clothing, shelter, and even the chemical medicines they used to protect themselves from chemical poisons.

Eliade's nomination for the "best" is what I am calling the third definition: "Myth narrates a sacred history." It tells "how reality came into existence." Myth, he continues, is the "story of creation, of what we are, our nature, being, how we are human rather than non-human." Thus *myth,* in this sense, is about the "original, what it is and how to get in touch with it, how to restore it."

Eliade, of course, has his own theories of mythology, and some might think him thereby unqualified to write an objective definition for the *Encyclopedia Britannica;* but other sources confirm Eliade. The Thrall and Hibbard *Handbook to Literature,* for example, includes the following: myths "attempt to explain creation, divinity, and religion, to guess at the meaning of existence and death, to account for natural phenomena, and to chronicle the adventures of racial heroes." That's a good definition, but note the prejudicial word choice, *to guess,* a verb Catholics and Protestants would not use to define their own religion but might use when characterizing a religion based in devotion to the land.

Obviously, problems with the national consciousness behind our use of the words *myth* and *reality* are heightened when the subject is the American West. On one hand, westerners are citizens of the nation in their admiration of practical action. There is much praise for those who are down to earth and have horse sense and get the job done. When John Wayne refuses to balk at legal scruples and kicks the door down and handles the problem, many of us applaud in our hearts while watching cinematic implications we would never approve in our heads. Thus words common to the third definition of myth—*sacred, supernatural*—are held in contempt by stories of American heroes who plunge on to victory, stories that come to us from childhood on in history, propaganda, literature, and popular culture.

On the other hand, both in history and in literature, the

American West is pre-eminently a story of exploration and development; and the land being explored and developed was a pre-civilization land, original land, a place not created by human beings. The historical and literary heroes and heroines who pioneered the West are not commonly thought of as sacred or supernatural. Debunking and exposing anyone who questions the authority of reason, in fact, is a favorite American activity. Still, pioneers in history and as imagined in literature are cast—however reluctantly or unconsciously—in the role of the supernaturals. They are the ones who live in the national psyche as the first people in a new land, *new* in terms of Anglo prejudice for its version of civilization over any other version of civilization.

And it is probably true—though difficult to demonstrate—that there is a connection between the ancient belief in knowledge of the original as power and the widespread American fascination with the West. If we knew what it was like to move into a frontier wilderness, if we understood the original as the mountaineer experienced it, then perhaps we would be in better control of our present day self and world. The connection, certainly, is advocated in an impressive number of works including *Walden, The Track of the Cat, Lord Grizzly, People of the Valley,* and "Big Two-Hearted River."

Essays in vocabulary—especially when claiming to be remarks on the national consciousness—should be modest. Words are never adequate to what we dream of saying, and comments on the deep consciousness of the American people are always in danger of being comments on the consciousness of one citizen.

And little will be gained by berating one another over differences in vocabulary. Political rights aside, critics who believe that myths are illusions have an intellectual right to say so. Religion aside, critics who believe that myths are the truth have an intellectual right to say so.

I have, therefore, no solution to offer, no dictionary entry to propose. Instead, I suggest a few guidelines for consideration.

It would be helpful, certainly, if we reminded one another from time to time that clarity and content would be improved if we identify our viewpoint when using—sticking to the task at hand—the words *myth* and *reality*. I am not suggesting an internal essay in vocabulary each time these and other troublesome words are used. I am suggesting that all of us—myself included of course—need to be more aware of the possibilities when using a word that slides all the way from illusion to fact to ultimate truth.

Edwin Corle's *Fig Tree John,* for example, has been rapped on the grounds that the mythic materials in the novel are not authentic. The word *myth,* in such a study, is being used in what I have called its second sense and refers to organizing stories of cultural history.

But the range of possibilities here is not confined to the simplistic opposition of authentic or not authentic. Mircea Eliade, C. G. Jung, and many others have described four stages of myth: the spontaneous birth of a myth, the organization into a ritual with definite patterns, the selfish manipulation of the myth for the personal benefit of a few, and the loss of faith in the validity and power of the myth.[2]

If we are aware of some of the varieties of the word *myth,* we read *Fig Tree John* with questions not confined to the assumption that a myth never changes. Why, for example, does Agocho go to town and ogle the pretty white woman, which, he thinks to himself, is a violation of his own tribal beliefs? Why does he settle by a dead land, allow his wife to be murdered, and fail in revenge? Why does this religious man become so destructive to his own family and to himself? Agocho's failures may come to seem internal as well as external; and, if that is a valid possibility, what then of the myth? Has Agocho's religion—acted out in his devotion to the land—failed him? Has he failed his religion? Or perhaps we have here a poignant and paradoxical and universally relevant story of the human heart and a value system working in reciprocity, each giving strength and even existence to the other, each failing and even destroying the other.

This one possibility—of myth as truth but losing power and moving toward illusion—is also suggested by a surprising number of major works representing a variety of American regions. Sinclair Lewis's Babbitt loses energy, toys with betrayal of his own value system, complains that his devotion to the businessman's credo is not returned, flirts with antic misbehaviour and dreams of a nostalgic return to wilderness as efforts in the restoration of power and unity, and ends with the hope that his son can achieve a better connection between the self and the world. William Faulkner's Quentin Compson obsessively berates the South, bangs the table to insist that he does not hate the South, is unable to believe in the South or to reject it or to find strength and identity in any other value system, and ends his life by suicide.

In western American fiction, stories of mythic powers undergoing change are perhaps even more recurrent. One characteristic motif consists of heroes who cannot assimilate their value system, or systems, and who therefore deliberately make a wrong and terrible decision. In *Mountain Man,* Vardis Fisher's Sam Minard leaves his wife alone in an isolated cabin even though he himself agrees with John Bridger's statement that leaving her there alone is not safe. In *A Very Small Remnant,* Michael Straight's Wynkoop rejects the offered colonelcy and accepts a position as Indian agent. As a full colonel, Wynkoop could give his devoted wife the life she has patiently waited for and have the authority necessary for helping the Indian in the way he wants to help. As a civilian agent, he will take his good wife to yet one more miserable outpost where he will have no power to carry out the mission he has assigned himself. Shortly before this decision, Lieutenant Soule has walked into an ambush and been murdered even though he had been told and already believed that the trap was set and that he would be killed.

In Frederic Manfred's *Riders of Judgment,* Cain Hammett loses his animal instinct and waits for death to take his brother and, finally, himself. In Harvey Fergusson's *Grant of Kingdom,* Conrad Richter's *The Sea of Grass,* and Willa Cather's *A Lost Lady,* the frontier hero loses the love of his wife and loses his land, the spiritual decline within tracking the historical decline of original energies associated with the land.

A. B. Guthrie's *The Big Sky* and Walter Van Tilburg Clark's *The Track of the Cat,* I believe, are primarily studies in truth moving toward untruth, or a myth in the process of betrayal, but certainly something more complex and mobile than a fixed true or a fixed untrue.

In addition to recognizing the dramatics of mythology, we need to increase our awareness of the tendency to use the same word for opposite meanings. By the first definition, a *myth* is false, an untruth, and the purpose may be to entertain merely, to propagandize, or to indoctrinate, and the results may be more or less innocent, more or less vicious. By the second definition, a *myth* is the organized and shaped values of a people, a part of history and culture; and the possibilities include Zeus as well as Hitler, the Southern Confederacy and the American Cowboy, Coyote Man and Christianity. By the third definition, a *myth* is a religion, a special type of religion in which history, philosophy, literature, and religion are one; and Anglo contemporaries especially need to remind one another that, just now, religions based in devotion to the land seem much more reasonable and practical than any philosophy or religion thought to be among the hallmarks of what we call civilization.

Such suggestions do not imply a formula or exhaust the possibilities or describe a program; but they do indicate, I hope, a few techniques of clarification and the importance of clarification. If the word *reality* is responsible only to facts and yet is assumed to mean the truth, if the word *myth* is used to describe both the fiction of Walter Van Tilburg Clark and the films of John Wayne, then a few signposts along the rhetorical way would be helpful to readers.

NOTES

[1] See David Bidney, "Myth, Symbolism, and Truth," in John B. Vickery, ed., *Myth in Literature* (Lincoln: University of Nebraska Press, 1966), pp. 3-13.

[2] Erich Neumann (*The Origins and History of Consciousness*), Irving Massey (*The Gaping Pig*), and others emphasize the range of mythic energies from power to weakness, from good to evil.

Also seeking clarity of definition, **Harold P. Simonson** probes the meaning of western primitivism, contrasting the man-over-nature paradigm outlined by Frederick Jackson Turner with myth-as-sacred history as seen in the experience of the mountain man of history and literature. Using William Everson's *Archetype West* (1976) as a point of reference, he examines the philosophical-cultural implications of "pantheistic apotheosis" whereby man attains truth by returning to primitive consciousness. Is this the essence of American experience, the shaping force of the American character, and is the West a microcosm of America? Is the western writer the modern frontiersman who has penetrated the wilderness and speaks sacred truths? Without denying the possible validity of this West-as-myth and indeed affirming the sacred, mystical relationship of self to nature, Simonson also reminds us of other cultural inheritances which impinge upon our views of the West.

Simonson is the author of *The Closed Frontier: Studies in American Literary Tragedy* (1970) and *Radical Discontinuities: American Romanticism and Christian Consciousness* (1983), as well as books on Zona Gale, Francis Grierson, Jonathan Edwards, and theories of literary criticism. Other publications include essays on Ole Rølvaag and John Muir. With advanced degrees from Northwestern University and the University of St. Andrews, Scotland, he is a professor of English at the University of Washington.

The West as Archetype

Harold P. Simonson

Frederick Jackson Turner failed to push his frontier thesis far enough, stopping at the point where the frontiersman donned buckskin moccasins and took scalps in "orthodox Indian fashion." He said little about the Indians themselves—too little, according to Ray Allen Billington, who thought that Turner regarded them only as retarding the advance of civilization, and only as compelling the whites to organize and consolidate their frontier settlements (*Frederick Jackson Turner: Historian, Scholar, Teacher* [1973], p. 454). As for the deeper levels of primitivism Turner did not speculate. The frontier, he said, was a safety-valve for the civilized albeit restless American, but Turner did not confront what the safety-valve opened unto. He was experientially ignorant about this deeper world, and was satisfied to say only in theoretical terms that the frontier allowed a brief exposure to primitivism, a momentary sampling of it, as if this return to ancestral well-springs would offer the psychic charge needed to thrust the evolutionary process even higher. Turner saw the frontier as a microcosm where man's history from primitivism to civilization could be re-enacted. The pattern itself, however, was inviolable: from primitivism to civilization. Such was to be the meaning of Progress. A little primitivism would remind the nineteenth century frontiersman of his mercantile errand and martial obligations.

Of course Turner went on to say in 1893 that the frontier was now closed, but he missed the irony in his announcement. To him and his heroic frontiersman, including the settler and the entrepreneur who came later, the frontier had never been open, not in the full sense and meaning of primitivism. Neither had it been open to the Parkmans, the Irvings, and the Twains who journeyed out to have a look at it. For the frontier was not merely a dividing line to be described with demographical statistics, as Turner had theorized it could be, nor was it an anthropological museum of Indian customs that Parkman condescendingly enjoyed examining, nor was it the land of tobacco-chewing prospectors. The point has to do with deeper significances, with levels of human experience that nothing short of the term "mythological" can satisfactorily serve to describe. In this sense primitivism and mythology come together. Whatever Turner and the others suggested about this deeper union, they sadly lacked an adequate vision of it. In short, they missed seeing the archetypal West from which Turner's West issued, and the mythological experience that the term "frontier" signified. One could argue that in this failure Turner missed seeing the real America, even though he intended his frontier thesis to explain the very roots of the American character.

It cannot be said that Turner had neglected his philosophical homework. Taking important ideas from the Concord Transcendentalists, he posited a world of God, man, and nature in which man has final dominion to transform what he cannot assimilate and in the process to hail himself as Captain if not Creator. Although Turner did not celebrate the ego as the ultimate reality, this notion is implicit in his view of the liberated frontiersman who, in reaching his full measure, is, according to Turner, "reborn," meaning re-energized and re-challenged to dominate nature, to organize and utilize it. In the end the true frontiersmen were Rockefeller, Hanna, Carnegie, and all the other captains of capitalism whose achievements over nature testified to the self as being the supreme creative force.

Perhaps this paradigm does capture the essential American character. If so, the American is essentially Romantic; his sovereign ego encompasses the divine and rules nature. To be sure, it is a far different paradigm from those engendered by the Enlightenment and an earlier Puritanism, both affirming important distinctions in the cosmic scheme of God-man-nature. Try as we will to capture the essential American spirit, it is elusive enough to allow sturdy arguments to be made for these other paradigms that also define the philosophical groundwork in which America's roots have grown. Who is to say, for example, that Oppenheimer and Faulkner were not inheritors of these other world views?

But we return to the question of the West as archetype and as primitive experience unique to the West alone. Again the paradigm includes God, man, and nature, but instead of any one having dominion over the others, the primitivism integral to the western experience finally rules out all distinctions among the three. The three become one in cosmic unity. It is this unity, some say, that informs the American character at its heart. "Pantheism," says William Everson in his provocative study, *Archetype West: The Pacific Coast As a Literary Region* (1976), is "not only the basic Californian or western point of view, but is essentially American . . . indeed *the* characteristic American religious and aesthetic feeling" (p. 7). So we have still another proposition as to what constitutes the American essence. Here the argument concerns pantheism as the root-force, the primal and authentic impulse in the American consciousness. Pantheism, we know, dispels the separateness of God, man, and nature: none has separate existence, none has sovereign authority, but each is part of the combined totality. The ultimate or constitutive reality is the universe, not the Mind or human personality as Emerson had argued. The universe is the All, the cosmos. According to Everson, its microcosm is the West . . . the West as archetype . . . the West as *the* essential American experience . . . the West as true primitivism and myth.

Before we look more closely at Everson's book—and it is upon this book that I wish to bring these thoughts into final focus—something needs to be said about the westerner who, even though he had never heard of pantheism and would have cared nothing about it if he had, nevertheless lived amid the mysteries of the land, sensing in unconscious but collective ways his psychic relationship to it. I am not referring to Turner's frontiersman whose contact with primitivism served to quicken his self-affirmation and strengthen his resolve to take the land. The reference instead is to the mountain man, portrayed by such writers as Vardis Fisher, A. B. Guthrie, Jr., and Don Berry and studied by historians and critics alike. As depicted, the mountain man of the Rockies donned buckskins and took his share of human scalps. Although he subsisted on what he received from furs that he trapped, he existed within the deeper rhythms of nature, as the original inhabitants, the Indians, had done for ages before his arrival. His concern was less to control nature than to be alert to it for his next meal and higher truths. The mountain man was different from the settlers who followed after him because he could hear in nature what others could not and see what to others was invisible. Delinquent in matters of societal laws, he was keenly attuned to nature's laws not only for his survival but for a sense of belonging. Granted that a certain mythical heroism colors the interpretation I am making. I know, for example, that Bernard DeVoto, Ray Allen Billington, and Henry Nash Smith have seen the mountain man as daring but degraded, fleeing to the frontier because he was unable or unwilling to conform to social restriction. Others have interpreted him as the expectant capitalist—hard-driving, ambitious, acquisitive, eager to gain wealth. This pragmatic judgment, however, fails to capture the whole truth about him. The mountain man *was* a different breed, and the difference lies in the fact that he lived in a world that had not yet been demythologized. He sensed the Indians' consciousness of this pantheistic world and to some degree wanted to make it his own. As for the Indians, he was no more interested in Christianizing or civilizing them than he was in imposing his will upon nature. The mountain man best represents the westerner who sought the ultimate merger with the ways of nature and the ways of the Indians, whose shamanistic culture made nature sacred and whose tamanawas experience made them one with this sacred, mythological world. Again, the effort was to know experientially this other dimension, even to touch the "original" truth, though being wary of ever claiming to possess it. One way was to marry Indian women. Another was to assimilate Indian dress, crafts, art. The most audacious way was to have a tamanawas experience: to go into the forests or the moutains, to fast, to hallucinate if necessary, in order that in a visionary moment some natural object might take on individual sacramental meaning and thus serve as a link forever after between one world and the other. The tamanawas became the transformed object itself—a bird, a river, a tree—as well as the religious experience upholding the transformation. It was in this experience that the white man merged with nature and truly became one with its aboriginal inhabitants. Racial distinctions were dissolved. So too were distinctions between nature and God. The cost to the initiate was nothing less than everything, including his ego. But the reward was the peace that passes understanding and the certainty, as Don Berry says in his remarkable novel *Trask* (1960), that "this tree wishes you no harm. Go around it in peace" (p. 365). To kill the tree would be to kill a part of oneself. This is hardly the knowledge that comes to Frederick Jackson Turner's frontiersman. It is, however, the knowledge inherent in the primitive experience—the experiential knowledge that a person exists in a relational world, indeed that existence itself is relationship, not dependency, certainly not separateness, and least of all dominion.

To William Everson the West is archetype. It is the original and unfallen unity. Had he written a longer book he probably would have developed his definition and thus balanced the term more satisfactorily with his other key term, "apotheosis." Everson is more intent upon the experience of apotheosis than upon a philosophical analysis of archetypal reality. It is clear, however, that he wants nothing to do with the old God-man relationship in which God is sovereign and man is dependent, nor does Everson find meaning in John Winthrop's famous definition of true liberty as restricted liberty. Hierarchical structure is anathema and non-western. Furthermore, Everson does not probe the tragic implications of the sovereign self which wars against God, against moral restraints, against nature; which sees all reality outside itself as antagonistic and all existence as consisting of polarities, encounters, struggles. Everson is as unMelvillian as he is unEdwardsian. In neither does he find what is essentially American. His archetype is a pantheistic West devoid of hierarchy, fallenness, polarity, ambiguity—in short a region "suffused by the presence of the Other" (p. 21).

Everson's *bête noire* is Edmund Wilson who, as a thoroughgoing easterner, had little sympathy for and even less understanding of western writing. Yet it was from Wilson and his ilk that the western writer had to gain approval. According to Everson, creativity constitutes the power of the West, and judgment constitutes the power of the East. The western writer is fated to stand before the eastern seat of judgment. It's like a prophet's destiny, says Everson. "Christ left Galilee to suffer crucifixion in Jerusalem. The western artist in New York can expect nothing less" (pp. 118-119). Everson is referring specifically to Jack Kerouac, Allen Ginsberg, Lawrence Ferlinghetti, and Michael McClure, but his more important point has to do with the uniqueness of the western experience as being understandable only to one who participates in it. This participation at its fullest he calls apotheosis—the full appropriation of the archetype into one's being. Not surprisingly, Everson associates the Beat and Hippie movements of the 1960s with the western archetype. The beads, buckskins, and long hair were its archaic signature. The movements struck at the center of the American experience, and at this center is pantheistic apotheosis.

The word "apotheosis" invariably reminds me of Melville's conclusion to chapter 23 of *Moby-Dick*: "Take heart, take heart,

O Bulkington! Bear thee grimly, demigod! Up from the spray of thy ocean-perishing—straight up, leaps thy apotheosis." Or of Brueghel's Icarus plunging into the sea, the uprising spray taking the shape of a crown that heralds the tragic self, still profoundly independent even in the very death-maw of the sea. This is not what Everson would call a western apotheosis. Rather than the ambiguity of victorious defeat or of what Hawthorne in the *Scarlet Letter* calls "triumphant ignominy," Everson speaks of "gigantic visions," the "primacy of discovery," and, in quoting Josephine Miles, the relationship of " 'the gods of the solar system to the gods of the solar plexus' " (p. 152). In what he calls "the Westward-hungering consciousness" (p. 152) Everson synthesizes a region and a state of being, making each serve the other in a charismatic wholeness . . . transcendence . . . quintessential truth . . . vertical accent (p. 10). Western comes to be synonymous with mystical, primal, archaic, religious, and cosmic.

In some respects Everson's book is old hat, warmed-over Whitman, exotic Big Sur stuff. But it is also provocative in its strident argument for the western archetype and the western artist as its embodiment. Not the mountain man, definitely not the pioneer, but the western writer is the real frontiersman.

> What attests to it is the scale of imagination, the repudiation of received forms, the eruptive intensity of the energy, the monumental output, the aloof, transcendental passion, the overwhelming pantheistic vision—all these are the unmistakable evidence that the force so long abuilding has at last found its voice. (pp. 75-76)

Everson believes the voice was that of Robinson Jeffers. Joaquin Miller was the archetype's inceptor and Edwin Markham its amplifier, but Jeffers was its embodied apotheosis. Such western writers as Bret Harte, Mark Twain, and Richard Henry Dana were only "birth-pangs." In sheer Dionysiac energy Frank Norris, whose *The Octopus* Everson calls the West's *Moby-Dick,* came close to Jeffers. In his portrayal of the artist Presley in *The Octopus,* Norris caught the immensity of the western imagination and mythical consciousness. But after Jeffers, according to Everson, western writing faded into reductionism, with writers like Jack London and John Steinbeck too afraid to allow their pantheistic passion to develop, and someone like William Saroyan too willing to "humanize" it. Abrose Bierce, H. L. Davis,

Walter Van Tilburg Clark, and Wallace Stegner achieved a certain brilliance but stand outside the scope of what Everson calls "the primary archetype . . . its protogenic emergence and its subsequent evolution" (p. 91). Not until the writings of Kenneth Rexroth, Kerouac, Ferlinghetti, and Gary Snyder did the archetype once again have its "constellated" voice. For example, in Rexroth's "The Phoenix and the Tortoise" the archetype "rises to redeem the deracinated intelligence" which was T. S. Eliot's legacy (p. 105). In *The Dharma Bums* Kerouac "became for a magic interval the archetype's chosen voice" (p. 113). In Ginsberg's "Howl" the dark element introduced into the archetype by Jeffers "thrust down to a deeper, more explosive level" (p. 116). Everson's assessment of Gary Snyder borders on rhapsody: "Jeffers had looked westward to the vast expanse of water, and Kerouac and Ginsberg both responded to the sweep beyond, but more than any other American poet Snyder has followed that gaze to its conclusion. This oriental insemination makes him, among the young, one of the most influential poets writing today" (p. 141). As for Ken Kesey's work, especially his novel *Sometimes a Great Notion,* Everson finds the archetype revealed with more force than with any development since Steinbeck. Indeed Kesey's characters inhabit a vast and forbidding terrain, even though Kesey denies "the higher register of the archetype, the evocative pantheism, the sense of transcendental sublimity in the vastness of Western landscape" (p. 130). Everson thinks this denial is centered in Kesey's fear of nature: " 'that river is no buddy of mine' " (p. 124). Consequently, Kesey is deaf to "the religious note in the Western archetype"; he leaves western fiction "at a point of impasse" (p. 129). In denying transcendence he supposedly has nowhere to culminate his vast energies.

The frontiersman today is the artist to whom the mantle of heroic consciousness has been passed, enabling him to achieve the apotheosis that can awaken modern man from his spiritual somnolence. This is Everson's faith. Little matter that that consciousness feels a penchant for violence one moment, a disquieting lassitude the next, and frequently a preoccupation with death. It need only be noted that California's official flower is the poppy, that its most popular magazine is *Sunset,* that the western archetype has a dark strain, a death-pulse, which writers like London and George Sterling knew too well. The thrust of Everson's argument is that certain western artists have penetrated into the wilderness, there to discover the frontier to be a passage leading to fuller existence best described as primitive, pantheistic apotheosis. Those who achieve this existence are able to identify the myth of the West with salvation, including their own.

Although not new, this thesis forcefully reminds us once again of the primitivism that yet resides in the American character despite three centureis of alien ideologies that would work to expunge it. Among the many exciting interpretations this fact elicits, one must be the centrality of the western experience that includes the full mythical sense of sublime wholeness. A corollary suggests that this wholeness is our destiny, to be reached not in going along the upward way charted by social evolutionists but by going back to truths intuited by primitive consciousness. Unfortunately, the nagging problem Everson fails to recognize is that, like one's hearing a fly buzz at the moment of transcendence, even the most rapturous vision emanating from primitive consciousness never completely expunges America's other inheritances, including the dark shadow emanating from Jerusalem and slicing through the western archetype.

PART TWO:

WRITING ABOUT THE WEST:
HISTORY, REALISM, AND MYTH

Readers of western literature often expect either careful attention to authentic detail (when authors use historical materials) or a simplistic, literarily unpretentious adventure narrative (when authors write "Westerns"). A western writer who utilizes historical sources but goes beyond them and beyond simple narration to explore psychological and philosophical realities may draw criticism from an audience reluctant to grant the same fictive freedom to western writers that it expects more traditional writers to exercise. Moreover, western novelists have themselves too often limited their fictional possibilities by a too facile allegiance to what **Stephen Tatum** calls "historical realism."

What happens when a writer seeks to work with known historical evidence without violating it, yet using it for fictional purposes? If he writes about an infamous, legendary historical figure with the intent of not going beyond the line of accepted history, what problems does he face? Can he create successful characterization? **Stephen Tatum** addresses these questions within the larger critical framework of the relationship of historical realism to the literary imagination by examining Charles Neider's *The Authentic Death of Hendry Jones,* a novel based on the life of Billy the Kid. Undergirding Tatum's analysis is the conviction that an author should work with his own contemporary values when dealing with historical subjects, for only by examining what *is* can he achieve some insight into human destiny.

A native Southwesterner, Tatum is a member of the University of Utah English faculty. He has published articles on Frank Norris, the Australian poet Judith Wright, the Hollywood Western, and the British periodical view of the American frontier experience. He is the author of *Inventing Billy the Kid: Visions of the Outlaw in America, 1881-1981* (1982).

Historical Realism and the American West: The Example of Charles Neider's *The Authentic Death of Hendry Jones*

Stephen Tatum

> The crucial obligation of art is to be faithful to the real because it is in the real that people must live.
> —George Levine, *The Boundaries of Fiction,* 1968

> Every true novel is a historical novel.
> —Paul Horgan

Among certain philosophers of history the nature of the relationship between history and literature is as central a concern as the question of historical causation or even the epistemological question of our ability to know the past at all. On the most fundamental level, these philosophers supplement Aristotle's notion that poetry occupies an ideal mean between the extremes of philosophy and history with the belief that history, in its combination of scientific investigation and artistic formulation of narrative, occupies the frontier between the disciplines of art and science. As Peter Gay remarks in *Style in History,* "historical narration without analysis is trivial, historical analysis without narration is incomplete."[1] The successful historian, in order to recreate the "feel" of the human condition in the past universe—whether at Hastings or the Little Big Horn—and to prevent his analysis from being incomplete, necessarily employs the narrative powers and the imagination of the novelist in selecting, interpreting, and presenting his material.[2]

Just as the historian claims access to literary techniques to entertain as well as to inform his audience, so too the literary artist creating fictional narratives about the American West often employs historical events as the lifeblood of his narrative, as does Thomas Berger in *Little Big Man.* Such artists, furthermore, often include detailed observations of a social milieu, as in

Wallace Stegner's novels, which both reveal historical authenticity and also fulfill what George Levine conceives to be the crucial obligation of art. The affinity between art and history is such that some novelists or poets cannot operate without the spur of history to jolt their imagination into action, and such that idealist philosophers of history like Dilthey or Collingwood cannot conceive of the historian proceeding without the intuitive understanding of characters and environment commonly demanded of the novelist or poet.

If in this larger, theoretical context the historian can sometimes be labelled a prose artist and the prose artist can sometimes be labelled a historian, we in western American studies should not be surprised. Just as Clio is also one of the Muses and historians are also eligible for the Nobel Prize in Literature, so too the close interrelationship of history and art remains a central aspect defining a regional culture. Certainly we are familiar with western history as literature and western literature as history. We have experienced the narrative power of historian Dale Morgan's *Jedidiah Smith*, and the Dickensian comic genius of novelist Don Berry's *A Majority of Scoundrels*, an informal history of the Rocky Mountain fur trade. On the other hand, we have witnessed—to choose from a lengthy list—Vardis Fisher's use of the Donner party ordeal in *The Mothers*, Frederick Manfred's use of the Hugh Glass episode in *Lord Grizzly*, and John Neihardt's portrayal of historical trappers in *The Mountain Men* poems. Above all else, perhaps, we recognize Paul Horgan's distinguished career as both novelist and historian, and we praise Wallace Stegner's inspired use of the historian-narrator in his novel *Angle of Repose.*

Characteristically, the writer of western prose fiction appears faithfully devoted to presenting the "real" in which we all have to live, but it is the carefully rendered sense of the past universe in which our ancestors lived and died. The writer takes care to portray man speaking to man, to be sure, but also—in the manner of a historian—offers his audience the results of his research as well, offers his audience documents speaking to man. To employ one of Henry James's analogies, this from his preface to *The American*, the author documenting a western narrative ensures that the rope tethering the hot-air "balloon of experience" and the "commodious car of the imagination" to the solid earth remains more secure than a tight piggin' rope around a heifer's legs. Thus we view on television the world's most popular author of Westerns declaiming, while standing before his well-stocked personal library, the vices and virtues of the "real" old West and advising his audience that historical accuracy of dates, names, and places is the hallmark of his work. Thus we hear of Frederick Manfred retracing his wounded trapper-protagonist's crawl for life in order to understand more fully the event. Thus we study scholarly efforts to identify the western novelist's sources, and thus we become familiar with those readers and critics who balk at considering a novel worthy of the label "Western" unless the work in question sports some authentic nineteenth-century historical paraphenalia—appropriate to time and place—like beaver traps, buckskin leggings, and branding irons.

[Because of this close kinship of history and literature in the West, and because of a critical demand for what we may term a historical realism based on a standard of authenticity, the problem confronting any imaginative artist who explores the ontological and cultural meanings inherent in western settings is that the result of such an effort must endure—it cannot truly evade—withering critical volleys from all sides of a critically muddy street.] An author delving into the life of a historical western figure faces a critical backlash from actual and would-be historian-readers who chastise inaccurate historical accounts of the figure's career. Typical of this sort of critical response is Walter Prescott Webb's criticism of Emerson Hough's *North of 36* for its submission "*to the demands of fiction* and to the possibilities of the moving pictures," and Webb's praise instead for Eugene Manlove Rhodes, who "made his stories *true to life in the cattle country* rather than to the eastern notions of what the life there ought to be."[3] On the other side of the street the author interested in the western historical figure faces critical condemnation from reviewers who decry any authorial lapses into high seriousness due to the presence of sophisticated literary techniques.

These responses, however superficially opposed, similarly serve as obstacles to the development of a fully-imagined historical western figure in a sophisticated fictional work. The one response insists the author present both straightforward, elementary human characters with uncomplicated motives and fast-paced adventures from opening complication to closing act of violence. In this view western fiction is best seen as escapist entertainment essentially irrelevant to contemporary concerns of readers and writers. The other response insists the author's primary task is to immerse himself in the past via historical research in order to establish his authority as one who has been there and can thus speak the authentic truth about the way it was. In this view western fiction, reassuringly based on historical facts, is valuable because it makes history "come alive." Together, both types of response share a characteristic preoccupation in the study of western American letters: the study of western fiction as anything but fiction, as anything but an artifact whose literary values can communicate a searching exploration of the human condition regardless of time and place.[4]

The obvious point here is that it would seem unimportant, finally, whether the novelist accurately renders the border shift or exposes Billy the Kid as a right-handed gun. The problem is that such responses ask writers and readers to believe that the accumulation of historical details and laconic characters will add up to fiction—as if, to paraphrase G. K. Chesterton, letters produced letters, newspapers produced litters of little newspapers, and six-guns sired families of little derringers. It would seem more to the point to suggest that any explanation of Billy the Kid's *reality* would depend less upon authenticity and more upon how completely the author discloses the human meanings implicit in the welter of historical events and constructs a narrative that yet captures the texture of actual persons, places, and events.

Yet the insistent demand for authenticity persists, regardless of the efforts of scholars and critics to declare the problem no longer exists.[5] Such a demand underlies what Sanford E. Marovitz has recently labelled "the contemporary crisis in the study of Western American letters."[6] Although his phrase is perhaps overstated, Marovitz tellingly argues his verdict by discussing how ambiguous and contradictory definitions of key terms, how the neglect of serious western fiction's literary values, and how the demand for rigorous historical authenticity have produced much heated debate—but little in the way of serious, specific consideration of fundamental questions. One such question Marovitz believes is too often assumed as a "given" is particularly germane to the shortcomings in critical responses accorded such historical novels as Charles Neider's *The Authentic Death of Hendry Jones*: "When Western romancers heavily emphasize the authenticity of their details and backgrounds in presenting history, anthropology, and landscape," Marovitz asks, "while yet taking great liberties in rendering character and action, *how real is their realism*?"[7]

Such a fundamental question underscores a critical problem simply because critical attention to western fiction has neglected sustained explanations of how authenticity and verisimilitude in western American fiction have been transformed in specific works into a heightened reality. Of course, one essay on one literary western fiction such as *Hendry Jones* will not dissolve any "crisis" in western American letters. Still, by understanding how novelists like Neider employ factual sources we can move profitably toward understanding the literary (not mythic, sociocultural, entertainment, or historical) values of a western novel, toward clarifying the relationship of authenticity and realism, and toward discovering the consequences of authenticity in western fiction.

Published in 1956 during a revival of interest in Billy the Kid, Charles Neider's *The Authentic Death of Hendry Jones* reinterprets the Kid's story by removing its setting to Old California, by changing the names of its historical characters, and by adopting a sophisticated narrative technique to detail its successive acts of violence.[8] Narrated by one Doc Baker, fictitious surviving friend of Hendry Jones (the Kid), Neider's novel records the Kid's capture by Dad Longworth (Pat Garrett), his confinement and escape from jail, his reunion with his gang, and his travels along the California coast before he is shot by Longworth and buried on a barren point called Punta del Diablo. Although *Hendry Jones* was favorably received when it appeared, some reviewers—seemingly believing that Will Henry, not Henry James, is an author to emulate—lamented "some literary flourishes here and there," as well as "an annoying vestige of literary erudition in the book."[9]

Despite these criticisms, the novel is noteworthy for its presentation of the human consequences of violence. Wirt Williams declared the novel "the greatest 'western' ever written" since Neider, "apparently free of the usual, fatal pre-conditioning," synthesized the best qualities of both popular fiction and first-rate works of serious literature.[10] While Williams seems to be praising Neider's fresh perspective on the Kid's story, he nevertheless admiringly describes the extensive "pre-conditioning" Neider contributed to his novel: interviews with old-timers; library research on the Kid's career; the fact that Neider "wore everywhere a holstered handgun tied low to his leg for a good fast draw."[11] For Williams, the central factor defining "the greatest 'western' ever written" appears in the final analysis to be *authenticity,* a factor that emerges in the novel when, for instance, Neider's outlaw realizes, during a stay in jail, that his awkward stride is the result of having to learn how to cope without a hefty six-gun and holster strapped to his thigh. Yet, the major questions in need of discussion, once again, are these: does such authenticity make for more compelling fiction? Does such "pre-conditioning" guarantee or even contribute to realism? Because Neider's novel explores—but does not duplicate—Billy the Kid's story, *Hendry Jones* provides an excellent example for a close study of what happens when a novelist uses his apparent freedom from exacting authenticity during a discussion of such a timeless human reality as the confrontation with death.

Examining Neider and his primary sources at the point of Hendry Jones's death near the novel's conclusion provides a convenient entry into the discussion of these questions. Eugene Cunningham's chapter on Billy the Kid in *Triggernometry* serves as an excellent companion-piece to Neider's novel. As an objective recorder of events, Cunningham characteristically debunks various legends in his study and follows a sparse outline of the events on the Kid's last night. This historian's Billy the Kid is startled by the presence of two strangers—Garrett's fellow sleuths—lounging on the long veranda of Pete Maxwell's residence. Concerned about his safety, unarmed except for a butcher knife he carries to slice some meat for a meal, and caught, furthermore, without his boots on, the Kid retreats into Maxwell's bedroom to find out who the strangers are. Expecting to find only Maxwell and instead perceiving two shadowy shapes in the darkened bedroom, the Kid nervously asks a question:

> "Quien es? Quien es?" he cried. Maxwell whispered gaspingly to Garrett:
> "That's him."
> And Garrett threw himself to the side, for he expected a shot at any moment. He jerked out his own gun, levelled it, fired at the Kid.
> He heard the thud of the body striking the floor, heard a rattling, gasping noise, then silence.[12]

Historical Realism and the American West 37

Except for the debate over whether or not the Kid was armed with a revolver at the moment Garrett shot him, little disagreement exists among reliable historians about the sequence of events in Maxwell's bedroom that night in July 1881.[13]

Neider's novel focuses on the Kid as a weary, prematurely-aging outlaw who fatalistically sees his "luck" change as a catastrophic series of events brings him closer to his rendezvous with Longworth in Hijinio Gonzalez's (Pete Maxwell's) bedroom. The image of the carefree, humorous, defiant Kid is replaced in narrator Baker's account by a preoccupation with the Kid's troubled state of mind. Worried about a rising young gunslinger in another town, about his relationship with his mistress, about the jinx another member of his gang has put on him, the Kid, scared by the presence of two strangers, darts into the darkened bedroom and, in much the same manner as Cunningham's account, asks a question. At this point,

> The Kid felt something moving there and covered the crouching figure with his gun, retreating rapidly across the room and crying, "Quien es? Quine es?" as if it was the devil himself.
>
> And then Longworth [Garrett] drew and fired and threw his body to the left and fired again from close to the floor, lighting up the room, and sprang up and ran outside and pressed himself against the wall at the side of the door, looking pale in the moonlight.
>
> The Kid probably never knew what hit him. Coming out of the moonlight into that dark room, he was aware only of darkness and of his own danger and of how tired he was and of how tired of loving he was and of how he would have to get himself down to old Mex. And then the red flame sprang at him and the fortyfive ball crashed into his chest and it was as though a tree had hit him trunk first and then he heard the roar like the roar of the sea and found himself face down on the dirt floor, wondering how he had got there, and he was gasping and gurgling, and he said faintly, "Mother. Help me. I'm strangling."[14]

The essential issue here is not whether the Kid should be armed with a pistol, but whether or not this is a fully-developed account of what happens to a man harboring a death wish in his being and who finally experiences its fulfillment. Or, is this merely an accurate account of what happened to one man in a certain year who was surprised and shot dead? We have, in the last paragraph describing the Kid's death throes, provocative possibilities for development which heighten the bare authentic facts of Cunningham's text. Ultimately, death has become a release for the Kid in the novel: tired of running and of loving, he wonders how he finally came to be in this situation. In the long sentence with the lovely repetitions of the coordinating words "and of how" Neider resurrects earlier concerns of the novel—the change in the Kid's personality; the Kid's conflict over the decision to stay in Mexico or return to California—and discloses insight where historians and biographers have customarily refused to tread. As the Kid evolves from a prisoner of life to a free man in death, the text's light imagery moves from moonlight to darkness, which contrasts with the earlier jailbreak scene's movement of imagery from darkness to light. Such technique suggests that any meaning in the event arises from the author's creative imagination, not his "pre-conditioning." Such meaning also succeeds even if there is no way anyone can document the Kid's authentic last words.

Yet the entire experience, however faithful to the authentic facts, is not richly developed. On the most basic level, the novel's title is intended to contrast with the 1882 Pat Garrett-Ash Upson *The Authentic Life of Billy, the Kid.* One of Neider's main concerns is thus to explore the meaning of an *authentic* death, which would not precisely be the fact of the Kid's death but rather the imaginative experience of death which exists beyond what the visual eye records. To be more specific, there would seem to be a complexity of thought and feeling running through a scared, hunted fugitive—standing in the dark in his stocking feet and holding an ineffectual butcher knife—which is not opened up to understanding. Is the Kid, through the narrator's brief image, perhaps conjuring up religious guilt about his violent life into a confrontation with the devil? Why did the Kid in both history and this novel for once continue to ask questions instead of defending himself as he had done in the past? And if the Kid is "tired" of his violent life, then why did he return from Mexico? To go beyond a dependency upon previous accounts, Neider would need to do more than introduce the lure of an attractive woman. The point here is that it seems superfluous to change character names and the story's setting if one is content to present the familiar ambiguities surrounding the Kid's last days.

On another critical level, given the necessity of discovering the meaning of an *authentic* death, it seems surprising that Neider did not treat the scene by means of shifting point of view. The beauty of his version of the earlier jailbreak scene is due partly to his presentation of the event from three different viewpoints. Here in the Kid's death scene, one is curious to know what courses through Gonzalez's mind as his loyalties to either the Kid or to Dad Longworth are put to the supreme test. One is also curious to know what the sheriff was thinking when he realized that the high-pitched voice in the dark was the voice of his assassin—unless the sheriff acts quickly and efficiently. Given these considerations, which could be developed to the extent one wished to explore the characters, the author and reader could fully grapple with such additional thematic concerns as loyalty, friendship, and duty—concerns as enduring as the conflict between Cain and Abel in Biblical times.

One can argue that Neider left these questions and images undeveloped for several reasons. In the first place, death is an inscrutable experience, and no living author can ever completely penetrate the experience. Nevertheless, this did not prevent Neider's narrator from fully exploring a character's psychological reactions to death at an earlier point in the novel. One could also argue that since Doc Baker as narrator cannot plausibly examine the Kid's mental state, his use of the word "probably" in the third paragraph of the above passage is entirely appropriate and justifies the opaqueness of the passage. Yet the shield of ambiguity or decorum in characterization is not relevant here: this same narrator, for instance, verbalized the Kid's mental processes during earlier passages in the novel.

In order to free the writer from the tight reins of realism, one must demand that the writer explore certain originally tentative points in order to raise or symbolize realities unbounded by historical verisimilitude, realities that declare a state of consciousness transcending the distinctions between past and present, writer and reader. In this context, the Kid's death certainly raises interesting questions about the meaning of the words "safety" and "life." The Kid clearly could have chosen to play it safe by staying in Old Mexico; yet he also possessed a personal ideal that transcended a concern with mere safety. Indeed, any failure to measure up to his ideals could be considered philosophically a form of death, while—on the other hand—integrity to these personal ideals could be considered, even in the face of death, a form of life. All we need remember here is Sarpedon's speech to Glaukos in *The Iliad*. With this renewed focus, larger human truths may usher forth from a configuration of such personal values, and Neider's Kid *potentially* could travel with an Antigone if such an ethical conflict was developed through image and context to transmute any initial concern with historical authenticity. However much as we historians may applaud Neider's vividness in embroidering an account of the Kid's death that is yet, by means of reliable sources, still responsible to history, we as readers and literary critics should be disappointed that the boundaries of history and literature coincided at this important point in the novel. Vestiges of literary erudition are not annoying because of their presence, finally, but because of their absence. Neider's exploration of Hendry Jones's death is historically authentic, possesses verisimilitude, reveals common sense realism—yet is not *real*.[15]

As writers and readers we at times overlook the necessary and valuable distinctions between history and the novel, between a literature devoted to the illusion of truth and a literature devoted to truthful illusion. Every novel is a historical novel, as Paul Horgan states, in the sense that we are presented a coherent group of statements about particular settings and groups of characters who live at a particular stage of historical consciousness. Yet any demand for literary erudition on the novelist's part implies that he speak not only with the assurance and tone of a historian seeking truth, but that he transform the givens of a historical story into a meaning both personal and "universal"—personal because the story is localized in space and time and attempts to define the implicit meaning of a particular cultural moment; "universal" because the story involves the hopes and fears of humans in a world in which we all must live and, inevitably, die. As a means of accomplishing this task the novelist has the freedom to render his character's inner thought processes, to detail a number of perspectives on his material, and to impose a shape upon and to endow meaning to a life in the making, not a life already made. Whereas to my mind Neider failed to move beyond what Max Westbrook has called "facsimile authenticity"[16] during the death of Hendry Jones, Neider does achieve in another important scene literary success that is *both* authentic and real. I am referring here to Neider's rendition of the Kid's escape from jail, an event in the novel which closely follows the historical version of the Lincoln County jailbreak of Billy the Kid.

About the historical sequence of events during the Kid's escape from the Lincoln County jail there has been one major question: how did the Kid obtain the gun he used to kill the deputies on duty? In his *The Saga of Billy the Kid,* Walter Noble Burns advances the least credible theory: the Kid quite simply jumped the guard during a game of monte, obtained the gun, and was subsequently forced to shoot the deputy attempting to warn the town. Although we shall probably never know exactly how the Kid managed to get the drop on his guard, Maurice Fulton's theory that Billy found a gun waiting for him in the jail's outdoor privy, as advanced in Frazier Hunt's *The Tragic Days of Billy the Kid,* is accepted as the most thoroughly researched and, therefore, the most plausible explanation.[17]

Until Fulton's research was published, however, most interpreters of the Kid's career followed the tradition represented by Pat Garrett's *The Authentic Life of Billy, the Kid.*[18] Garrett's reconstruction of the escape has the outlaw, on his return from the outhouse in the back corral, outdistance his unsuspecting guard, reach the jail's gunroom, seize a six-shooter, and kill the deputy climbing the stairs in pursuit. Between the publication of Garrett's book, ghost-written by Ash Upson, in April 1882 and the publication of Hunt's biography in 1956, Garrett's version was followed by such notable authors as Jack Thorp and Neil Clark, in their *Pardner of the Wind,* and Eugene Cunningham, in his *Triggernometry.*

Writing before Hunt published the results of Fulton's research, Neider disdains Burns's description of events and follows instead the Garrett-Thorp-Cunningham version. For the purposes of this discussion it is necessary to quote at length Cunningham's version of the jailbreak:

> Coming back the Kid walked ahead. The chain connecting his shackles was long. He walked fast, entered the building and, momentarily out of sight of Bell, raced up the stairs, whirled at the landing, leaped up the last flight and hurled himself at the door of a small room used by

> Garrett as a sort of armory. That door was locked but the ram of the Kid's shoulder burst it open. He snatched up a loaded six-shooter and ran back to the stairhead. Bell, still unalarmed, had just reached the landing. The Kid fired at him and missed, yet did not miss. His slug struck the wall twelve feet below almost at Bell's side, ricocheted and pierced the deputy Sheriff's body. Bell spun about and half fell back down the stairs to the yard, staggered a few steps and fell dead.[19]

Although Neider's deputy is named Pablo, the lawman receives the same fate in *Hendry Jones* that Bell does in *Triggernometry*: both men are unalarmed at first; both men receive the Kid's shot, fall down the stairs, and die exposed to the sunshine—not the shadows of the jail's interior. Like the Kid in history and in *Triggernometry*, Neider's Kid also hobbles up a stairway, breaks open a door, obtains a six-gun, and shoots his guard from the top of the stairs.

If this were the extent to which Neider examined the event, then as literary critics and readers we should be disappointed because the meaning of an *authentic* death is not portrayed. However, Neider does fill in the outline of what happened during the jailbreak by rearranging events and shifting the point of view. Neider first transforms a known historical fact—that Bell allowed a few select persons to visit the Kid during his captivity—into scenes which portray Pablo's family paying respectful visits to the Kid. These visits develop Pablo's character during the hours prior to the Kid's breakout, revealing the deputy's love for his family, antipathy to racial prejudice, and developing friendship with the man he guards.

This expansion of fact and preparation of characterization accomplishes an effective variation in narrative point of view. Instead of an objective glance at Bell's physical actions when the bullet strikes home, Neider probes, at length, the deputy's mental processes as his life ebbs away:

> Then Pablo heard the shot and he knew the ball had hit him. He tried to rise but couldn't, there were chains and shackles on him, pinioning his arms and legs, and great weights holding him down. There was no pain but he knew he was dying and he wanted to get outside to die out there. So he got to his hands and knees and, like a

blind bear, crawled and scuttled onto the grass, saying nothing, not even groaning, not even feeling the hot flow of blood across his chest, hardly seeing anything, and he scuttled out of there to avoid a second shot, but the second shot did not come, and he scuttled out onto the plaza which was so full of golden light. But the plaza looked as though evening had come on it and he thought it was night in Ensenada and that the fishing was good and that Maria Jesus was visiting her sister and he crawled a little way south in the direction of his house on the Calle de Estrada on the way to the mission, leaving blood on the long grass, and when he had gotten about as far as the first window it occurred to him that it ought to be morning and that there ought to be plenty of light on the plaza and he wondered if this were the plaza and why he was lying down and then suddenly he thought: They ought to use some of that lumber to make my coffin, and it seemed important that he tell somebody that and he tried to crawl as far south as he could, going diagonally across the plaza, and suddenly he saw the mission and the altar and the sun blinded him and, sobbing "Dios me perdone!" he died.[20]

Unlike the objective, "unvarnished" account authored by Thorp or Cunningham, Neider details a man's conscious actions as his life ends: the fading eyesight which perceives day as night, the hopeful exclamation to an unseen God, the desperate attempt to reach home and family. The lengthy coordinate sentences—highlighted by the repetition of conjunctions and verbs, and the juxtaposition of mission, altar, and blinding sunlight—appropriately convey the complexity of thought and feeling in a dying, utterly isolated man torn between devotion to life and family and a devotion to life's work, a man both crawling and scuttling his way toward his ancestral and familial home—and toward a hopeful salvation. Pablo's character assumes tragic proportions not only because the symbols of law and religion are unable to nurture him—he dies within view of the mission and the lumber to be used to construct the Kid's scaffold—but also because he is "dead" no matter which way he turns: if he obeys the Kid's orders to submit, to stay alive, he will then be considered an untrustworthy "greaser," an outcast to his Anglo neighbors; if he tries to warn the town, as he did, he then physically dies from a bullet in the chest. Neider's deputy not only falls dead but metaphorically becomes a prisoner of death just as his murderer becomes a prisoner of life after the jailbreak. By developing Pablo's character to reveal his love of family and sensitivity to racial slurs, Neider's internal narration maturely unfolds what may happen with an objective phrase like Cunningham's "staggered a few steps and died." Thus, Neider's faithful adherence to and transformation of the facts as presented by his sources here illustrates just how *real* such realism can be.

One might argue, however, having read Burns's account of the same scene, that a mere change in point of view does not necessarily validate Neider's transcendence of "facsimile authenticity" in reporting the scene. "In fact," as Kent Steckmesser writes, "Burns established certain conventions for novelistic treatment of character and events. For example, . . . we get an inside view of the thoughts of J. W. Bell and Ollinger before the Kid kills them."[21] Nevertheless, unlike Neider, Burns's biography casts aside the interior monologue strategy at the moment of death: "The bullet struck Bell beneath the left shoulder blade, cut through his heart, and buried itself in the wall beyond. He pitched forward on his head, crumpled over in a somersault, rolled down the few remaining steps and lay lifeless at the bottom, his limp body half out the courtyard door."[22] Burns does not presume here to expand the event in psychological time, although he does devote more attention to the event than does Cunningham's later version. Both Cunningham and Burns, however, similarly depict the incident without distorting the time sequence of the historical event. Such a fleeting moment of physical action is precisely what the successful novelist seizes and explores in form and content, whether it be Neider here in this novel or, say, Melville in the conclusion to his early novel *White-Jacket*.

To criticize the novel, as some have, for its graphic and leisurely depiction of bloodshed is to miss the point that Neider is concerned with relaying the existential reality of violence in a manner more humanly felt than an antiseptic body count or objective photograph or external narration. In this sense, the authentic death of Hendry Jones is not precisely his physical death from a gunshot wound, but is rather the imaginative experience of death which constitutes the entire narration. While the outlaw's death is announced in the novel's first sentence, the reality of the outlaw's authentic death is not apparent until narrator Doc Baker and we as his audience experience the entire narrative process, its stops and starts, its digressions and repetitions, as Baker examines the human encounter with death from as many angles as possible. An *authentic* death is realized only when the imagination can probe the personal meanings that exist beyond what the visual eye records; an *authentic* death in *authentic* western fiction successfully presents the reality of the human encounter with death by imbuing the realistic portrayal of the facts with significant human meanings.

In a novel so dominated by the main character's concern with "luck" and the violent acts necessary to ensure a continued string of "good luck," we should expect Neider to explore imaginatively Hendry Jones's confrontation with death in at least as much depth and symbolic richness as in his treatment of Pablo's waning moments. Yet, as we have seen, Neider's portrayal of the outlaw's death reveals an imaginative shortcoming as his narrative more closely resembles his sources. On the other hand, his portrayal of a minor character's death indicates what can happen when a novelist penetrates through the surface of historical realism, through an allegiance to "facsimile authenticity," and discovers a fictive world of meaning and passion that demands our involvement. And if one questions whether an "adenoidal moron" like the Kid, as one person has described this outlaw, is appropriate subject matter for the serious novelist, we need only remind this person that the complex relationship between an individual's sense of the law and society's legal definition of justice is as natural a theme for development in a western setting of sagebrush and sand as in Sophocles's Greece or Thoreau's New England. The Billy the Kid discovering John Tunstall's bullet-riddled corpse *can be* a figure fraught with as much complexity as an Antigone finding Polyneices's unburied corpse outside the gates of Thebes.

For both the novelist and historian to reach their goal of tapping an audience need to experience imaginatively the possibilities and limitations inherent in human life, both writers and readers must recognize that realism of "facsimile authenticity" is a responsible, but not a final, step in the right direction. With this recognition we remember that the real we must live in, as well as the real we look for in the novel, is the real of both past and present—as much as we need to know how it was, we need to know how it is. Thus to ask the novelist to refrain from imposing his own values upon the hard-won balance between individual will and environment forged in the last century is effectively to close the door to the creative imagination. Forgetting that, as Peter Gay writes, "truth is an optional instrument of fiction, not its essential purpose,"[2,3] we often watch the critics' words roll off the pages and achieve a reality as fixed as the historian's belief that the past can be captured: "fidelity to fact"; "fidelity to reality"; "true to life"; "verisimilitude"; "authentic re-creation." As our discussion of *Hendry Jones* and its sources reveals, the consequences of realizing and not realizing the impact of these words can be both disheartening and exhilarating for both reader and writer. As we continue to study western fiction as fiction, we shall continue to discover that authentic western fiction may or may not be realistic—but it certainly will be *real* whenever the novelist opens the text for the reader by showing how reality is *not* synonymous with or reduced to a concern for the referential nature of language.

NOTES

[1] Peter Gay, *Style in History* (New York: Basic Books, 1974), p. 189.

[2] For an extension of this point see Paul Hernardi, "Clio's Cousins: Historiography as Translation, Fiction, and Criticism," *New Literary History,* 7 (Winter 1976), 247-257.

[3] Walter Prescott Webb, *The Great Plains* (New York: Grosset & Dunlap, 1931), pp. 462-463.

[4] For more on this preoccupation's consequences see Jack Brenner, "Imagining the West," in Merrill Lewis and L. L. Lee, eds., *The Westering Experience in American Literature* (Bellingham, Washington: Bureau for Faculty Research, 1977), pp. 32-47; and Don D. Walker, "Criticism of the Cowboy Novel: Retrospect and Reflections," *Western American Literature,* 11 (1977), 275-296. Just how pervasive this preoccupation is can be indicated by noting that C. L. Sonnichsen's *From Hopalong to Hud: Thoughts on Western Fiction* (College Station: Texas A & M University

Press, 1978) opens with his declaration that his is "not a book about Western Literature."

[5] A recent article by Jackson K. Putnam declares that because of the criticism published by Don D. Walker and Max Westbrook "one need no longer argue with the holdouts of the authenticist school who continue to assert the primacy of fact over imagination." See his "Historical Fact and Literary Truth: The Problem of Authenticity in Western American Literature," *Western American Literature,* 15 (1980), 68. Putnam's essay, however, reopens the problem, for his remarks offer no evidence that the situation has changed for either most literary critics or historians: he argues that the novelist should submit himself to Clio's demands or else risk perdition, and neglects to answer the central question of the essay: "Is there not . . . some necessary relationship between factual authenticity and aesthetic truth in a novel, whether the novel is historical in character or one of contemporary life?" (p. 19). The problem of authenticity is discussed best in Max Westbrook, "The Authentic Western," *Western American Literature,* 13 (1978), 213-225; Don D. Walker, "Can the Western Tell What Happens?" *Rendezvous,* 7 (Winter 1972), 33-47.

[6] Sanford E. Marovitz, "Myth and Realism in Recent Criticism of the American Literary West," *Journal of American Studies,* 15 (1981), 97.

[7] Marovitz, p. 97. My emphasis.

[8] Charles Neider, *The Authentic Death of Hendry Jones* (New York: Harper Brothers, 1956). Between 1953 and 1961 the following efforts signalled the renewed interest in the story of Billy the Kid: Edwin Corle, *Billy the Kid* (1953); Gore Vidal, *The Death of Billy the Kid* (1955); Frazier Hunt, *The Tragic Days of Billy the Kid* (1956); William Keleher, *Violence in Lincoln County* (1957); *The Left-Handed Gun,* dir. Arthur Penn (1958); Jack Spicer, *Billy the Kid* (1958); William Lee Hamlin, *The True Story of Billy the Kid* (1959); *The Tall Man,* television series (1960); *One-Eyed Jacks,* dir. Marlon Brando (1961). Brando's film is loosely based on Neider's novel. For more on these and other visions of the Kid since 1881, see my *Inventing Billy the Kid* (Albuquerque: University of New Mexico Press, 1982).

[9] Lewis Nordyke, *New York Times,* 26 August 1956; Martin Levin, *Saturday Review,* 29 September 1956, p. 16.

[10] Wirt Williams, Introd., *The Authentic Death of Hendry Jones* (New York: Harrow Books, 1972), p. vii.

[11] Williams, p. ix.

[12] Eugene Cunningham, *Triggernometry* (New York: Press of the Pioneers, 1934), p. 166.

[13] Ramon Adams's *A Fitting Death for Billy the Kid* (Norman: University of Oklahoma Press, 1960) surveys the major misconceptions con-

cerning the accounts of the Kid's death.

[14] Neider, pp. 189-190.

[15] By way of sharpening my terms, let me provide definitions of two terms that I find synonymous with my use of the terms historical authenticity, verisimilitude, and common sense realism: "conscientious realism" and "facsimile authenticity." Damian Grant, in order to distinguish kinds of realism in his *Realism* (London: Metheun, 1970), defines "conscientious realism" as a realism which "arose out of an appeal to the evident truth of the external world" and which believed that not only could truth be verified by reference to that external world, but that it was literature's obligation to submit to the real world and ballast the imagination with the weight of facts, statistics, and density of texture. Believers in this kind of realism possess "the conscience which protests when it [literature] neglects or disparages external reality, and seeks to draw sustenance from, and exist for, the disengaged imagination alone." Max Westbrook, in his aforementioned essay, stipulates two definitions of authenticity in order to distinguish the kind of authenticity that promotes the creative act from the kind of authenticity that inhibits the creative act. My use of the above-named terms corresponds to his term "facsimile authenticity," which is a restrictive concept that grants the artist permission to create on the condition that "the specifics, all details which have a counterpart in the actual world, must qualify by meeting the factualist standards" ("The Authentic Western," p. 215).

My use of the term "reality," on the other hand, is to identify what results when the novelist transcends a merely faithful and informative account and imbues the described event with knowledge, sympathy, imaginative power, and a moral vision that enables the reader to participate fully in the event. Just how and when this happens is the burden of my discussion of Neider's novel at the point of the Kid's jailbreak—not his death.

[16] Westbrook, p. 214.

[17] Walter Noble Burns, *The Saga of Billy the Kid* (New York: Grosset & Dunlap, 1926), Chapter 17; Frazier Hunt, *The Tragic Days of Billy the Kid* (New York: Hastings House, 1956), p. 288. See also Maurice G. Fulton, *History of the Lincoln County War*, ed. Robert N. Mullin (Tucson: University of Arizona Press, 1968).

[18] Pat Garrett, *The Authentic Life of Billy, the Kid* (Norman: University of Oklahoma Press, 1965), pp. 87-88.

[19] Cunningham, p. 163.

[20] Neider, pp. 78-79.

[21] Kent Ladd Steckmesser, *The Western Hero in History and Legend* (Norman: University of Oklahoma Press, 1965), pp. 87-88.

[22] Burns, p. 245.

[23] Gay, p. 191.

Historical Realism and the American West   49

Even historians, seeking to illuminate the past, may reach questionable conclusions. **June Underwood** begins her essay by claiming that neither fictional nor non-fictional accounts of midwestern pioneering experience support Walter Prescott Webb's assertion that the Plains exerted a more maddening effect on the women than on the men. Discounting this "myth" (invalid stereotype), she shows how fiction and non-fiction of the Plains portray madness as a phenomenon common to both men and women, rooted not simply in reactions to nature but in cultural backgrounds and the difficulties of cultural adaptation. Both diarists and novelists work with the same materials; do they differ significantly in the ways they portray madness in their works? Did the all-too-common phenomenon of madness in the pioneering Plains period provide material especially adaptable to the fictional purposes of novelists? Underwood explores these questions in the following essay.

The author completed her doctorate at SUNY-Stony Brook and is now Associate Dean of Liberal Arts and Sciences at Emporia State University (Kansas), where she also teaches an occasional course on western literature and women in the American West. She scripted and narrated an award-winning television show, "Blessed, Blessed Mama," on a Plains mother and daughter and has published historical studies of women's organizations in Kansas. She is currently working on a book-length study of Kansas women's groups, 1880-1920.

Men, Women, and Madness: Pioneer Plains Literature

June O. Underwood

The Plains, with its wind, sand, and extremes of space and temperature, has a very bad reputation. Rølvaag in *Giants in the Earth* entitles Book II, Chapter 4, "The Great Plain Drinks the Blood of Christian Men and Is Satisfied."[1] Walter Prescott Webb says, "The Plains exerted a peculiarly appalling effect on women. . . . The wind drove some to the verge of insanity and caused others to migrate."[2] In Sandoz's *Old Jules* there are, by rough count, eleven different points in Jules's life when the "monotony of the hills . . . broke through the crust in lawsuits, fights, suicide, murders, and insanities."[3] In short, the environment of the Plains is blamed by all kinds of writers for a whole host of mental instabilities. Novelists use Plains madness as a way to build tension and create character contrast; diarists and memoirists record its effects on everyday lives.

In this study I am deliberately using "madness" in its vaguest sense. The inability to cope, accompanied by slow changes of character and habit, is the simplest criterion for madness. Suicide, an extreme inability to cope, obviously involves mental instability. Depression, traditionally suffered by women and seen in fits of crying, slovenly dress, and an aversion to family and community gatherings, is also a sign. Critics of western literature do not identify violence as a symptom of madness. Some of the violence in the literature is mere lawlessness, but that which breaks out under the pressure of blizzard-beseiged huts, for example, and is accompanied by other symptoms and causes, must be seen as mental breakdown. Personality and cultural factors often underlie the aversion to the harsh land to produce loss of control. In other words, the Plains sometimes exacerbates outbreaks of "lawsuits, fights, suicide, murders, and insanities," but the primary cause is found elsewhere. Causes for mental breakdown range from economic frustration, personal displacement and loss of identity, to guilt and isolation. All these are parts not only of a physical environment but of a mental landscape.

Life on the Plains was tough. Men and women alike faced the limits of their capabilities. Many won out over the environment, forcing it to allow their habitation. Others succumbed to it, going home, going mad, dying. Webb says that women were responsible for the numbers of pioneers who retreated from the Plains. Nothing in the literature bears this thesis out. The American folksong, "Sweet Betsy of Pike," has Betsy telling her fearful Ike, who wants to go home, "You'll go by yourself if you do." In the pulp fiction, *The Soddy,* by Sarah Comstock, Terry, the wife, stays on the claim when her husband leaves. She says, "Dexter has a delusion. . . . I've read about delusions—they come when you're worried and worn past what you can stand. He'll get well—I know it. . . . He'll come back! I'm holding on to the soddy till he comes."[4] Among the diaries and memoirs, as many women as men insist upon staying at critical moments of despair.

Leaving is generally thought to be a sign of defeat, especially by those who stay. John Ise, in *Sod and Stubble,* records the sight of people being driven out by drought in 1880: "The discouraged settlers trekked out of the drouth-stricken country. Day after day they passed by, grizzled, dejected and surly men; sick, tired, and hopeless women."[5] Yet in many of the memoirs and diaries, moving out seemed, like corn mush, to be an accepted part of life. Mollie Dorsey Sanford follows her husband from eastern Nebraska (where she has moved from Indianapolis) through many mining towns and army posts in Colorado before they settle in Denver.[6] In *There Have to Be Six,* by Amelia Meuller, the family moves from Kansas to Texas to Oklahoma and back to Kansas, sometimes in defeat but more often in optimism.[7] Sonora Babb's family of *An Owl on Every Post* moves from Oklahoma to 360 acres in eastern Colorado where they live in a sod hut and then move to southwestern Kansas, where they settle in town. All this takes place over a scant two or three year time span.[8] In Nannie T. Alderson's *A Bride Goes West,* she says, "In all my years of marriage, I never had trees over my head; they could have been planted, but we never lived long enough in one place for them to grow."[9] Moving around seems not only a way to stave off starvation (although that enters into it), but also a way to act, to control. Whole families went further west or east, rented other farms or moved to town, and by this activity circumvented madness.

For those who stayed in place, stability maintained itself in one of two ways. One way was to recreate as closely as possible an older culture. This was of particular importance to women, whose roles, especially if they were married and had children, were generally modeled after the cultures from which they came. In Cather's *O Pioneers!*, Mrs. Bergson, Alexandra's mother, "had never quite forgiven John Bergson for bringing her to the end of the earth; but now that she was there, she wanted to be let alone to reconstruct her old life in so far as that was possible. She could still take some comfort in the world if she had bacon in the cave, glass jars on the shelves, and sheets in the press."[10] In *An Owl on Every Post*, the one effort the father makes to get the sod hut ready for his wife and children is to erect two cedar clothesline posts. The morning after their arrival, his wife kerosenes (to get rid of the bugs) and washes all the bedding in the hut. Both her husband and father-in-law had lived with the bugs for years without bothering to kill them.

This mode of retaining sanity, given conditions in the Plains, was difficult. Neither the kind of farming nor the mode of housekeeping was conducive to an easy application of old ways. Women were hard pressed to maintain the image of the frail Victorian while washing clothes on a scrubboard, chasing pigs, and killing bed bugs. Nannie Alderson notes, "As a guide to housekeeping in the West I had brought a cook book and housekeeping manual which our dear old pastor at home had given me for a wedding present. This book, written by a southern gentlewoman for southern gentlewomen, didn't contain a single cake recipe that called for fewer than six eggs" (p. 38). The section on doing laundry began, "'Before starting to wash, it is essential to have a large, light airy laundry with at least seven tubs.' I had one tub, a boiler, and a dishpan" (p. 38).

Given the nature of the difficulties, many of the pioneers found it saner to actively engage the new conditions rather than attempt to maintain or re-erect the old. Per Hansa, Morissa Kirk, and Alexandra Bergson, to name some fictional characters, all meet the challenges actively. Per Hansa, for example, is ill at ease with the Plains only during the winter when he has no activity to engage in. Men, or women like Alexandra who are unaffected by the Victorian myth about women's place, could work outside, becoming part of the landscape rather than fighting it. Alexandra is only happy outside; the land "seemed beautiful to her, rich and strong and glorious. Her eyes drank in the breadth of it . . ." (p. 65). Alexandra's house is "unfinished and uneven in comfort. . . . You feel that, properly, Alexandra's house is the big out-of-doors, and that is is in the soil that she expresses herself best" (p. 83-84). Morissa Kirk, of Sandoz's *Miss Morissa* (1955), not only is the first doctor in western Nebraska, but also begins one of the first gardening and farming operations in the region.

This active engagement, accompanied by a change of old values and expectations, appears not only in the characters of fiction but also in the non-fictional memoirs. Alderson says, "Back home . . . my stepfather . . . wouldn't dream of going into the kitchen, even to carry a pail of water, and all the men were the same. But in Montana that first spring there would always be three or four in the kitchen getting a meal—Mr. Alderson, Mr. Zook, one of the cowboys and myself" (p. 40). In *Memories of the Old Emigrant Days in Kansas 1862-1865*, Mrs. Adela Orpen reminisces about homsteading with her father and aunt. The family allows the 9-year old Adela a great deal of freedom—she wears bloomers and has her own horse—but the aunt, of course, is tied to old customs. Auntie suffers a breakdown. "She was found crying. . . . She was crying because everything was hopelessly ugly, and even the kitchen floor was always dirty, and it was useless to wash it." Adela's father recognizes Auntie's depression and prescribes a radical action to re-establish her sense of control. "This would never do, so my father straightaway bought her a pony. She must fare forth riding, and go down to the creek and see water there, when there was any. At all events, Auntie must get out of the house and refresh her mind and body with riding."[11] Auntie recovers quickly.

Thus the dangers of mental instability on the Plains were averted in two ways: the first was to re-establish, as closely as possible, the way of the home from which one came. The second was to actively wrestle with the environment, to immerse oneself in it wholly. However, maintaining the old ways, as we saw with "Auntie," was fraught with certain dangers.

The re-enacting of the old ways often magnified the contradictions between expectations and reality; the baggage of an outmoded or inappropriate culture sometimes caused madness. Beret of *Giants in the Earth* feels tremendous guilt for leaving her parents; Letty of Scarborough's *The Wind* has been trained as a genteel southern lady and is helpless when confronted by West Texas homesteading. Mr. Schimerda of *My Antonia* has to leave behind the gaity, music, and companionship which he valued so highly. Frank Shabata (*O Pioneers!*) is forced into a role as farmer which frustrates all his city ways. Guilt, caused by one's early training, isolation from people like oneself, frustration growing out of an inability to adapt, and displacement from one's expected role all serve to drive the characters of pioneer literature mad.

Rølvaag's Beret is the classic case of madness on the Plains. She is frightened by the new life and feels its threats as punishment. She goes into a depression, not caring for her appearance, withdrawing from her family and their meager social life. Her depression, in spite of Rølvaag's ambivalence about the Plains themselves, is the result of the force of her faith. She feels she has sinned against God and thus the Plains wait to punish her:

> Ever since she had come out here a grim conviction had been taking stronger and stronger hold on her. This was her retribution! Now had fallen the punishment which the Lord God had meted out to her. . . . She had been gottenwith child by Per Hansa out of wedlock; nevertheless, no one had compelled her to marry him. . . . Her parents, in fact, had set themselves against the marriage with all their might. . . . Whenever she had been with him she had forgotten the admonitions and prayers of her father and mother. . . . He [Per Hansa] had been life itself to her. . . . Had there ever been a transgression so grievous as hers! (216-217)

This strong sense of religious duty is clearly a part of her culture; others in the Norwegian community suffer as she does. Both Tönseten and Per Hansa tremble when the preacher arrives, for they fear they have committed unforgivable sins: Tönseten by marrying a couple (he is justice of the peace) who badly need marrying and Per Hansa by naming his child Peder Victorious. Both men fear they have committed sacrilege and both weep at discovering God (in the form of the preacher) is not angry with them. The strength of the religious training and consequent possibility for tremendous guilt is clear. Beret's attempts to build a life like her old one lead to impossible contradictions.

Scarborough's Letty suffers from an inability to cope with a new kind of identity. The life she yearns for, the life she has led in the past, is so drastically different from that which she has come to that she has no resources with which to cope. She is totally unprepared to deal with the realities of Plains homemaking. "She realized her shortcomings as a housekeeper; she couldn't put her heart into the work, and then too, she had never any training for it. At home Mammy had treated her like a child that couldn't wait on itself properly."[12] In addition, she had loved the gentle Virginia countryside from which she had come and had passionately wished to be allowed to stay there. As her sanity slips, she daydreams about the world:

> She lived a dual life . . . sun-scorched plain . . . waste of sand . . . leafless mesquite bushes, dead swords of the yucca [and then] a far off land, a gracious smiling country . . . where magnolias opened their waxen petals in lovely curves to show their golden hearts, where yellow jasmine climbed up into the trees. (p. 273)

When Letty is rudely taken from her Virginia life she responds with the lady-like coquetry she has been trained to; her cousin and most of the cowboys she encounters fall in love with that image and it, as much as anything else in the novel, is her downfall. She is an unthinking product of a stereotyping society, but no one, not herself nor the men around her, are aware of this. When she is seduced by Wirt Roddy, the villain, it is merely the finishing blow to her romantic idealism. She kills him and runs into the windstorm, committing suicide.

Both these authors are ambivalent about the role of the Plains in the breakdown of the women. Rølvaag analyzes Beret's religious and familial guilt, but also feels the land causes madness. In the chapter entitled "The Great Plain Drinks the Blood of Christian Men and Is Satisfied," he begins with a description of "the strange spell of sadness which the unbroken solitude cast upon the minds of some. Many took their own lives; asylum after asylum was filled with disordered beings who had once been human" (p. 413). Scarborough depicts Letty as weak and her upbringing as totally inappropriate. Yet she begins *The Wind:* "The wind was the cause of it all. The sand, too, had a share in it, and human beings were involved, but the wind was the primal force" (p. 1). Both authors see the physical environment as a force with which puny humans must reckon. However, each shows those humans as molded by cultural factors which determine their mind set.

Willa Cather is hardly ambivalent about the exaltation she (and a number of her characters) feel in the land. She does not blame the land for madness, but recognizes that some people can't face its rawness. In *My Antonia* Mr. Shimerda's suicide comes during a blizzard, the first terrible winter of his life on the Plains. He, like Letty, cannot forget the world he has left behind. Antonia tells Jim Burden, "My papa sad for old country. . . . My papa he cry for leave his old friends what make music with him. He love very much the man that play the long horn."[13] Mr. Shimerda kills himself, unable to cope with a world in which it seemed "peace and order had vanished from the earth" (p. 86). Antonia establishes, after much struggle, her own "peace and order," and through her Cather makes a statement about the land and possible ways of relating dynamically to it.

Another Cather character, Frank Shabata of *O Pioneers!*, is dealt with in more detail. He kills his wife and her lover in what seems to be a relatively simple act of jealous rage. But his stability has clearly been shaken much earlier. When Marie married him, Frank had been the "buck of the beer-gardens—with his silk hat and tucked shirt and blue frock-coat, wearing gloves and carrying a little wisp of a yellow cane" (p. 143). After Frank's marriage the couple move to a farm and when Carl Linstrum meets him, "he was burned a dull red to his neck band and there was a three days stubble on his face" (pp. 139-140). He becomes infuriated over small things: "One of the Goulds was getting a divorce, and Frank took it as a personal affront. . . . The more he read, the angrier he grew. . . . Marie thought it hard that the Goulds, for whom she had nothing but good will, should make her so much trouble. . . . Frank was always reading about the doings of rich people and feeling outraged" (pp. 148-149). Frank's instability builds up over the years; his erratic temper is frightening to everyone. His displacement, removal from the life in which he felt comfortable and from an identity which he felt was his own, leads to his breakdown and Marie's and Emil's murder.

These four examples of acculturation and identity madness are literary. They are plot-centered, traumatic, extreme. In historical records, however, the breakdowns seem to be accepted as part of the normal burden of life. The diaries and published memoirs show madness as a temporary element in the life of most of the pioneers. Women became depressed and silent for finite periods of time; men became violent and acted out their rage and frustration and then subsided. In *There Have to Be Six,* Meuller speaks of a period in which her mother is "unwell." "Mama be came ill with the flu. Long after her temperature was back to normal and she no longer had to stay in bed, she continued to be listless and despondent. To Hilda and me it seemed as though she did not want to get well; that she had lost all interest in living" (p. 222). The mother refuses to join the Christmas preparations and celebrations and at one point screams frantically at the carol-singing family to be quiet and leave her some peace. In the next chapter she seems to have recovered. Mrs. Orpen depicts her "Auntie," who cried over nothing (or everything) until she got her horse. "Sir, Looney," in Babb's *An Owl on Every Post,* seems to have suffered and survived a lengthy breakdown, without aid from anyone. He lived afterwards in a dugout, fondling his dead wife's hair, eccentric, but able to cope. Sometimes depression or breakdown was cured, or at least modified, by time. At other times, moving or a change in habit acted as a cure.

A distinction needs to be made between the active, long brewing madness of Beret or Frank Shabata, and the temporary loss of control caused by conditions on the Plains. The soddies, trapped in their 14-by-14 foot huts for days during a blizzard, must have had many moments of insanity. Per Hansa says, "In the dead of winter, of course, when the blizzards are raging and we don't see any other folks for weeks at a time, she [Beret] has days when she seems to go all to pieces; but I hardly reckon that as the disease—that sort of things happens to a good many of us, let me tell you" (p. 378). Madness breaks out when the environmental pressures increase. Old Jules points out the result of a drought: "Water was all they needed. . . . [They could remain] a year or two longer,—at the best,—with more of them hanging from the ridgepoles by ropes and getting free rides to Norfolk to the crazy house" (p. 151).

Those who survive such onslaughts of instability seem to do so either by force of their own character, a life-loving tenacity, or through an alliance with someone who waits them out. Romantic men often chose to come west; they sometimes were lucky enough to bring or find hard-headed women to sustain them. This theme of men as dreamers is quite strong in both the fiction and non-fiction. Old Jules's fourth wife, initially a dainty, pretty woman, becomes the hardheaded stabilizing force in Jules's eccentric romantic vision. Sarah Comstock's Terry works in the fields and, when she is too pregnant to do that any longer, drives a medicine wagon, hanging on to the homestead until charismatic but unstable Dexter returns. Sarah Donnelly Wooley, in Fred Trump's *Uphill in the Sun* (1973), marries a music lover and an adulterer, has eight children, and manages to support all of them, including the husband, through much of her life. One of Avis Dungan Carlson's grandparents, in *Small World, Long Gone,* taught her husband to read and regretted it long after, since he became an educated dreamer, but not a farmer. Carlson says of this grandmother, "she bore ten children, the last when she was forty-three and raised seven of them. She cooked with a wood fire, scrubbed with lye soap, washed clothes on a board, raised her own poultry, and grew her own vegetables, made the family's soap and clothing, even to the men's overalls."[14] To come West, someone had to have the vision, the romance, and the force of character to pull others (wife, husband, family) into that vision. But to stay there after they arrived took perhaps opposite qualities.

Thus far, fact and fiction, biography and novels, have been liberally mixed. But in order to understand the role of madness in the pioneers' lives it is finally necessary to separate the two literary modes. In the factual writings, madness seems to be more prevalent and more complex. It is not a single thing; it derives both from the environment and from acculturation; it comes with bad weather, with money troubles, with moving around. It appears and disappears, is minor or major, sometimes tragic, sometimes, alas, merely tedious. It appears in male and female alike and is conditioned by a great variety of factors, including character, company, and the Plains themselves. It is generally not fatal; it is mostly a part of the difficulty of living. At times it makes small dramas in a monotonous life; at other times it simply exists among other things of the quotidian.

However, in the fiction, madness has a simpler and a more dramatic role. It serves as an excellent device for arousing conflict and tension. Beret's struggle against what she feels is the menace of the Plains is vivid and becomes more acute as the novel progresses. That madness, like the madness of *The Wind*, serves as a major plot device. The drama in both cases works itself inexorably toward tragedy.

Madness also serves to highlight the heroism and strength of those who encounter it or actively battle against it. Per Hansa's superman skills and fearlessness are given focus and clarity when contrasted to Beret's passivity and fear. Letty's inability to cope is directly contrasted to Cora's "unwomanly" management of her romantic husband, her household and the land itself. Terry's saving of the homestead is a dramatic and heroic adventure and works partly because of Dexter's weakness.

The violence which marks the fictional insanity is useful to literary plots. Frank's murder of Emile and Marie precipitates Alexandra's realization that she needs Carl Linstrum. She takes on human qualities in her suffering, and thus madness serves to bring greater awareness. As a device to serve literary realists, the brutality of madness is effective; Hamlin Garland in particular depicts the harsh effects of the endless hard work and hard environment.

In short, while madness in non-fiction is complex and woven into narratives bearing other themes, the madness in the fiction often serves as a major dramatic device, for plot, for contrast, or for awakening a character to new possibilities. Fictional madness is perhaps more vivid, yet more simple, than that which occurred in real life. Madness in both worlds brings out the difficulty, the horror, of the Plains environment for some people. It also shows the strength and resilience and insight of others—their love for, rather than fear of, the land. Madness, for men and women alike, was an ever-present part of their existence on the Plains.

The Plains has perhaps gotten undeserved blame—or credit—for causing madness. Like other parts of the human condition, madness seems to accompany the human personality, taking on local coloration as conditions change. It was neither caused by the environment, nor did it refuse to allow blizzard, drought, grasshoppers and sand to aid it. Madness seems to have had as many resources as the settlers themselves.

NOTES

[1] Ole E. Rølvaag, *Giants in the Earth* (1927; rpt. New York: Harper and Row, 1955), p. 413. All further references are to this edition and are included within the text.

[2] Walter Prescott Webb, *The Great Plains* (Boston: Houghton Mifflin Company, 1936), p. 506.

[3] Mari Sandoz, *Old Jules* (1935; rpt. Lincoln: University of Nebraska Press, 1953), p. 410. All further references are to this edition and are included within the text.

[4] Sarah Comstock, *The Soddy* (New York: Grosset and Dunlap, 1912), p. 251.

[5] John Ise, *Sod and Stubble* (Lincoln: University of Nebraska Press, 1936), p. 126.

[6] *Mollie: The Journal of Mollie Dorsey Sanford in Nebraska and Colorado Territories 1857-1866* (Lincoln: University of Nebraska Press, 1959).

[7] Amelia Meuller, *There Have to Be Six* (Scottsdale, Pennsylvania: Herald Press, 1966). All further references are to this edition and are included within the text.

[8] Sonora Babb, *An Owl on Every Post* (New York: The McCall Publishing Company, 1970). All further references are to this edition and are included within the text.

[9] Nannie T. Alderson, *A Bride Goes West* (Lincoln: University of Nebraska Press, 1942), p. 241. All further references are to this edition and are included within the text.

[10] Willa Cather, *O Pioneers!* (Boston: Houghton-Mifflin Company, 1913), p. 30. All further references are to this edition and are included within the text.

[11] Adela Orpen, *Memories of the Old Emigrant Days in Kansas 1862-1865* (London: Harper and Bros., 1928), pp. 51-52.

[12] Dorothy Scarborough, *The Wind* (New York: Harper and Bros., 1925), p. 230. All further references are to this edition and are included

within the text.

[13]Willa Cather, *My Ántonia* (Boston: Houghton Mifflin Company, 1918), p. 90. All further references are to this edition and are included within the text.

[14]Avis Dungan Carlson, *Small World, Long Gone* (Evanston, Illinois: The Schori Press, 1975), p. 17.

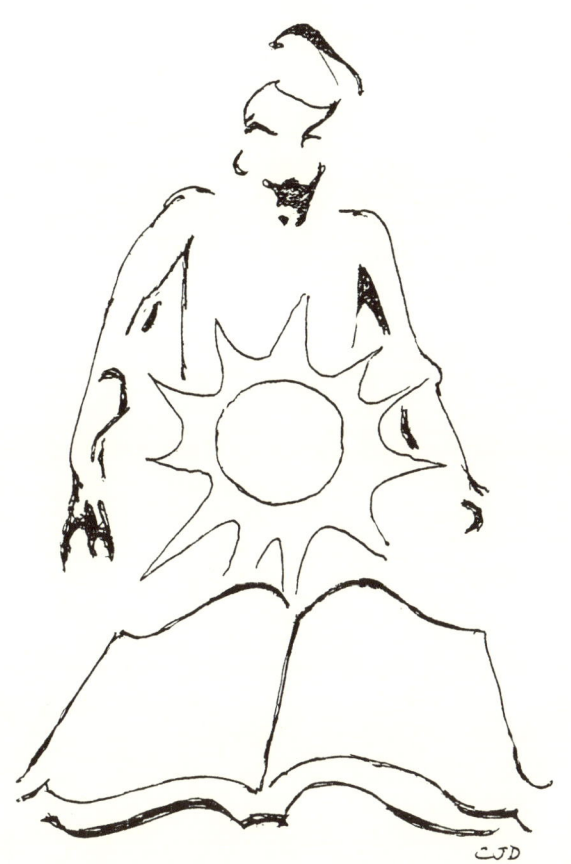

L. L. Lee examines still another way in which the historical realities of the West present both challenges and problems for the writer. Drawing upon Richard Chase's distinctions between the romance and the novel and relating these to the myth of the West-as-Paradise, Lee suggests that we might expect the Mormon presence in the West to inspire realistic novels dealing with society, specifically the family unit. Refusing to dodge the issues by claiming that the Mormon Hawthornes and Melvilles have not yet been born, he points out particular problems faced by novelists who would portray characters in a Mormon society and applies these perspectives to a review of the work of one such novelist, Virginia Sorensen.

Lee has written two pamphlets in the Western Writers Series (Boise State University Press), on Walter Van Tilburg Clark and Virginia Sorensen (co-authored with Sylvia Lee). He is the author of *Vladimir Nabokov* and co-editor of *The Westering Experience in American Literature* and *Women, Women Writers, and the West*. He teaches English at Western Washington University (Bellingham).

Western Myth, Mormon Society

L. L. Lee

That the myth of the West has shaped us Americans and our literature is, I think, a universally agreed-upon truth. Myths are the value systems of our cultures in symbolic order; literature is either a particular embodiment of the myth or a criticism of it.

We can see our western myth expressed in our whole literature, from the first American Western, Sir Thomas More's *Utopia*, written no more than twenty-five years after Columbus' first voyage, to Edward Abbey's *The Monkey Wrench Gang*, published in 1976. These two books may be taken as the limits of the myth, which is the myth of paradise. *Utopia* found a secular paradise in America, whereas *The Monkey Wrench Gang* finds paradise lost. That is, they say that the West is a place where we can be saved or lost, either through a purified social order or by rejection of a corrupt social order. And so the treatment of the myth tends to divide on the values of order and dis-order. More's view, the view of the Europe of his time, was social: in the New World there could be a New Order, like but better than the old. Abbey, post-industrial and post-Rousseau, is romantic and, so, rebellious against industry: the New Order has failed; up with a New non-Order.

But, too, the treatment of the myth tends also to divide on formal matters as well as on matters of value. Abbey's book is basically a romance, an ignoring of society except as a force; *Utopia* is, although fantasy, in a way more "realistic," for it attempts to reflect a societal structure, the source of our realistic novels.

Abbey's book more exactly fits the myth as it usually has been realized in our literature: when we speak of the Western myth we most of the time mean something that celebrates the natural man—who is always an individual and likely to be against society. One must add one thing: Abbey's book is not postpatriarchal—it is almost exclusively masculine in the values presented. Indeed, romantic literature in America has tended to reflect masculine values.

I do not wish to suggest that the idea of the family as reflected in the literature of social order is feminine as opposed to the idea of the individual as masculine. The idea (ideal) of social order can be and usually is masculine also. But it can have a real place for women, not just women in their place. There is no such place in the non-order—order imposed by the romantic individualists of the West (Abbey's book, for instance, presents a girl activist, but she's more a dream of sex than a real person—and that is the almost inevitable type of such novels and perhaps of actualities based on such value systems).

Our type hero, then, is Natty Bumppo, the strong, self-reliant male who is, at least in part, escaping the traditional East. And the East is civilization, cities, and, in particular, the family. What was Cooper's real wish? D. H. Lawrence asks rhetorically. To be Natty Bumppo. And, Lawrence continues, rather nastily, deep inside Cooper preferred Chingachgook to his own wife.

However, the *actual* movement west was not simply a matter of mountain men, cattle drives, etc. Squarely in the West is Utah, the stronghold of a family-worshiping, group-forming, conformist—even if somewhat revolutionary—religious community. One cannot ignore the Mormons, or, more exactly, the members of the Church of Jesus Christ of Latter-day Saints. They too are the West. But what can, did, literature do with their experience, especially a literature that follows the prevailing myth?

The Mormons' own myth (based indeed upon truth) was of group action and group suffering in search of paradise. There were individual Mormon heroes, of course. But the major act in Mormon history was communal, the journey west—a long-continued exodus from New York to Ohio to Missouri to Illinois—and then the great and terrible leap to Utah. They created their stories *together.*

Their religious beliefs were no doubt the source of the group. They began that way. And the Church was and is authoritarian. Mormon dogma insists on the primacy of the family because the family, continuing in the after-life, is the very basis of existence. (One might note that the male is the *head*—women in the after-life will depend utterly upon men.) Too, the early

Mormons preached a kind of religious communalism; in the 1870s this idea was most fully realized in practice in Orderville, Utah, with a functioning religious-communist settlement. When the Mormons met the mountain-man, Jim Bridger, in Wyoming, they did not regard him as a heroic figure but, at best, as an unreliable guide and bad counselor, and, at worst, as a source of disorder. *His* family was ill-defined; his loyalties were vague.

In brief, the Mormons in the actuality of their experience turned one end of the prevailing American myth upside down—although I must admit that they kept the other straighter up than might be imagined. For there were Mormons who approximated Bumppo, Boone, and Bridger in ways, men of action who still accepted the group: the one-time famous or infamous Porter Rockwell, for instance. And Wallace Stegner calls the rather remarkable J. Golden Kimball, the representation of the Mormon *heritage,* "a salty combination of zealot and frontiersman."[1]

Still, at the very center of the Mormon experience, and so necessarily of a literary *treatment* of that experience, is *society,* not the individual. Now, societies usually offer a rich material for the novelist: the English novel depends absolutely upon English society. And Mormon society has a history that seems to hold a tremendous promise. Indeed, the history of the society has been the center of almost all literary treatments of the Mormons—it is only now that that history seems less important.

Perversely, though, the representation of Mormons in fiction has seldom been successful. One can name the novelists who have done something good on almost one hand: Vardis Fisher, Virginia Sorensen, Maurine Whipple, some things of Richard Scowcroft, a couple of books by such non-Mormons as Halldor Laxness, Mark Harris, and Diane Johnson, in which Mormonism has a function. A few others—and that is all.

There have been guesses why: the Mormon Hawthornes and Melvilles have not been born (all young societies—and Mormonism is still young—take time to grow into literature); or the Mormon experience is fatally divided, and no author can find an adequate form in which to embody the division (how does one dramatize the strange mixture of dull Puritan moral attitudes and anti-Puritan celebrations of life in Mormon culture?).

Yet these are not complete explanations, certainly. Let me expand. The major reason for the failure of the Mormons to be realized in literature is *because* they are a society. For the society is not, or so it has seemed to its writers, really rich enough for the kind of novel that it requires. It does not offer the class awareness, class conflicts; the complex variety of high and low culture; the nuances of interrelationship; does not offer, most strangely, the sense of history. Mormon history, all-engrossing as it is to Mormons, is not long and is not complex.

However, the romantic novel of the individual is surely not the way of seeing the Mormons. For the society will intrude, assert itself. If the individual is a believer, he can only be, if historical, a rather melodramatic figure fighting the society's enemies, human or physical. He must conquer or be conquered—and that is melodrama. If he is not a Mormon, he is also certain to be melodramatic, the outsider against the monolithic community. If he is simply a modern believer, he will be dull. If he's a modern rebel, he's going to be a rather narrow rebel, for his society does not offer him the opportunity to struggle against much except an intense social pressure to conform—his mind will not be much involved, especially if he is an intellectual, as such rebels must be. One can answer that Joyce's Dedalus is interesting and that he was rebelling against a narrow society. But Dedalus is interesting in part because he rebels against a long, involved history, one that engaged the mind as well as the emotions.

What has been done, then, if a novel about Mormons is necessarily about the society—and the religion? The average author, i.e., a writer incapable of dealing with the complexities of the religious experience, seizes upon the externals of the society, ignores possibilities, and takes societal sides. And that makes for bad myth and bad literature almost inevitably. Most nineteenth and twentieth century works by non-Mormons, for instance, on the Mormon experience are rabidly, or foolishly, anti-Mormon; social values crowd out language. The Mormons tend to be demonic, but asininely demonic—or they are stupidly comic. They are destroyers of the family, but for the purposes of building up their own totalitarian community (the image of the Mormon family is too strong to be ignored and so must be attacked). The Mormons obey orders almost without question, a trait that is the very antithesis of those of the lonely frontiersman who resists authority and has his private code of honorable existence.

Neal Lambert cites a story in *Harper's Weekly* of December 12, 1857, that is beautifully representative.[2] The Gentile hero (all non-Mormons are Gentiles to Mormons) overhears his wife talking to a man who orders her to come with him. The man is a Mormon; she has been converted. She asks for time, but the Mormon replies, "I can not. . . . My chief orders me to join him." And then, as she bemoans the husband she must leave behind, the Mormon cries, "You have no husband. . . . Your husband in God yet awaits you. You will yet be blessed with the true spouse." The wife does not leave, but she is rejected by her husband who can not believe "that any one who has allowed the Mormon poison to enter their veins can ever be cured."

There are dozens of stories and novels expressing much the same attitudes. A fairly well-known example would be Sir Arthur Conan Doyle's *A Study in Scarlet,* in which the villainous Mormons, supported by their church, raven after nubile young ladies. And there is Zane Grey's *Riders of the Purple Sage*: here the struggle is between the strong individual, Lassiter—who is good—and the evil Mormons who function together to seduce and ruin young women. (In actuality, sex—as opposed to marriage—was not that important to the nineteenth century Mormon society.)

The novel about Mormons written by committed Mormons themselves is no better literarily: it is likely to be pious, preachy, with characters who are only dreadfully good or dreadfully bad types. A character may waver in his faith, but there can be no real dilemma for him. Such novels do usually embody the value system of the family and the community: order is better than anarchic individualism, which leads to the destruction of material and spiritual goods. But there is no real sense of the complexities of the world or of, for that matter, the Mormon society itself. The social order being by definition pure, those inside are safe; those outside are not. If the individual is not a member, he is at fault.

The best novels about Mormons have been written by Mormons or ex-Mormons who are not violently prejudiced. Such novelists have been, first, artists, not propagandists; they have been able to keep a balance between the image of the individual and the fact of the community, to create living people in a world that, seen with a *discerning* eye, can be found complex enough for the realistic work. Their people are people, not abstractions to be saved or lost.

And, but not strangely, most of the good Mormon novels have been written by women. And there is a reason. Virginia Sorensen is perhaps the best of these novelists. Unlike most

Mormon novelists, she has not limited herself to the historical, although Mormon history is ever present in her works, just as it must be. For the past is always with us, especially if we live in concert with others, i.e., in a community. But her attempts have been to see the society whole.

Now, Sorensen's major characters are usually women. And that is because she has seen the paradoxically central place of women in the Mormon experience. Men created the society, dominated the society. But they have lived it rather abstractly. That is, they have lived in it either as parts of a machine, the obedient servants, or as rebels against it; but their experience has been in action. It is the women who have *felt* the society. Or at least Sorensen has created, vividly, such women.

True, she has had major male figures in her works. Erik Eriksen of *On This Star* (1946) is perhaps the most important: he is the standard rebel, the artist whose creativity is stifled by a too narrow culture and so must escape. Erik, though, is not quite a cliché; if nothing else, he does not find the whole Mormon world repellent. Indeed, he feels its attractiveness - and I use the word "feel" deliberately here, for the male artist has always been somehow more "feminine" (androgynous?) than other men. Still, Sorensen has to turn to melodrama to resolve this novel, perhaps because she concentrates too much on the male characters and their value system: Erik, who loves his half-brother's wife, accidentally kills the half-brother; another half-brother kills Erik. Sexual jealousy was, is, a powerful element in Mormondom, of course, and so the actions may be psychologically accurate; but the novel, reflecting a society that is ambiguous about physical violence, becomes strained. Mormonism is man-centered theologically; practically it is not "macho."

Sorensen does much better with her women, because she does not make them pursue heroics. The major character of her first novel, *A Little Lower Than The Angels* (1942), Mercy Baker, also suffers from sexual jealousy (her husband takes a plural wife) and also dies as the book ends—and she is a kind of rebel. But her struggles with her religion are intricately tied to her personal life, to her family life, to her inherited values; she is, in brief, a round character, not simply a series of actions.

In *The Evening and The Morning* (1949), perhaps the finest of her works, Sorensen gives us three generations of Mormon women, a history from Brigham Young into the nineteen twenties. There is the grandmother, Kate Black, who has lost her faith and rejected the society; the daughter, who has questioned the faith but tried to accommodate herself to the society; and the granddaughter, entering her adolescence, who becomes aware of the possibility of evil in the world around her. These three women are intensely sensitive to that world; they can see how the religion is not the society and yet how it is. The novel's plot is not melodramatic but elegiac, the nearest thing to an English novel that any Mormon novelist has created.

I do not mean that Sorensen presents only positive women, that is, those whose values the reader is expected to accept automatically. For instance Kate Black is not always morally admirable; she can be selfish and insensitive. But she is, thereby, the more human.

Yet Sorensen's works represent the end of one way of seeing the Mormon world. Mormonism, as a society, has undergone important changes in the last forty years. And with those changes have come changes in the myth. One can see the possible future in such a novel as Douglas Kent Hall's *On The Way To The Sky* (1969). It is about Utah and Mormons also, the Utah of the 1950s. But the Mormon church has very little function in it; moreover, the novel almost ignores Mormon history (although there is a standard "salty" old reprobate Mormon in it). We are, in short, seeing a new kind of Mormon novel, one without history and so without the restrictions of history, one about the society as it is now with its changes.

In these last forty years, Mormon society has become less inward looking, become, one might say, more secularized, less a society that is defined in terms of itself. In a sense, it is becoming more American. One can speak of the conservatism of the Church, but that is an American conservatism, not necessarily a Mormon one. The Mormon novel, in the old sense of a novel reflecting a single, peculiar culture, may therefore be dead (new ones on Mormon history will simply repeat what has already been done). What we may expect as really new is a Utah novel—which will be different, yes, from a Wyoming novel, but it will not be just a Mormon novel. There will be a loss of variety in our literature, no doubt, but I think it is unavoidable. Still, the Utah novel will inevitably be a novel about *society,* even if the kids still sometimes ride horses without saddles.

NOTES

[1] Wallace Stegner, *Mormon Country* (New York: Bonanza Books, 1972), p. 197.

[2] Neal Lambert, "Saints, Sinners and Scribes: A Look at the Mormons in Fiction," *Utah Historical Quarterly,* 36 (Winter 1968), 64-65.

In an essay sharply critical of western fiction, **Madelon Heatherington** traces failure to its roots in unrealistic depiction of female characters. Utilizing Northrop Frye's theories of the romance, she claims that the archetypal pattern leading to salvation of the people and restoration of fertility to the wasteland is not achieved because the male characters' ignorance of women leads to adventure for its own sake (not salvation) and an asexual (sterile) resolution. Fulfillment of the archetypal myth, according to Heatherington, demands realism of characterization.

Heatherington's essay first appeared in *The Georgia Review* (1979). She has also published articles on John Donne and Homer's *Odyssey,* as well as textbooks on composition and linguistics. Formerly specializing in seventeenth-century British literature and linguistics at Montana State University and the University of California at Los Angeles, she works now for The Burroughs Corporation in San Diego.

Romance Without Women: The Sterile Fiction of the American West

Madelon Heatherington

In recent years, virtually every art form dealing with the American West has become fashionable, profitable, and therefore to some extent respectable—every art form, that is, except fiction. Most novels and short stories about the West are still regarded as merely "pulp" trash, widely read but rarely taken seriously. Ph.D. candidates have written dissertations on western music, films, sculpture, and painting, but in many universities the fiction still limps along on the academic blacklist, lower than Women's Studies or Science Fiction. I propose that a significant reason for this respectability gap, as it might be styled, is that unlike other art forms taking the American West as their source or subject, the fiction has for the most part stayed at the simplistic level of its dime-novel origins and its early popularizers (Owen Wister, Zane Grey, *et al.*), especially in characterizations, and has therefore failed to take into account the complexities both of human behavior, actual or fictional, and of the Western's own genre, the romance.

An important manifestation of Western fiction's arrested development occurs in its treatment of women characters. Even the best of recent fiction about or based on myths of the West, like Kesey's *One Flew Over the Cuckoo's Nest* and Berger's *Little Big Man*, has generally continued to perpetuate a puerile fantasy—by males, about males, for males—that has restricted most such novels to a realm of escapism in which Hawkeye, Shane, or Hud grows solitarily gray, hunting and fishing, building forts and shooting Injuns, happily removed from all adult women forever. Not merely such formulaic pulp novelists as the likes of L'Amour, but often the most respected of Western writers still manufacture the same dreary female stereotypes as Wister and Grey did (types who are by no means confined to fiction about cowboys and Indians, but who appear in some form in virtually all literature): the basic division of women into the purely good and the utterly bad, the virgin and the bitch, Northrop Frye's "the lady of duty and the lady of pleasure,"[1] the Princess and the Poison Queen.

But simply to identify such characterization as shallow, or to disparage it as merely another form of male chauvinism, is to overlook more salient consequences in favor of an equivalently simplistic revisionist-feminist attack. It is a commonplace among students of literature, especially of Westerns, that women have received short shrift in the fiction, that most fictional women are flat and peripheral, and that even when a woman is a central figure (like Catharine the shrew, tamed in one of the few Westerns written by a woman, Marilyn Durham's *The Man Who Loved Cat Dancing*), she is handled in a manner so predictable as to be formulaic. It would be equally commonplace to observe that such treatment is unfair, a shame, a gross misrepresentation, etc. More important, I believe, is the examination of two further consequences arising from limited characterization of women in Westerns: the basic dynamics of romance are aborted in these novels, and therefore most fiction of the American West has never allowed itself to explore and develop its own full potential.

II

Doubtless one of the reasons that much Western fiction remains at best a problematic genre for most critics is that the West itself is still ordinarily seen, even by many who live there, as an uneasy mixture of mythic fantasy and social inertia. The region itself is vague, uncertainly located somewhere over the Mississippi and south of Philadelphia. What "the West" means is even less clear. To many Americans, it stands for the last U.S. frontier, final refuge of the disaffected, inspirational locus of true Marlboro *macho* where people and things are simpler, cleaner, and wiser than in the East. To others, the West is a cultural desert littered with radioactive sheep and half-ton Chevy pickups bearing bumper stickers which vow, "You can take my gun when you can pry my cold, dead fingers off the trigger." The same schizoid response appears toward art about the West, long dismissed by most critics as regional sentimentalism which only the proletariat favor, presumably moving their lips and stroking their Winchesters the while. But suddenly Wall Street brokers wear Justin boots, and all of the arts except fiction have acquired a WASP-ethnic cachet.

Western fiction has earned its lack of status, however, for much of it is still as limited as it was seventy years ago—a striking contrast with what is happening in the other arts about the West. The others have so managed to adapt Western formulas as to have it both ways: they are keeping pace with a more sophisticated (or perhaps a more realistic) apprehension of history and of human beings, but they have also continued drawing on the Western's traditional resources of romance myths. Consider country-western music as an example—a hybrid of country and western, granted, but sharing enough of the Western's resources to participate in its myth. It is clear that at least some of this music has changed in recent years. David Allen Coe wrote a song in 1977 with these lines: "I was drunk the day my ma got out of prison / And I went to pick her up in the rain"—a deliberate parody of the hillbilly's preoccupation with Mama and prison and being drunk, as Coe's lyrics cheerfully declare. Or take Jerry Jeff Walker's "Up against the wall, redneck mother,/ Mother who has raised her son so well"—a play on the radical sloganeering of the 1960s, as well as an ironic treatment of the conventionally syrupy portrait of Mother by such singers as Roy Acuff and the Carter Family. A few other female stereotypes are changing in the music, too: along with Tammy Wynette's conventional injunction to "Stand By Your Man" or Wylon Jennings' eulogy of the "Good-Hearted Woman," loyal as a hound, there is also Loretta Lynn snarling "Don't Come Home A-Drinkin' with Lovin' on Your Mind" or the Amazing Rhythm Aces' sardonic vignette, "Third-Rate Romance."

These sorts of transformations are slow to appear in Western fiction, which for the most part still gives us shallow demitypes of no complexity whatever. Not even stereotypes, much less archetypes, most Western women characters are so formulaic, so diluted, so single-dimensional that their functions in various novels are usually as interchangeable as assembly-lined carburetors. To be sure, there are a few exceptions. Sissy in Robbins' *Even Cowgirls Get the Blues,* Susan in Stegner's *Angle of Repose,* and (to choose an earlier character) Beret in Rølvaag's *Giants in the Earth* are examples of exceptions. None of these women could be removed or exchanged with another female character without seriously damaging each novel's effectiveness and impact. All of these women's presences and perspectives are crucial in the development of their novels. Sissy's spacy gallantry as a focus for Robbins' philosophical meanderings makes her the focus of the whole picaresque book; every character in it functions because of some connection, however tenuous, to her. Susan's and Beret's struggles to come to terms with the frontier, Susan more successfully than Beret, form such an essential part of each work that what Stegner and Rølvaag were saying about human life under alien, often hostile circumstances could not have been so fully realized without these women. But Sissy, Susan, and Beret are exceptional creations.

Much more common are the legions of faceless women who service, follow, or prompt the men—motivators, not actors, important only to the plot, which is primarily concerned with the maneuverings of males. Note, for instance, the roster of "good woman" demi-types customary in the fiction, led by Molly Wood's Schoolteacher in Wister's *The Virginian:*

> The Transplanted Lady: White's *These Folded Hills,* Guthrie's *These Thousand Hills,* Goldman's *Butch Cassidy and the Sundance Kid*
> The Indian Virgin: Fisher's *Mountain Man,* Manfred's *King of Spades,* Guthrie's *The Big Sky*
> The Farm Wife (often combined with The Earth Mother): Guthrie's *The Way West,* Schaefer's *Shane,* McMurtry's *Leaving Cheyenne*

Who can name more than a few of the main female characters in these novels? And these are not the pulps; these are the good books, among the best in Western writing. But even here, the ladies of duty blend into a single creature, whose fictive function is to swell a procession, to gather firewood, to keep the children out of the way and the dishes unbroken in the flour barrel, to minister to her man's marital advances, and occasionally to be abducted, raped, or murdered in order that the men might avenge her. On the whole, the good demi-types are no more distinguishable from one another than are Isolde the Elder and Isolde White-Hands in *Tristan.*

Curiously, neither are the bad demi-types, even though naughty women are ordinarily more distinctive in literature since they cause more trouble; their comparatively greater freedom of action makes them more of a threat to the homeostatic well-being of the heroes than are the dutiful ladies. In our wider literary typology, for every St. Anne, Griselda, Ophelia, or Marmee March, there are half a dozen memorably wicked women like the Apocryphal Judith, Lady Macbeth, Amber St. Clare, Scarlett O'Hara, Carol Kennicott, Jo March, Lady Chatterley, Isadora Wing: rebellious figures, one might almost say "masculine" in their ingenuity, self-sufficiency, and assertiveness. But the appearance in Western novels of even demi-typed Poison Queens is much rarer than in the rest of our fiction. Indeed, there is only one type, The Outlaw Girl. Sometimes she is a literal felon like Cat Ballou or Etta Place, sometimes a perverse Earth Mother like Ma Grier in Clark's *The Ox-Box Incident,* but most popularly, she is The Soiled Dove (a/k/a The Dance-Hall Girl), as in Schaefer's *Monte Walsh,* Steinbeck's *East of Eden,* or Guthrie's *These Thousand Hills.*

Now contrast these indistinguishable figures with the full-blooded archetypes, of which most women in the Westerns are but featureless copies. The good woman can be identified in Jungian terms as the beneficent *anima,* the soul mother objectified as a goddess adored from a distance: Isis, Athena, Mary, Beatrice. Whether as Leslie Fiedler's "Blue-Eyed Protestant Virgin"[2] (i.e., a true Princess) or as the domesticated Princess (the Earth Mother), the good woman stands for transcendence of human baseness, the incarnation of virtue, chastity, mercy, and no bad habits or internal organs. She is the antithesis of the hero, his secular pipeline to the other world of divinity. The bad-woman archetype is more complicated, in part because she does share some wicked ways with the hero, particularly sensuality, and in part because her power over him can interfere with his mythic function as hero, the attempted mediation between savagery and civilization. The Poison Queen is the destroyer of men's souls and the ruination of their bodies, Jung's maleficent *anima,* the seductive castrator feverishly chased but despised once had: Ishtar, Aphrodite, Lilith, Magdalene, Morgan le Fay. Her encouragement of the hero's sensuality (i.e., secularity) can doom him unless he establishes his dominance over her—and over those impulses in himself which she represents—for if he does not de-fang her with his magical, symbolic weapon, he cannot go on to save the world in the name of righteousness, the Princess, and manifest destiny.

Given these two points of comparison (the small number of exceptional female characters in Westerns, and the romance-myth archetypes on which Westerns draw), the trail of flattened women in most Western fiction is faint indeed. The paradox is that the vehicle of romance by which these demi-types are carried to readers is potentially quite powerful—but not if it is limited by internal constraints. Assuming that Stanley Fish is correct, the best "self-consuming artifacts" are designed to push their readers beyond the text and beyond their own minds. Good books, that is, do not merely affirm what a reader already believes, but induce in him a disequilibrium, a happily anxious quest that carries him out of his own assumptions, in fact, past the book itself.[3] But most Westerns are self- and reader-affirmative; they reassure the reader that his attitudes are right and just, that he need not bestir himself to question them. Worse, many readers of Westerns, especially of the pulps, believe that those novels are almost telling the literal truth, as if they were honest-to-God historical case studies about the way the West really was, including the way men and women really were—and possibly should be still. By appealing to this kind of search for affirmable bias, and by fixing characterial "truth" at the level of Barbie and Ken dolls, most Western novels have left unexplored the non-literal, ambivalent, but nevertheless far more powerful truths of their own origins in romance.

III

Even the most conventional Westerns rest on a foundation of romance mythology that can sometimes elevate novels above the limits of formula. This mythology is both received and created about the nature of America, of the West, of good and evil, of solitude and solidarity, of heroism and salvation, of savagery and civilization—and of men and women. In his important study of Western American fiction, *The Six-Gun Mystique,* John G. Cawelti has observed that good Western novels "can be seen as the embodiments of the archetypal pattern of the hero's quest which Frye discusses under the general mythos of romance."[4] As Frye notes, romance is characterized by "its extraordinarily persistent nostalgia, its search for some kind of imaginative golden age in time or space," and by its ritual quest or chase structure, the whole set in an idealized universe removed from the ordinary, real world (p. 186). The Western, we know, is ordinarily located in some region of the West (*Cuckoo's Nest* in Oregon, *Little Big Man* in the Dakotas), usually takes place in the past (roughly 1830 to 1890), and nearly always involves a chase of villains by the hero, with civilization—the Princess, the town—as the prize. Like all romances, too, the Western usually is stripped of mundane concerns like hemorrhoids or excise taxes which might distract the hero from the ritual tests and confrontations required by romance as prelude to deliverance.

Deliverance, the romance/Western hero's principal duty, can be subdivided into two related and sequential tasks. First, the hero must confront evil, usually by undertaking an arduous journey during which he encounters several preliminary sources of conflict before he meets and slays the symbolic dragon which has been ravaging the Princesses, ruining the crops, and generally rendering the landscape sterile. So the romance-hero's social obligation is to eliminate the savagery that has disrupted the community. His second task is to return the community—however illusorily, however momentarily—to the purified, prelapsarian, neoplatonic paradise from which souls are expelled when they are born into this ordinary world of bills, beans, and boredom. The hero's anagogic function, then, is to give us a glimpse of what we could be if we were better than we are.

The point here is that in order to carry out this two-stage process of deliverance, any hero of romance, and therefore of a Western, must accept and conquer various initiating challenges which prepare him for the task ahead. It is because of the initiatory tests that he progresses first to mastery of himself and his world and thence to the salvation of lesser mortals from sterility and despair. In the romance mythos, women play a crucial part in this preliminary testing and therefore in the preparation for deliverance, for because of his encounters with various female archetypes, the hero learns to accept various aspects of himself. He must undergo confrontation and acceptance so that he can recognize the synthesis of those archetypes in what Joseph Campbell calls "the goddess of the world," figures like Gē or Parvati or H. Rider Haggard's "She," and then he must symbolically marry the goddess, metaphorically becoming or absorbing her and thereby multiply enhancing his own powers. At that point, says Campbell, the hero will have achieved "total mastery of life; for the woman *is* life, the hero its knower and master."[5]

Suppose, however, that the hero cannot or will not attempt confrontation, assimilation, and mastery: then he has three less acceptable (because more restrictive) choices. As one, he may project his lack of fulfillment, his insecurity, and his concomitant self-loathing directly onto women, seeing them as figures of the sexuality in himself which, being unacknowledged and untested, has therefore destroyed him. This first choice forces him to fixate on woman as Poison Queen, whom he now sees as an enemy. To some extent, McMurphy takes this stance in *Cuckoo's Nest*. As a second choice, the hero can take the opposite tack and deny his fear and rage about his own reluctance to encounter the goddess; he then projects an overcompensatory reversal of loathing onto woman and now sees her as his antithesis, the Princess, an icon. Most fictional cowboys may seem to have made this choice—Jack Crabb appears to have done so in *Little Big Man*—but I suggest that in most Westerns, the hero's awe around women stems less from throttled rage disguised as reverence than from his having made the third, and worst, choice: the denial that women exist in any significant way at all.[6] This attitude is the worst because if a hero tries to proceed on his task in ignorance of women and what he can learn from them, his capacity for deliverance is severely weakened because *he* is. He becomes vulnerable to unexpected assaults by enemies who take advantage of his ignorance, as Ishtar does in her first encounter with Enkidu or as Brunhilde does with Siegfried. Thus undermined, the hero becomes essentially powerless to effect his primary task of salvation, so he wastes his regenerative energies in mere adventure for its own sake.

Sadly, this is what has happened with most fiction about the West, even the best novels. Hugely and deservedly popular (and not just with readers of the pulps), wonderfully ironic in tone and in their manipulation of Western formulas, provocative and perceptive works in nearly all respects, *Cuckoo's Nest* and *Little Big Man*—representative of the best of Western fiction— still avoid confrontation with the goddess, still use female characters as narrowly and peripherally as Wister did in 1902, and consequently still deny their heroes full romance status.

Kesey's novel is a marvelously complex anticipation of psychiatrist R. D. Laing's proposition, rather like Scaramouche's, that insanity is the only sane reaction to a universe gone mad. Everything in *Cuckoo's Nest* compels us to deal with the clash between individuality and conformity, between self-definition or self-discovery and institutional prescription, even between the East and the West: East Coast technology *versus* West Coast naturalism, the Promised Land re-created by all writers of Westerns. As Kesey advances these oppositions in order to argue for their synthesis, he invokes and then inverts nearly every tradition of Western fiction: the Promised Land becomes an insane asylum, the Lone Ranger helps the Indians to win, the Lone Ranger himself (Randle Patrick McMurphy) is enormously compelling but still a wheel-spinning con man dodging the work farm.[7] Through such inversions and resultant ambiguities, Kesey shows us that the contest is not a simplistic one between McMurphy and the Combine, libido and super-ego, good and evil, Dionysiac rebellion and Apollonian restraint. Granting McMurphy's powerful appeal, granting his vigor and his necessary potency as an antidote to the entrenched sickness of the asylum, nevertheless, Kesey's central point is that balance rather than extremes produces health, and McMurphy is as unbalanced in one direction as Big Nurse is in the other. Were McMurphy's iconoclasm and self-indulgence left unchecked in the world outside the asylum, he would be as dangerous there as the nurse is inside.

But despite her status as the hero's opponent, and therefore despite the necessity of her individuation as part of Kesey's Hegelian argument, Big Nurse gets nothing like the artfully distinctive treatment which Kesey affords the male characters. True, she is made a formidable antagonist. No single character so clearly stands for regimented oppression as does Nurse Ratched, always surrounded by mechanical imagery as harsh as her name: the tools she supposely carries in her purse, her switchboard nurse's station, her black "robots," even her incongruously maternal, implausibly sexual breasts, as machined as the rest of her, "skin like flesh-colored enamel" (p. 11). But hers is basically a one-dimensional evil, for her power is largely derivative, not something she has earned or can exercise on her own; she only symbolizes the impersonality of power. Significance does not reside in her, but merely manifests itself through her. Consequently, when McMurphy attacks her, his act is primarily a political one, a defiant trust-busting assault on the Combine she represents. The Chief implicitly recognizes the political nature of McMurphy's charge when, using Western-formula terms, he describes the scene prompted by McMurphy's responsibilities to his constituents: "We couldn't stop him because we were the ones making him do it. It wasn't the nurse that was forcing him, it was our need. . . . We made him stand and hitch up his shorts like they was horsehide chaps, and push back his cap with one finger like it was a ten-gallon Stetson, slow mechanical gestures" (p. 267) directed against a mechanical woman.

In demonstrating that the Western paradise no longer exists unless people deliberately create it, Kesey shows the danger of imposing a single perspective onto reality, even McMurphy's. But in not allowing Big Nurse any more complexity of characterization than Trampas got in *The Virginian* or Big Brother in *1984*, Kesey thereby weakens the mythic confrontations and the promise of salvation in *Cuckoo's Nest*. The cardboard characterizations in *Little Big Man* have the same effect. Because this *tour de force* could be said to turn Kesey's tragic-comic vision into unbridled satire and demythologizing, the force of romance is dissipated, its generative power sapped, and its salvationary function aborted. Like many contemporary novels, *Little Big Man* focuses on deconstructive process more than on certification of any product. For example, Berger plays with our preconceptions about heroes and heroines throughout the novel, mixing the generic assumptions in figures like Caroline, so that none of the women is taken seriously because few of the characters-in-general are. Consequently, neither of Berger's Princess types has even the little substance that Kesey's Poison Queen did. Amelia and Mrs. Pendrake simply invert the Princess model.

The original Western Princess, Molly Wood, is "spunky," Wister says, so her innocence and virginity—the *sine qua non* of Princessdom, as experience is of Queendom—become valuable symbols of virtue and self-control. Her eventual submission to the Virginian may be retroactively predictable, but nevertheless, the submission is a gallant, self-determined act of completion: "She knew her cow-boy lover, with all that he lacked, to be more than she ever could be with all that she had."[8] With their chaste union, the robust West is given authentication and value by the refined East, a typical "civilizing" role assigned to women in Westerns/romances, but in Wister's book a profound act. Amelia and Mrs. Pendrake, however, are as ephemeral in their influence on Crabb as each is shabby in her origins: Mrs. P. impeccably blue-eyed and a minister's wife to boot, but a closet Soiled Dove who has taken on nearly the whole town; Amelia the Dance-Hall Girl whom Crabb fancies just long enough to give him time to learn shooting from Wild Bill Hickock. Like

Molly and most Princesses, both women are unattainable, but here, they are out of reach through Crabb's choice, not their own. He says he was only interested in Amelia because "all my life I had yearned for a bit of class, and I purposed to achieve it in this niece of mine,"[9] but once she has attained classiness, Crabb abandons her to the lawyer in the Kansas City Hotel. Similarly, he runs away from Mrs. P, not because of anything so personal as queasiness about her behavior or his, but because he was "just worn out with the whole business" (p. 158) of living among Caucasians.

Thus, what these two represent to Crabb is approximately what Molly represented to the Virginian, but the concept of civilization that the two books examine has degenerated considerably since Wister's time. Where Wister was attempting to redefine American society in terms of the code of the West,[10] Berger's hero first can "see no sense to it [civilization] whenever Mrs. P wasn't around" (p. 145) and then later, through Amelia, translates "civilization" into all those useless arts for which Amelia had showed no talent in the saloon: piano playing, refinement of accent, lifting the pinkie while drinking tea. The point is not merely that Molly stood for something powerful thinned out to silliness by Amelia and Mrs. P; rather, it is that both Wister and Berger feel that civilization is approximately equal to manners, gentility, or fashion, behaviors to be studied rather than ideas or ethics to be learned—in short, trivialities women are as well suited to symbolize as Big Nurse symbolized an equivalently shall evil. Once understood, the evil is overcome an equivalently shallow evil. Once understood, the evil is overcome as easily as is the useless good forgotten.

IV

In *The Virginian, Cuckoo's Nest,* and *Little Big Man*—the fountainhead of Westerns, and two of the best Westerns in recent years—the women are significant in a catalytic, supportive fashion, but not as characters. They are props in front of whom the men may snarl or strut, but from whom little independent action is expected or required. Molly feeds the conflict of the Virginian with Trampas, but as another representative of good, not as a participant in the conflict with views of her own. Big Nurse is not much more than the figuration of the Combine;

Amelia and Mrs. P are toys. Even love, a most natural response between hero and heroine in a romance, plays no significant part in the major conflict of such Western novels as these, for few fictional Western males ever feel their hats, horses, or sleep—much less their world—well lost for love.

Should the usual Western hero fall in love, and particularly should he marry any woman but an Indian, he is automatically removed from the action. If he does not voluntarily take himself out, as the Virginian does, then his cronies will remove him. To cite only three representative examples, Crane's "The Bride Comes to Yellow Sky," Schaefer's *Monte Walsh,* and Guthrie's *These Thousand Hills* show that in most Westerns, a married man figuratively becomes a gelding, appallingly sensible and unheroically grounded—literally as well as metaphorically, for a woman takes a man off his high horse.[11] Marriage virtually unmans a Western hero, removing him from truly masculine pursuits, which are essentially celibate and therefore perhaps more holy as well as more fun than those accessible to domesticated males. So a "real" Western man, like a horseback Simon Stylites, lives, works, and plays alone or with other males, saving his *virtú* and his *preux* for roping calves, shooting scoundrels or strangers, and swatting flies on the bunkhouse wall.

That is to say, like most protagonists of heroic literature, the Westerner is typically unmarried and earns respect in the eyes of other would-be heroes through his self-sufficiency and his expertise with the weapons of his trade. Unlike the others, however, the usual Western hero *stays* unmarried, uncommitted, arrested at an adolescent level of sexual and psychological development. He does so possibly because the risks in attempting further maturation would be frightening, certainly because its attainment would exclude him from the atmosphere of pubescent play hovering behind even the direst straits of a fictional cowboy's life.[12] When the Western hero stutters and stumbles like a thirteen-year-old in the presence of a woman, his ineptitude is only partially the result of naïveté, only partially an outsider's unease with the little known, the seldom seen, the rarely realized. His discomfort is also a symptom of his own (or his creator's, or his readers') repressed fears about himself, fears too alarming ever to be consciously acknowledged and therefore impossible to overcome, because nobody—not character, nor writer, nor readers—admits the fears are real.

But the cowboy's is not a homosexual panic at all; it is

an *a*sexual panic, a terror at the possibility of any kind of full emotional sexuality lurking anywhere. A Western hero might get his ashes hauled in Dodge City, if the book were written after 1950, but a committed and loving attachment to even a stereotyped Princess or Poison Queen is usually beyond not only his ken but his impulses as well. Any woman is a threat to the Westerner's monastic playground; so, as much as possible, he simply ignores women altogether. There are exceptions here, too—the Virginian, for example, spends so much time courting Molly that we are obliged to wonder how he gets his chores done—but the more common case in a Western novel is that only men have status or respect and the chance to earn the same, from other men, because only men are familiar threats, externalized versions of the hero himself, predictable, safe, known.

The bulk of fiction about the American West, then, does something virtually unparalleled in romance: it vigorously celebrates the *divorce* of psycho-sexual maturation from growth, heroism, and ultimate salvation. Instead of encompassing, restorative fertility, the typical Western novel supports an erotic ignorance, a debasement of that "chaste" Edenic love labeled by Frye as the "erotic innocence" characteristic of romance (p. 200). The taboo against sexuality in any form is deeply hidden in most Western fiction beneath paeans to the charms of rugged individualism and to the moral enlightenment supposedly inherent in an amorphous "code of the West" derived from nineteenth-century industrial/expansionist dogma and hellfire theology. But as a result of repression, the quest of a typical Western hero almost never takes him deeply into himself by way of significant contact with a woman, since what she might teach him is more dangerous than his willed erotic ignorance. Consequently, almost never does a Western novel free itself from psycho-sexual stagnation.

"Translated into ritual terms," Frye writes, "the quest-romance is the victory of fertility over the wasteland" (p. 193)—but the Western romance is designed precisely to keep fertility at bay. The Western version has little or nothing to do with rejuvenation or with civilization and, like Natty Bumppo, its hero becomes attenuated, even dangerous, once the town has arrived. This literary West, the American version of Avalon, the Hesperides, the Isle of Cockaigne, is a dry land in more ways than one, for in order to keep his own narrow myth of autonomy intact, the Western hero has been forced to refuse the responsibility of furthering the community's needs, and has thereby niggardly withheld fulfillment not only from himself but from all the barren land. Constrained in his quest before he even begins by his inability to accept the most frightening challenge of all, the typical Western protagonist has neglected his best chance of saving his soul and encasing eternity in his mortal lifetime.[13] As a hero, he has been sold short because he has not been allowed to take the one risk that can bring him true salvationary stature: the risk of losing his soul, not to a Princess or a Poison Queen, but to a woman.

END NOTES

[1] Northrop Frye, *Anatomy of Criticism: Four Essays* (Princeton: Princeton University Press, 1957), p. 196. All further references to this work appear in parentheses in the text.

[2] Leslie Fiedler, *Love and Death in the American Novel* (New York: Stein and Day, 1973), p. 294.

[3] Stanley Fish, *Self-Consuming Artifacts: The Experience of Seventeenth-Century Literature* (Berkeley: University of California Press, 1972), pp. xi-xiv.

[4] John G. Cawelti, *The Six-Gun Mystique* (Bowling Green, Ohio: The Popular Press, 1974), p. 30; cf. pp. 68-70, 83.

[5] Joseph Campbell, *The Hero with a Thousand Faces* (Princeton: Princeton University Press, 1968), p. 120.

[6] Larry McMurtry has pungently observed of real, not fictional, cowboys that they are "an excellent judge of horseflesh, only a fair judge of men, and a terrible judge of women, particularly 'good' women." "Take My Saddle from the Wall," in *The Literature of the American West*, ed. J. Golden Taylor (Boston: Houghton Mifflin, 1971), p. 555.

[7] Ken Kesey, *One Flew over the Cuckoo's Nest* (1962; rpt. New York: New American Library/Signet, 1963), p. 17. All further references to this work appear in parentheses in the text. For a lucid analysis of Kesey's portrayal of women, see Joseph M. Flora's essay in *Women, Women Writers, and the West*, ed. L. L. Lee and Merrill Lewis (Troy, New York: Whitston Publishing Company, 1979), pp. 131-141.

[8] Owen Wister, *The Virginian* (1902; rpt. New York: Pocket Books, 1974), p. 306. All further references to this work appear in parentheses in the text.

[9] Thomas Berger, *Little Big Man* (Greenwich, Connecticut: Fawcett Publications, 1964), p. 306. All further references to this work appear in parentheses in the text.

[10] Bernard De Voto, "Birth of an Art," *Harper's Magazine* (December 1955); rpt. in *Western Writing,* ed. Gerald W. Haslam (Albuquerque: University of New Mexico Press, 1974), p. 10.

[11] McMurtry has pointed out that the identifying symbol of the real cowboy is as much the horse as the gun: "The gunman had his place in the mythology of the West, but the cowboy did not realize himself with a gun. Neither did he realize himself with a penis, nor with a bankroll." (In Taylor, pp. 555-556; cf. Cawelti, p. 57.)

[12] This observation has been made by many critics, e.g., Leslie Fiedler, *The Return of the Vanishing American* (1968); D. E. Wylder, "The Western Hero from a Strange Perspective," *Rendezvous* (1972); Cawelti, pp. 49, 61-62; and McMurtry, in Taylor, p. 567.

[13] The phrasing here is borrowed from Campbell: "The meeting with the goddess . . . is the final test of the hero to win the boon of love . . . , which is life itself enjoyed as the encasement of eternity" (p. 118).

PART THREE:

MYTHOLOGIZING IN THE WEST

"Mythic realism," as **Ann Moseley** uses the term, means a blend of realistic subject matter (in Cather's novel, midwestern pioneering experience) with mythic patterns. These patterns derive from vegetation myths of the ancient Greeks and Pawnee Indians and from Jungian archetypes. Never forsaking the realist's concern for credible depiction of sense experience and accurate representation of the human struggle for material well-being and fulfillment of self through love, Cather structures her narrative according to mythic forms and explores human destiny in terms of the realities of spirit or psyche. Her work, claims Moseley, exemplifies a realism of universal truths best expressed in mythic terms.

Moseley's doctoral dissertation (University of Oklahoma) was a study of myth in the fiction of Willa Cather. She has published several articles and presented conference papers on Cather and other midwestern authors. Now teaching at East Texas State University, she is director of the Writing Center.

Mythic Reality: Structure and Theme in Cather's *O Pioneers!*

Ann Moseley

Willa Cather's own definition of realism recalls James's assertion that each writer must be granted his own *donnée*, for to her realism is "more than anything else an attitude of mind on the part of the writer toward his material, a vague indication of the sympathy and candour with which he accepts rather than chooses his theme."[1] This definition also implies, however, Cather's non-traditional and perhaps non-Jamesian idea that there are powerful but unknown forces behind the author's choice of this *donnée* or theme. These forces—mythic, historical, and psychological in origin—combine to determine the writer's choice of his material, and the way in which he responds to these forces determines his artistic success.

Cather herself spent a long apprenticeship period during which she experimented with various subjects and themes—many of which showed Jamesian influence.[2] However, by the time she wrote *O Pioneers!*—which she considers a "first novel"[3] even though it was written after *Alexander's Bridge*—she was ready to "accept" her true subject: the land and people of the Midwest. At this time she was also ready to treat this subject with mythic "sympathy" and realistic "candour," with the unique and yet inherently western approach which I call "mythic reality." In *O Pioneers!* this mythorealistic approach to the land and its people is expressed in both form and theme—in the novel's cyclical structure and in its treatment of man's archetypal quest for unity.

I

Sarah Orne Jewett once told Willa Cather that she should abandon old forms and create a new "kind of writing"[4] which would faithfully portray the land and people close to her heart.

In writing *O Pioneers!* Cather follows this advice, using the tools of reality and experience to unfold a myth about the land and the people of the midwestern prairie. This "myth" is concretely revealed through what Richard Slotkin has called the "myth-artifact," which is either an "actual tale or some sacred image or object connected with the myth" and which "symbolically embodies the mythopoeic perception and makes it concrete and communicable."[5] Narratives from Greek and Pawnee mythologies are inherent in *O Pioneers!*, but the most important artifact in the novel is the land itself,[6] which, through its unique composition as well as through the myths associated with it, forms the basis for the structure of the book.

That the composition of the land serves as a basis for form and structure in *O Pioneers!* has been revealed by Cather herself, who answered Elizabeth Sergeant's complaint that the novel has no "sharp skeleton" with the defense that the land has "no sculptured lines or features. The soil is soft, light, fluent, black, for the grass of the plains creates the type of soil as it decays. This influences the mind and memory of the author and," she concludes, "so the composition of the story."[7] Thus, Cather sees the materials of creation—both in nature and in art—as being originally formless, raw materials to be molded according to the appropriate creative vision. Moreover, she sees both art and nature as being part of a cycle—a cycle which must include death as well as life. Just as the soil uses dead and decayed grass as well as new seeds to create new life, so does she combine in *O Pioneers!* the themes of death and life, destruction and creation. The novel, in fact, is a synthesis of two originally separate and sharply different stories—that of "Alexandra," a positive story about life and creation, and that of "The White Mulberry Tree," a tragic story about the death and destruction of two young lovers. Cather reports that as she wrote *O Pioneers!* these two stories came together for her in what she called a moment of "inner explosion and enlightenment," bringing with it "the inevitable shape that is not plotted but designs itself."[8] This shape—which corresponds to the shape of the land—is based on the universal, and also particularly western, archetype of natural cycles[9]—cycles of the seasons, of human life, and of civilization itself.

The cycle of the seasons is not only basic to the progression of events in *O Pioneers!* but also symbolically appropriate to the action. Like a Shakespearean play, the novel is divided into five parts, reaching its climax in Book IV. Book I begins in the heart of winter, which is the appropriate setting for the death of old John Bergson, Alexandra's father; after covering several years, this book ends in late summer with Alexandra's new understanding of the land and its spirit. Book II, which describes Alexandra's successful farm and narrates the budding romance of her brother Emil and her married neighbor Marie, begins in June and ends in later summer with Alexandra's friend Carl and Emil both leaving the Divide. Book III is set in the winter and, with Emil and Carl both gone, is a period of loneliness and dormancy, much like the quiet that precedes the storm in Shakespearean tragedy. Book IV corresponds structurally to Book II, for it also begins in June and ends in late summer or harvest time. However, whereas Book II tells of the marriage of Emil's friend Amédée and of Emil and Marie's innocent discovery of their love, Book IV describes the funeral of Amédée, the illicit consummation of Emil and Marie's love, and the lovers' tragic death at the hands of Marie's irate husband Frank. Finally, Book V corresponds structurally to Book I, for, although Book I begins in winter and Book V begins in October, the opening scenes in both are bleak and dreary. On the first page of Book I, for example, "low drab buildings" huddle on a "gray prairie, under a gray sky,"[10] trying not to be blown away by a snow storm; and on the first page of Book V an afternoon storm brings "black clouds, a cold wind, and torrents of rain" (p. 275). Moreover, both Books I and V emphasize Alexandra's subconscious search for truth and wholeness, both of which she seeks outside of her conscious self. This search, in fact, leads Alexandra to an understanding and identification with death, for in Chapter I of Book I, she goes "deeper and deeper into the dark country" (p. 19), an image which recalls both the subconscious and death, and in Chapter I of Book V, she goes out in the dark and the rain to seek communion with Emil at his grave site.

The emphasis on the seasons and on related events in *O Pioneers!* recalls a similar emphasis in primitive land and vegetation myths, and there are, in fact, several important parallels between the novel and these myths. With such myths in mind, it seems no coincidence that the deaths of Amédée, Emil, and Marie all occur at harvest time—the season during which ancient sexual and sacrificial rites were performed to insure continued fruitfulness of the land.[11] Indeed, the imagery surrounding Emil and Marie's final meeting emphasizes the harvest setting and Emil's impending death. As he approaches the orchard where he finds Marie, Cather writes that "Everywhere the grain stood ripe and the hot afternoon was full of the smell of ripe wheat" (p. 257). He felt separated from himself, and it seemed to him that "His life poured itself out along the road before him as he rode to the Shabata farm" (p. 258), an image which sharply foreshadows the tragic sacrificial/murder scene in which the blood of both Emil and Marie is spilled, staining the pure white mulberries on which they are lying just as the blood of Pyramus and Thisbe had darkened the white mulberries surrounding Ninus's tomb.

While the universal vegetation cycle in *O Pioneers!* is reminiscent of many related land myths, two of these seem more closely related than others to the specific events of the Bergson family story: the Pawnee creation myth and the Greek myth of Demeter and Persephone. The Pawnee myth visualizes all life as stemming from the primal union between Father Heaven and Mother Earth. According to Hartley Alexander, this myth assumes that "The power in the earth which enables it [the corn] to bring forth comes from above. . . . The kernel is planted within Mother Earth and she brings forth the ear of corn, even as children are begotten and born of women. . . ."[12] In the novel, the union of Heaven and Earth is suggested by the dream union of the heavenly spirit or Genius of the Divide and Alexandra herself, who represents both humanity and the land. Implying this union, Cather writes that when Alexandra returns to the Divide from the river country, she looks at the land with "love and yearning" and is in turn answered by the "great, free spirit" of the Divide bending to her "lower than it ever bent to a human will before" (p. 65).

Moreover, according to Pawnee mythology, birds are important intermediaries between the sky and the earth, and in *O Pioneers!* birds play a correspondingly important role. For example, Ivor, the prophet of the Divide, attracts ducks, a crane, and even a seagull to his cave in the hill; Alexandra and Emil watch a wild duck soar into the heavens; and Alexandra alone gazes after a hawk as it flies up into the brilliant blue sky. Alexandra is representative of the land and the earth, but as suggested by her relationship with the birds and the spirit of the Divide, she also looks for meaning beyond her cornfields. Her comprehensive view of life is reflected in the success and wholeness of her farm, where the country "seems to rise a little to meet the sun" (p. 76) and where "The air and the earth are curiously mated and intermingled, as if one were the breath of the other" (p. 77).

In *O Pioneers!* the Genius of the Divide is a deeply complex mythic figure. On one level, he is representative of celestial or spiritual forces; on another level, however, he is representative of the land itself and of all phases of life enacted within the land, including that of death.[13] In this role, the spirit of the Divide recalls the ancient god Pluto, or Hades, who is best known as the god of death, but who is also a fertility god reputed to enrich men "with the abundance of the field and the fecundity of the flocks."[14] And while the Genius of the Divide recalls the figures of Hades, Alexandra and the major events of the novel are even more reminiscent of the related myth of Demeter and Persephone.

According to this myth, Persephone was picking flowers in a meadow when Hades, god of the underworld, suddenly appeared and abducted her. For nine days and nine nights, Demeter mournfully sought her daughter, until finally the sun told her where she was. After this, Demeter made all the land barren until Zeus forced Hades to allow Persephone to return to the earth for two parts of each year. Thus, as Fox has recognized, both death and life, the full cycle of growth and decay as well as the rebirth of spring, are symbolized in the mother and daughter, who are actually dual goddesses,[15] both of whom are necessary to represent the complete cycle of nature.

In the novel, Alexandra combines characteristics from both goddesses. With her reddish yellow coloring, she is unmistakably related to yellow Demeter, the corn goddess of the Greeks. Like Demeter, she rules over the farmland of the Divide, and it is largely her strength and ingenuity that cause its abundant productivity. Moreover, she is loved by a fertility god, a god associated with the sky and the land, just as Demeter was loved by Zeus, whose dual functions as god of the heavens and god of fertility[16] make him the appropriate father for Persephone. Also, just as Demeter sadly seeks her daughter throughout the world, so too does Alexandra haunt the graveyard, the land of the dead, in a futile attempt to recover Emil, the lost brother who was like a child to her.

Alexandra, however, is allied not only to the life and growth associated with Demeter, but also with death and decay as associated with Persephone. For example, when the novel opens, her father's terminal illness and the gloom of winter prompt her to voice a tentative death wish: "I wish," she says, "we could all go with him and let the grass grow back over everything" (p. 16). Also, just as Persephone, having eaten the pomegranate seed, willingly lives in the world of the dead for a third of the year, so does Alexandra spend most of her time in the bleak season following Emil's death in the Norwegian graveyard where he is buried. Once, after she has been caught there in a rainstorm, she tells Ivar "I think it has done me good to get cold clear through like this once. . . . After you get cold clear through, the feeling of the rain on you is sweet. It seems to bring back feelings you had when you were a baby. It carries you back into the dark, before you were born; you can't see things, but they come to you, somehow, and you know them and aren't afraid of them. Maybe it's like that with the dead. If they feel anything at all, it's the old things, before they were born" (pp. 280-281). Only after identifying with the dead in this way can Alexandra begin to understand and accept death.

Moreover, having once entered the land of the dead, Alexandra, like Persephone, longs to remain. After she returns home and goes to bed in the dark, "it occurred to her for the first time that perhaps she was actually tired of life. All the physical operations of life seemed difficult and painful. She longed to be free from her own body, which ached and was so heavy. And longing itself was heavy: she yearned to be free of that" (p. 282). As she lies there, she again has her old girlhood dream of the vegetation god—of the Spirit of the Divide—but this time her lover is quite obviously associated with death:

> He was with her a long while this time, and carried her very far, and in his arms she felt free from pain. When he laid her down on her bed again, she opened her eyes, and, for the first time in her life, she saw him, saw him clearly, though the room was dark, and his face was covered. He was standing in the doorway of her room. His white cloak was thrown over his face, and his head was bent a little forward. His shoulders seemed as strong as the foundations of the world. His right arm, bared from the elbow, was dark and gleaming, like bronze, and she knew at once that it was the arm of the mightiest of all lovers. She knew at last for whom it was she had waited, and where he would carry her. That, she told herself, was very well. Then she went to sleep. (pp. 282-283)

As this passage shows, Alexandra is resigned to the cold, wintry season and even to her own death, but the ever-revolving cycle of the seasons moves on, and, as she later tells Carl, her dream does not come true in the way she thought it would. Instead, after her subconscious visit to the world of the dead, she is reborn into a more fulfilling life than ever before, as illustrated by her magnanimous visit to Frank to assure him of her forgiveness and by her plans to marry her old friend Carl.

Thus continues the cycle of life, death, and rebirth which is so basic to the novel and which is symbolized throughout by the progression of the seasons. In *O Pioneers!* then, autumn and winter are shown to be seasons of harvest and death, during which it is easy to believe that in the "dead landscape the germs of life and fruitfulness were extinct forever" (p. 188). However, the events of the novel also show that the seeds of new life are only sleeping, that they will wake again to new life and beauty, and that the cycles of life will continue.

As the novel began, Emil and Marie were small children, and Carl, Alexandra, and her brothers were adolescents; as the novel ends, Emil and Marie have moved from childhood to adulthood to death, and Alexandra and Carl have moved from adolescence to adulthood to marriage and new life, with certain responsibilities toward several second generation nieces and nephews. The Divide itself has evolved from a primitive, undeveloped prairie to an improved farmland, and the social life of the Divide, under the stabilizing presence of a strong Church, has extended from the family to the community. Moreover, at the end of the novel, the prairie society contains such "advanced" social institutions as the university Emil attends and the prison where Frank is incarcerated for his crime. Thus, the novel implies that, just as the cycle of the seasons is inevitable, so too are those larger and less easily recognizable cycles of human life and civilization—in this case the microcosmic civilization of the American West.

II

In addition to being a basis for the cyclical structure of *O Pioneers!*, the land is also a basis for the theme of mythic power and unity. Moreover, the archetypal quest for unity which informs the novel takes both a personal form and a universal one. In the beginning of *O Pioneers!* Alexandra and her family are in conflict with the land, which is obviously the most powerful force on the Divide. Cather writes that "the great fact was the land itself, which seemed to overwhelm the little beginnings of human society that struggled in its sombre wastes," and that "the land wanted to be let alone to preserve its own fierce strength, its peculiar, savage kind of beauty, its uninterrupted mournfulness" (p. 15). At this time, the land is a "wild thing" with "ugly moods" (p. 20), unfriendly to man and his plow, whose imprint is thus far "insignificant" (p. 19) on its face.

Old John Bergson is intimidated and confused by the force of the land, but he is perceptive enough to realize that the problem might lie in the farmers rather than in the land itself. The prairie farmers' fruitless struggle against the land continues for several years after John Bergson's death, and indeed, not until Alexandra learns to love and submit to the land does it produce abundantly for her. When Alexandra does make her commitment to the high land on the Divide, Cather declares that "For the first time, perhaps, since that land emerged from the waters of geologic ages, a human face was set toward it with loving and yearning" (p. 65).

Thus begins a new relationship between Alexandra and the land—a relationship that has undertones of sexuality and overtones of mysticism. Alexandra's role in this relationship is an androgynous one. For example, under her masculine plough, the country "rolls away from the shear, not even dimming the brightness of the metal, with a soft, deep sigh of happiness" (p. 76), and the "frank and joyous" country "gives itself ungrudgingly to the moods of the season, holding nothing back" (p. 76). However, Alexandra also gives of herself to the land: there were "days when she was close to the flat, fallow world about her, and felt, as it were, in her own body the joyous germination in the soil" (p. 204). She understands that her success is a free gift from the land itself and that it stems from her love for and submission to it. She tells Carl that "We hadn't any of us much to do with it. . . . The land did it. It had its little joke. It pretended to be poor because nobody knew how to work it right; and then all at once, it worked itself. It woke up out of its sleep and stretched itself and it was so big, so rich, that we suddenly found we were rich, just from sitting still" (p. 116). Having learned to respect the power and order inherent in the land and in all nature, Alexandra is rewarded by being a recipient of nature's boons as well as by being made to feel that she herself is an integral part of nature.

From the moment that Alexandra does yield her life to the Genius of the Divide, her own personal and psychological existence becomes extremely complicated. Max Westbrook has said that "in Western realism the unconscious mind is primary,"[17] and indeed from this point in Alexandra's life her subconscious does seem more important than her conscious mind. In fact, she begins to feel an almost mystical identification with the land. During the winter, Cather declares, "Her personal life, her own realization of herself was almost a subconscious existence; like an underground river that came to the surface only here and there, at intervals months apart, and then sank again to flow on under her own fields" (p. 203).

The most vital part of Alexandra's subconscious existence is her dream life, for Alexandra has a recurring dream which closely matches Jung's description of the "big" or "meaningful" dreams which originate in the collective unconscious.[18] In her dream-like state,

> she used to have an illusion of being lifted up bodily and carried lightly by some one very strong. It was a man, certainly, who carried her, but he was like no man she knew; he was much larger and stronger and swifter, and he carried her as easily as if she were a sheaf of wheat. She never saw him, but, with eyes closed, she could feel that he was yellow like the sunlight, and there was the smell of ripe cornfields about him. She could feel him approach, bend over her and lift her, and then she could feel herself being carried swiftly off across the fields.
> (p.206)

In its similarity with the imagery of vegetation myths, this vision connects Alexandra's personal unconscious with the collective unconscious. Jung has declared that those important dreams stemming from the collective unconscious occur most often "during the critical phases of life in early youth, puberty, at the onset of middle age (thirty-six to forty), and within the sight of death."[19] It is significant, then, that Cather reports this dream to have occurred to Alexandra during her girlhood, when she is forty years old, and finally when, because of her brother's tragic death, she is indirectly wishing for death herself.

Alexandra's dream also performs a Jungian function in attempting to restore psychological balance by "producing dream material that re-establishes in a subtle way, the total psychic equilibrium."[20] That is, in her dream, Alexandra seeks the femininity that has been denied her in the basically masculine role which she has lived as a farmer who plows the land, as the head of a large household, and as a leader in her community. In her psyche, therefore, the *animus* or masculine side of her nature has become dominant. As Jung explains,

> ... The animus is the deposit, as it were, of all woman's ancestral experiences of man—and not only that, he is also a creative and procreative being, not in the sense of masculine creativity, but in the sense that he brings forth something we might call the *logos spermatikos,* the spermatic word. Just as a man brings forth his work as a complete creation out of his inner feminine nature, so the inner masculine side of a woman brings forth creative seeds which have the power to fertilize the feminine side of man.[21]

Subconsciously, Alexandra projects her *animus* onto the archetypal male figure of her dreams, a figure who represents and shares her own creative nature. In addition, she seeks psychological fulfillment in her relationship with Carl who, because of the weakness he shows in his struggle with the land and because of his sensitive and artistic nature, seems to be dominated by the *anima,* the spiritual or feminine aspect of his nature. The marriage of Carl and Alexandra, then, is a physical and emotional attempt to restore psychological balance to both characters just as Alexandra's dream is a subconscious attempt to restore balance to her own personality.

The search for unity which pervades the novel is reflected not only by Alexandra's personal search for wholeness in her relationship with the land and in her marriage to Carl but also by Cather's larger quest for cosmic unity and for a sense of oneness with nature, a quest which is reminiscent of such writers as Coleridge, Thoreau, and especially Whitman for whose poem the book was named. Like Whitman, Cather is concerned with the basic antiphonies of the soul and body, and like him, she is also optimistic about an ultimate mystical union of the flesh and the spirit, of man and nature. Her mystical hope for spiritual continuity after death is indicated in the novel, for example, by the symbolic presence of the two white butterflies which flutter over the blood-stained bodies of Emil and Marie, a scene which holds promise of an ultimate union of souls who were separated in their finite existence. The possibility of man's unity with nature is also suggested throughout the novel by Alexandra's mystical identification with the land. At the end of the novel, for example, Carl tells her, "You belong to the land . . . as you have always said. Now more than ever" (p. 309). And in this sense, Cather's conclusion is mystical and mythic rather than sentimental: "Fortunate country," she says, "that is one day to receive hearts like Alexandra's into its bosom, to give them out again in the yellow wheat, in the rustling corn, in the shining eyes of youth" (p. 309).

Implied in this conclusion is the fulfillment of the two major archetypes which are present throughout *O Pioneers!*: that of life, death, and rebirth as represented in the cycles of humanity, of nature, and of the country itself; and that of the universal quest for unity in multiplicity and for a sense of oneness in all nature. Cather's subject—the land and the people of the Midwest—is a deeply real one, and her treatment of this subject is a unique blend of myth and realism—in particular of western realism, which places more importance on realities of the spirit or the psyche than on physical or social realities.

Leaving ample room in the realm of realism for such unique and original approaches as Cather's, Henry James has recognized that "The house of fiction has, in short, not one window, but a million—a number of possible windows not to be reckoned, rather every one of which has been pierced, or is still pierceable, in its vast front by the need of the individual vision and by the pressure of the individual will."[22] Willa Cather has followed James's advice in developing her own brand of realism—a mythic realism which portrays universal archetypes and psychological truths. Through this approach, Cather is able—as she phrases it—to open a "square window" onto the world and let in the "fresh air"[23] of truth; in *O Pioneers!* she indeed finds her own unique vision, her own window in the house of fiction.

NOTES

[1] Willa Cather, "The Novel Démeblé," in *On Writing* (New York: Alfred K. Knopf, 1949), p. 37.

[2] For a perceptive discussion of some of the relationships between Cather and James, see James E. Miller, Jr., "Willa Cather and the Art of Fiction," in *The Art of Willa Cather*, ed. Bernice Slote and Virginia Faulkner (Lincoln: University of Nebraska Press, 1974).

[3] See Cather, "My First Novels (There Were Two)," in *On Writing*, pp. 91-97. It is also interesting to note that when Cather prepared her novels and stories for a complete edition, she made *O Pioneers!* the first volume.

[4] Willa Cather, Interview with Latrobe Carroll, *Bookman*, 53 (1921), 21.

[5] Richard Slotkin, *Regeneration Through Violence* (Middletown, Connecticut: Wesleyan University Press, 1973), p. 8. Much of Slotkin's discussion of myth is used on Philip Wheelwright's ideas as expressed in "The Semantic Approach to Myth," in *Myth: A Symposium*, ed. Thomas A. Sebeok (Bloomington: Indiana University Press, 1970).

[6] The fact that the structure of *O Pioneers!* is based on the land places it squarely in the western fictional tradition. John R. Milton has observed, for example, that novelistic form is usually "geared to the qualities indigenous to the region" and that the western novel in particular is "dominated by its landscape." See Milton, "The Western Novel: Whence and What?" in *Interpretive Approaches to Western American Literature*, ed. Daniel Alkofer and others (Pocatello: Idaho State University, 1972), p. 17.

[7] Willa Cather, quoted in Elizabeth Shepley Sergeant, *Willa Cather: A Memoir* (Philadelphia: J. B. Lippincott, 1953), p. 97.

[8] Cather, quoted in Sergeant, p. 116.

[9] James Miller has seen a similar emphasis on cycles in *My Ántonia*. See his article "*My Ántonia*: A Frontier Drama of Time," *American Quarterly*, 10 (1958), 476-484.

[10] Willa Cather, *O Pioneers!* (1913; rpt. Boston: Houghton Mifflin, 1941), p. 3. Future references to this source will be given within the text.

[11] James Frazer's comment that in primitive societies "illicit love

tends directly or indirectly to mar the fertility and to blight the crops" seems applicable to the almost sacrifical scene in *O Pioneers!* in which the young unmarried lovers Emil and Marie are murdered. Frazer further comments that many ancient societies held annual sacrifices to corn spirits and tree spirits, a ritual that seems particularly appropriate to the novel in view of Marie's propensity for talking to trees and of the lovers' tragic death in the orchard. See *The New Golden Bough*, ed. Theodore H. Gaster (New York: S. G. Phillips, 1959), p. 90.

[12] Hartley Burr Alexander, *North American Mythology*, Vol. 10 of *The Mythology of All Races*, ed. Louis Herbert Gray (Boston: Marshall Jones, 1916), 92. For further discussion of the Pawnee myth in *O Pioneers!* see J. Russell Reaver, "Mythic Motivation in Willa Cather's *O Pioneers!*" *Western Folklore*, 27 (1968), 19-25.

[13] For a Freudian discussion of the Love-Death struggle in *O Pioneers!* see Sister Peter Damian Charles, O. P., "Love and Death in Willa Cather's *O Pioneers!*," *College Language Association Journal*, 9 (1965), 140-150.

[14] William Sherwood Fox, *Greek and Roman*, Vol. I of *The Mythology of All Races*, ed. Louis Herbert Gray (Boston: Marshall Jones, 1916), 234.

[15] Fox, p. 231.

[16] Fox, p. 160.

[17] Max Westbrook, "Conservative, Liberal, and Western: Three Modes of American Realism," *South Dakota Review*, 4 (Summer 1966), 14.

[18] C. G. Jung, *The Basic Writings of C. G. Jung*, ed. Violet Staub de Laszio (New York: Modern Library, 1959), p. 373.

[19] Jung, p. 373.

[20] C. G. Jung, "Approaching the Unconscious," in *Man and His Symbols* (1964; rpt. New York: Dell, 1968), p. 34.

[21] Jung, *Basic Writings*, p. 179.

[22] Henry James, "Preface" to *The Portrait of a Lady* (1908; rpt. New York: Augustus M. Kelley, 1970), p. x.

[23] Cather, "On *The Professor's House*," in *On Writing*, p. 31.

Mythologizing in the West can take two forms: adaptation of old myths and creation of new ones. **James Saucerman** shows how the poet Thomas Ferril has done both, though Ferril's mythmaking poems seem to be more successful than those which draw upon classical sources. Perhaps the failure of convincing classical motifs is less significant to the evolving literary tradition of the West than Ferril's success in generating local myths from the realistic events, personages, and artifacts of the Rocky Mountain region.

A native Coloradoan, Saucerman is Professor of English at Northwest Missouri State University. His doctoral dissertation at the University of Missouri-Columbia was on Emerson's use of geologic imagery. He has published on Emerson, Twain, and western American poetry and has presented conference papers on a number of American authors.

Alien Myth and Natural Myth in the Poetry of Thomas Hornsby Ferril

James R. Saucerman

> He told me that the mountain idea got
> Mixed up with God and was hard to explain.
>
> "Orientation," Thomas Hornsby Ferril[1]

Realism is a necessary ingredient of the natural mythic consciousness of the American West. But while the American West is conspicuous in this circumstance it is not unique, for myths normally generate from the particular locale of the men and women creating them. Once established, however, they tend to become fixed; repeated in the same classical forms these beautiful stories dwell comfortably in a new environment. Job, Vulcan, or Apollo may be recalled for the sake of their exhibition of essential human values but perhaps not quite serve to effectually reactualize human mythic experience in the present. On the other hand, new myths generating out of our commonplace experiences, because of their realistic nature, may seem to lack the dignity of the formulated classical myths. Or they may be "hard to explain" (as the trapper suggests in the epigraph above) without the security of the familiar tale.

Thomas Hornsby Ferril experiments with both modes in his poetry. He borrows classical figures to enhance particular experience, and he allows myths to generate naturally as realistic actions fall into archetypal patterns that transcend cosmic planes. However, his attempts to interweave alien classical myths with western American landscape are less successful than his local myths that generate from the realistic events, personages, and artifacts of the Rocky Mountain region. Like the ancient Greeks, who humanized their mythic world by making "familiar, local habitation give reality to all mythic beings,"[2] Ferril finds in local historical experience the symbols of universal being.

I

The co-existence of two extreme time scales, the immediate historical past superimposed in the seemingly timeless geologic eras, in the same realistic locale offers Ferril a mythmaking freedom to range across differing dimensions of time while yet allowing his myths a local-color anchoring. Thus the Rocky Mountain region encourages him to harmonize with Mircea Eliade's identification of two aspects of time that separate the profane from the sacred: "The one is an evanescent duration, the other [the latter] a 'succession of eternities'" wherein existence of the ancient past surfaces in the present living moment to sacralize the natural event.[3]

His awareness of the same duality of time helps Ferril to escape what he identifies as the devitalizing "low-grade mysticism" frequently found in much of the literature of the Rocky Mountains. In an essay first published in *The Saturday Review,* Ferril writes that too often "the religious impulse, or mysticism, excited by landscape thwarts the poet and causes him to waste his time."[4] He faults otherwise successful poets for surrendering their talents to an abstract "God-finding" when they write about massive mountain landscapes; thus they move away from the function of poetry—Walt Whitman as he writes about the Colorado Rockies and Samuel Taylor Coleridge as he writes about the Alps. "The Indians were the last to write successful religious poetry about this region," Ferril writes; "had Coleridge and Whitman lived long ago in Walpi, their God need not have been 'The Invisible.'"[5] The appropriate solution is to use the literal landscape rather than adopting Garden of the Gods platitudes.[6]

Ferril, as poet, has the detachment with which to observe but not deny his own finitude. He is not overwhelmed by his environment primarily for three reasons: he is personally and historically at home there; he perceives the scientific nature of geologic process; and, finally, he makes the mountains and the plains become sacred ground. His natural myths revere the lives of people more than they adore distant gods. The people's lives are hallowed by a kind of original religious participation in life caused by the manifestation of spirit in their own lives. Ferril's perspective allows him to escape the inauthentic state of fallenness described by Heidegger as a state wherein man fails to distinguish his own Being from the nonhuman condition.

He recognizes the "radical duality between the human and the nonhuman," between the sense of his own existence and the surrender to that outer public necessity in which the "individual constantly obeys commands and prohibitions" of the outer public world.[7] This existential perception, the existential victorious use of anguish and suffering, is the human end of the radical duality described by Heidegger when he writes:

> That being that exists is Man. Man alone exists. Rocks are, but they do not exist. Trees are, but they do not exist. Horses are, but they do not exist.[8]

Ferril uses his locale in changing time dimensions to explore what it means to be human. The same existential consciousness that separates man from the "other" is also the locus of the mythic consciousness. For Ferril, as for Heidegger, "Man is the being who is immediately present to the world and who must live out his life in and through his inescapable relationship to the world."[9]

The poem "Blue Stemmed Grass" suggests this distinction between simply being present and existing in a Heideggerian sense. Analyzing parts of an individual stem of blue-stemmed grass does not help the narrator of the poem understand his being; the analysis is too much a part of the nonhumanness:

> There's blue-stemmed grass as far as I can see,
> But when I take the blue-stemmed grass in hand,
> And pull the grass apart, and speak the word
> For every part, I do not understand
> More than I understood of grass before.[10]

Even tracing the grass "through meadow beasts to men" is still merely describing the "mechanical economies" of the grass. Not himself like grass or cattle, he has detachment that allows him to witness and to speculate (as might Heidegger's authentic man) on his own finitude. It is a polarity because only his own infinitude can give him the power to recognize his finitude, to step back from his being-in-the-midst-of-the-world to view his Being-in-the-world. His very existence rests in this ability and it becomes the duty of the poet to articulate his position. Thus the poem ends with his rhetorically asking "if phosphorus or nitrogen / Can make air through lips mean hell or heaven."[11] There is, then, a distinction between particular forms as ends in themselves and those same forms as manifestations of a broader continuum of existence.

Ferril often uses commonplace images for the particular forms of his poetry, for they help to locate himself and his subject in actual place. In "High Passage" a honeybee (the first to travel farther West) is paralleled with the crushed, dried English rose in the pocket of the hunting vest (or in the mind) of an immigrant who is also "floating further West."[12] A single stem of wheat, the clotting blood in the heart of a freezing pronghorn antelope, the sound of "a pigeon's drumming" at Ft. Laramie all play a part in his thereness.

The brevity of duration combines with local artifact in a poem titled "These Planks" to form a brief comment on life and death:

> These planks that were a town
> Lie warping in the sun
> As if a barrel tumbled down the peaks
> Were shattered into staves.
>
> You always wish these wasted towns were older,
> It seems unreasonable for death to lack
> Experience and do so well so quickly.[13]

This poem is characteristic of Ferril for its use of the commonplace figure of barrel staves *and* for the death question.

In "Words for Leadville,"[14] the review of local history identifies a city which was once not so long ago filled with the sights and sounds and smells of a booming mining town: crimson gills of fish and tumbling gold in the creeks; the smell of spruces, beer, and burning fuse; the sound of clappers, axes, and "can-can drums for a tin-horn gambler's clink"; the tolling of church bells, and the shouts of miners. He remembers the "wincing of the earth / The spasms of the ranges" as he personifies the earth the miners dig into—the same earth that holds in its geologic formation not only the gold they dig but also the fossils of sloths and fish and mastodons laid bare by the erosion and the mining. But now, as in "These Planks," the noise has subsided, the houses crumble; the trees of yellow pine and silver spruce are old props that form a more sterile forest underground to hold up the now empty mountains. In the narrator's mind, the short historical duration and the longer geologic time merge with his own life:

> And you can count the beatings of your heart
> While roots of ferns are splitting particles
> Of time from granite and the corpuscles
> Of blood within you alter their confusion
> A tombward instant irrevocably. (p. 107)

Thus the two time scales necessary for myth-creating come together with the emphasis on historical duration and realistic artifact.

Two other poems, "Trial by Time" and "Time of Mountains," focus more intently upon man's relationship to geologic dimensions of time. The title poem of the 1944 volume, *Trial by Time*, demonstrates his use of geology. Here he places man in an eternal continuum rising "out of the old transgressions of the sea" and "out of the idle slime" with

> No vestige of beginning,
> No prospect of an end.[15]

These two lines have major scientific relevance in the history of geology. They crystalize an aspect of uniformitarian geology as it appeared for the first time in the late eighteenth and the early nineteenth centuries to form the basis of modern geology. Uniformitarianism represented a break from the catastrophist cosmogonies and instituted a new, and as some thought a more accurate, description of earth history which held that the earth's surface has been shaped by the continuing natural action of geologic processes presently in operation, and that the only way to understand the history of the surface of the earth was to observe current geologic process. Uniformitarian geologists saw the earth as dynamic rather than as a museum housing relics of past cataclysms. Thus the present, living moment becomes of vital concern, and the constant erosion and rebuilding of geologic process, more important than the particular forms. The two lines from "Trial by Time" cited above repeat, if not intentionally, a statement directly from James Hutton's first text of uniformitarian geology written in 1795, where he claimed that in the system of nature "we find no vestige of a beginning— no prospect of an end."[16] The term was repeated by Sir Charles Lyell, the major geologist of the nineteenth century, who in

1831 misquoted Hutton as saying, "'In the economy of the world . . . I find no traces of a beginning, no prospect of an end.'"[17] Ralph Waldo Emerson repeated Lyell's phrase in his lecture "The Humanity of Science" in 1836.[18] Henry Adams repeated the phrase again in his 1868 review of the tenth edition of Lyell's *Principles of Geology*.[19]

All this history of two short lines is to locate scientific concepts that underly Ferril's use of geologic forms and processes. Ferril perceives that the mountains do not represent permanence in their particular forms but only in the constant geologic processes. In the same mood that Emerson, under the influence of uniformitarian geologists, had called Monadnoc the "grand affirmer of the present tense,"[20] Ferril writes that "It is safer for the poet to be impressed by the erosion of the mountains than [by] their enduring qualities."[21] The constant geological processes, like the biological processes of the earth, cause particular individual forms to come and go as culminations each present moment but not confining life to any one particular form. Permanence is no more limited to the shape of one mountain, however majestic, than life itself is restricted to any one human being.

The earlier "Time of Mountains," from the second volume, *Westering* (1934), provides a fuller exploration of the freedom to compare man's existence to the geologic time of mountains and demonstrates especially well Ferril's control over his environment. The situation of the poem is his fishing for trout in a mountain stream.

> So long ago my father led me to
> The dark impounding orders of this canyon
> I have confused these rocks and waters with
> My life, but not unclearly, for I know
> What will be here when I am here no more.[22]

He knows "where the hills are going" as he feels the sediment against his ankles as the "solvent mountains going home to the oceans" (p. 7). As he pushes "uphill behind the vertebrate fish" (literally at that moment and evolutionarily as well), he knows life to be measured against the mountain's life; but neither he nor the mountains are eternal, only the moving force within both.

> But if I go before these mountains go,
> I'm unbewildered by the time of mountains,
> I, who have followed life up from the sea
> Into a black incision in this planet,
> Can bring an end to stone infinitives.
> I have held rivers to my eyes like lenses,
> And rearranged the mountains at my pleasure,
> As one might change the apples in a bowl,
> And I have walked a dim unearthly prairie
> From which these peaks have not yet blown away. (p. 8)

The mountains seem to locate the centering of his own life as he combines the scientific and the mythic importance of the present moment.

II

Existing in both kinds of time, historical duration and mythic "succession of eternities," provides the locus for Ferril's attempt to transcend time both by alluding to ancient alien myths and by allowing myths to generate naturally from the western American locale. The attempts to enhance experience by including Judeo-Christian or Greek figures are less successful. "American Testament" is developed primarily in two-line stanzas containing Judeo-Christian and Greek names. Their presence alone seems to transfer some mythic richness to the American soil. To the question "Where were the myths if these were beautiful? / Was Daphne there, beloved of Apollo?"[2][3] Ferril answers with the heroic but literal struggles of westward moving Americans bearing such names as Ezra, Isaiah, Ruth, and Job. But the Greek names by their counterpoise alone do not seem to enhance the more realistic Old Testament names. The religious heritage that causes these Americans to have Judaic names would take us beyond the scope of this poem, even though its title, "American Testament," alludes to Judeo-Christian history. Likewise, Old Ned Corbin in "From Saturday Evening On," who lived in Douglas County, Colorado, collected mountain lion bounty, and fished for trout, does not comfortably become King Priam. Ned's "love and agony" seem potentially powerful enough without the allusion, even though in remembering both him and Priam

> We argue back from lilies and from snows
> To lion meanings, timelessness and rapture.[24]

A more ambitious, more fully developed, but hardly more successful attempt occurs in "Bob Ford in Attica."[25] This poem attempts to combine the classical theme of Nemesis at Rahmnus with such local historical figures as Cole Younger, Quantrill, and Jesse James. The western Americans seem out of place in the Attic setting. As Robert Richards suggests,[26] their failure to become mythic may be a result of Ferril's own feeling that the modern media confine the mythic potential of popular heroes. Certainly the first stanza declares as much, for Ferril says these men "shall never ride again" because "wires and phonographs and fonts of type" classify and thus have already fixed the limits of their mythic possibilities. Their failure to become myths is perhaps due also to the fixity itself, the repetition of formula: while the mass media may have speeded the process, these folk heroes ultimately share with their Greek counterparts the problem of detachment from the dynamic present.

A more successful use of borrowed myth occurs in "This Foreman," which won the *Nation's* poetry prize in 1823.[27] The situation of the poem is a hearing or coroner's inquest where men, including the foreman, are testifying about the death of a construction worker who has fallen from the steel girders of a tall office building. Ferril's explication in the *Rocky Mountain Herald* of February 19, 1927, indicates his aims for mythic enrichment of the poem:

> "This Foreman" ... is a modern equivalent, perhaps, of the ancient God, Vulcan. He sings an ironic song suggesting that modern buildings are steel traps in which men, toiling for what they think makes life most worth while, are ensnared by their own folly. When the workman falls dead it symbolizes to the foreman the thousands of future occupants who will destroy themselves living their business.
>
> The poem might remind us of a tale told by Leucanae in Book IV of Ovid's *Metamorphoses* wherein Vulcan trapped his faithless wife Venus and her lover Mars in a net of invisible bronze chains, then called in the gods to laugh at his victims.[28]

The poem has been popular not only for the ironic juxtaposition of men against the steel net of their own business world but also for its modulated rhythms, the assonance, and the carefully balanced dialogue. Even so, granting the implied ridicule of modern values, Ovid's tale here is still alien; the mythic meaning comes from borrowed circumstance.

III

Ferril's more powerful poems are those in which his angle of vision extends back across the historical and geological dimensions of time to an eternal recurrence and allows him to see local human experience falling into archetypal patterns of establishing sacred ground, transcending time, and relating man to the Earth Mother. Many of Ferril's poems sacralize a particular spot of landscape. Here in this place, primordial mythic time may be made present,[29] offering freedom from mere duration and offering instead a "succession of eternities" appropriate to mythic use of sacred ground.

Locating one's own geographical and philosophical center is part of the process. The poem "Streets Due West" identifies just such a centering. The morality of "fables told in human span"[30] is juxtaposed to the mountains that rise from the west end of those streets, mountains that blend into the blue of the sky. Here where man's life span is measured against the seeming eternity of the mountain landscape, he can gain a mythic perspective on his own experience. According to Eliade,

> To settle a territory is, in the last analysis, equivalent to consecrating it. When settlement is not temporary as among the nomads, but permanent, as among sedentary peoples, it implies a vital decision that involves the existence of the entire community. . . . It supposes the choice of the universe that one is prepared to assume by "creating" it.[31]

Ferril's *Words for Denver* poems have as their subject the natural consecration of just such a place. The particulars of local color are important to the philosophical identity and centering of *his* Denver. But important, too, is the consecration of that "place." Although the line "You didn't know you came to make a city" recurs in two of the poems, the living, loving, and dying portrayed in the poems have the effect of consecrating the ground. The city is sacralized by the death, in the first poem, of a little girl drowned in a sandpit.[32] It is sacralized by the daily experience of settling and living: "people killing their meat and baking their bread." Life in the young city is consecrated by the appearance of a ghost-like Indian girl who wanders through like fate from beyond the settlers' experience in that place.[33] It is consecrated by the incense smell of "ammonia tang" of the barn at twilight where

> Fragrance of oats and harness are
> beckoning farther
> than October dreaming back
> long hills
> to the steeple fading out.[34]

It is consecrated by the intersections, not only of the city streets but of cosmic planes:

> There were intersections: Ambrose horizontal
> In the basket on the way on the embalmer.
> Criss-crossing points of time that zig-zag lines
> That generate the planes that form the wakes
> Each body leaves in space from here to there.[35]

The sense of the sacred place is most evident when a poem develops a mythic timelessness associated with one particular place. "The Prairie Melts" is only one of several poems that create a sense of thereness through realistic images but escape from the limitations of time. It begins with these lines:

> The prairie melts into the throats of larks,
> And green like water green begins to flow
> Into the pinto patches of the snow.
>
> I'm here, I move my foot, I count the mountains:
> I can make calculations of my being
> Here in the spring again, feeling it, seeing . . .

> Three granite mountain ranges wore away
> While I was coming here, that is the forth
> To shine in spring to sunlight from the north.[36]

There is a strong sense not only of place but also of geologic timelessness and of mythic identification of his own life with the blood of the Son of God "still ticking like a clock / Against the collar of my overcoat" (p. 15). "I can make calculations of my being," the narrator says, and one gets the idea that he could not make those calculations anywhere but on that prairie in that melting snow, with the visual imagery of magpies, sand lilies, and buffalo grass. His own sense of place and the eternal re-creating of his own being combine to make the beginning of mythic consciousness. The local color particulars become the symbols by which he expands to the universal in the micro-macro cosmic correspondence evident in his own participation in the natural world.

In another poem, "Life after Death," burial sacralizes the ground as did the death of the young girl in the sandpit in "Beyond the Ranges," the first poem in the *Words for Denver* set. It brings to mind the temporal/eternal nature of man. As the narrator returns from the graveyard, he moves in a world of elms and maples and the sensory particulars of

> The separate fragances of separate flowers,
> The prairie rattling in the summer lightning,
> The mountains musical with purple timber.[37]

But he distinguishes between alien myth and local myth as he says

> I have come widely with my spirit over
> The tombs of men, of prairies and of mountains:
> I can distinguish with clear precision
> The summer bones of winter-frozen steers
> From ribs of unicorns and jaws of centaurs. (p. 69)

Once that distinction has been made, against the backdrop of particular local sense impressions earlier in the poem, mythic metamorphosis has a more realistic, local veracity:

> I've changed no maiden to a mountain aspen,
> Though I might take you to a dappled grove
> Where graves are old and this is happening. (p. 69)

The literal process he refers to is commonplace enough, but it is the stuff of myth nonetheless. He returns in the closing lines of the poem to love and death, and to the archetypal patterns he has "seen in natural men, / In elms, in falcons, or in the coats of horses" (p. 69).

The event must be experienced by the individual or it rings hollow. The failure to live the experience, or in Thoreau's words to be fully awake, is the ultimate failure. In the 1974 poem "Metamorphosis: 1806" Ferril recalls Zebulon Pike's exploration and the depersonalization accompanying the subsequent excessive use of his name. Ferril seems to object to the overuse of Pike's name for much the same reason that Emerson objected to the sacrament of the Lord's Supper at Boston's Second Church. But the exciting element in the poem is the antelope which

> in a marvelous flash of sprung parabola
> white-rumped
> and disappeared forever.[38]

Pike, even, did not see the antelope, an emblem of the beauty of that region. Even worse, a modern American mother and child arriving by bus in Colorado Springs did not see the antelope the driver had pointed out as they crossed eastern Colorado. As they arrive at the bus station on Pikes Peak Avenue, the mother says

> I must have dozed off back out where
> the driver said we saw
> a beautiful antelope jumping over a bush. (p. 220)

To the child's question "Mama, did we see the antelope?" the mother echoes the sad failure to experience:

> We must have, dear,
> The driver said we did. (p. 220)

Mythic experience is more happily reenacted in particular human experience in "Children Coming Up the Stairs."[39] The children in the house reenact in particular the themes of the epigraph from Lucretius placed before the poem:

> Motions of atoms which tend, then, toward death
> and destruction can never have victory always, nor
> bury existence forever. (p. 54)

The children's particular experience tip-toeing through the old house is reinforced by primordial images of mountains grinding down, of dark forests, and of a roof that just as surely as the roof of temple or a tribal long house is emblematic of the vault of heaven. In the mythic dimension of centuries they renew experience as

> They slosh the tides that bathe and dry the slain
> In estuaries festering cenotaphs. (p. 55)

They *are* the morning; they reactualize human experience in their own particular paradigm.

Man's relationship with the earth in Ferril's poems is not only a scientific one; it often becomes a loving relationship with Mother Earth wherein actual women become symbolically associated with the mountains, or even mythically metamorphosed into a mountain. For example, in "Bride," the last poem in *High Passage,* the bride and bridegroom consecrate their sexual union by analogy to timberline and to the high mountains. To the bride's questioning how it feels to be at timberline, the bridegroom answers "One / Feels much as we do now."[40] The poem climaxes with these lines:

> "It's not so wild up there, you feel as though
> Something were finished. You're at peace with sky
> And earth, as we are now." She pointed where
> The peak seemed highest, whispering "take me there."
> (p. 50)

The blending of high mountains setting with the couple's sexual union suggests the characteristic mythic union of Father Sky and Mother Earth. The past creative activity of the gods consecrates the couple's own particular act in the present.

A later poem, "Waltz Against the Mountains," contains a classical allusion to Helen of Troy but gains most of its power from the mythic association of particular woman and mountain.

The situation is a New Year's Eve ball, that time of celebration and renewal and the microcosmic analogies that seem unavoidable then. As in "Streets Due West," human existence in the city lies within sight of the much older front range of the Rocky Mountains as if the city itself were conscious of how it "sweeps against the mountains" in cosmic dance. Instead of retreating with Bob Ford to Attica, enclosing the allusion in a durational time scheme, the narrator in "Waltz Against the Mountains" gives present mythic stature to the woman by the classical allusion and by the natural enhancement of her realistic place. He contrasts her to Helen:

> A woman on a high wall looking down
> Forever on the firelight of her kinsman.[41]

But his woman is "only a woman looking out of a window" (p. 51). However, for this very reason she transcends all time; she steps down *mountain* walls. She is beauty and life reactualized in the present "ceremony" of welcoming the new year. Even more, she is "the mountains changing into woman" and "a woman changing into prairie" (p. 52).

Ferril successfully combines local artifact, geological formation, and local history with his mythic consciousness in "Magenta." The setting of this poem is an abandoned mining town where the narrator finds a cast off dressmaker's dummy "on a pile of mining machinery over a graveyard."[42] Ferril unites actuality with the disembodiment symbolized in "Magenta" by the interplay between animate human bodies of the graveyard and the inanimate mining machinery from the same graveyard. The dressmaker's dummy as artifact reawakens the historic past, as does the ore bucket in which the narrator sets her to help her stand and to give her a skirt. He aligns a distant mountain with this artifact to form her head, and they talk of past human experience in that town. Ferril, the perceptive artist, has symbolically united past and present, historical fact and mountain, present location and distance, animate and inanimate relics to rescue Magenta from the entrapment, anxiety, and death associated with the lives the miners' wives led. In the morning, noon, and evening analogy to their lives, the wives died young, at noon.

Magenta becomes a transcendent Earth Mother figure as she symbolizes the feminine presence of whore and wife and of the mountains the miners tunneled into—as if loving mountain more than wife. Digging a grave for his wife, Magenta relates,

> "A miner would dig a grave with a pick and shovel
> Often a little deeper than necessary,
> And poising every shovelful of earth
> An instant longer than if he were digging a grave,
> And never complaining when he struck a rock;
> Then he would finish, glad to have found no color."
> (p. 40)

Magenta, as dressmaker's dummy, had been a symbol for the miners' wives also, a symbol of "things beyond the mountains and the mines" (p. 37), a symbol of the attempt to restore the miners' attention from the mountains to themselves. Magenta, herself symbol of the whores of that mining town, recounts her potential friendship with the miners' wives, but

> "These women wanted me to be their friend.
> I spent my mornings with them making believe.
> They'd sit around the mountains and the mines;
> Then they would get down on their knees to me,
> Praying with pins and bastings for my sanction." (p. 37)

The wives ultimately cannot compete with the lure of gold and silver ore nor outlast the whores whom the miners' minds fused with mountains into a single symbol. Magenta describes this metamorphosis:

> Some disappeared, some changed into curious songs,
> And some of them slowly changed into beautiful mountains. (p. 40)

One such mountain, Silverheels, in literal history named after a prostitute of that same mining town, is the mountain the narrator has been using for Magenta's head.

The resurrection of Magenta reverberates many directions. Here history and legend already fixed to the locale are reused to new mythic and aesthetic purpose. The conversation between Magenta and the narrator becomes a mythic paradigm of past human experience—of the role of women in that place, and of the symbolic association of woman and mountain.

A more comic Earth Mother figure is Lily Bull-Domingo. Although she is not as clearly identified with a particular mountain, she too transcends time to become mythic femininity in that place—from childhood, to sexual maturity, to ghost, but in reverse order. The conflict, vital to Ferril, between the abstract God-finding and the realistic use of environment is also a complementing central theme in "Report of My Strange Encounter With Lily Bull-Domingo."

Lily Bull-Domingo comes to us as myth out of the locale and the transcendence of time. The first few lines clearly establish the Colorado vernacular and location:

> If you want to know where it was,
> I stopped my car
> On the hump of Hardscrabble Pass up Hardscrabble Creek.[43]

In spite of the vernacular, the romantic narrative persona of the poem is one who shares with Whitman and Coleridge the abstract awe of the mountains. Clearly the reality of the place must be used to bring him down to particulars where natural western myth originates. Lily, a ghost from the past, is the pragmatic one, placed in ironic contrast to the "live" romanticizing narrator. The poem develops with several alternating passages contrasting the living narrator's abstracting with Lily's more pragmatic attitude.

> "The woods were God's first temples,"
> I said, "Don't break the spell!"
> And Lily Bull-Domingo said
> That she was sorry as hell
> If what she's said upset me
> And asked what my business was:
> "Insurance or electronics?
> Or maybe you peddle booze?"
> I was so stunned, the mountains fell.   (pp. 68-69)

His mountains could fall, of course, because they were merely ideal mountains, not part of the literal landscape at all. Almost midway through the poem Lily becomes more mythic as she is given characteristics of all women who helped settle the region—pillowing his head on a granite rock "As soft as eiderdown," washing his face, cutting juniper to build a fire, dynamiting a reservoir to kill trout, cooking flapjacks, pouring whiskey, and making love. When he asks Lily what it was like "up here a hundred years ago," she begins to talk of restoring the town for tourists, juxtaposing the original function of the buildings with the modern tourist function:

> "And let's restore the pesthouse
> And move a symphony in,
> And rearrange the slaughterhouse
> For Cello and violin.
>
> . . . .
>
> "And let's restore the whorehouse
> With costumed wax-work whores
> And let the girls from the Junior League
> Give two-dollar guided tours." (p. 71)

After his experience with Lily, the narrator drives down from the mountain to the town of Rosita to wander through an old cemetery where he finds an inscription that verifies the myth and brings him to tears of anguish:

> Lily Bull-Domingo
> Died at the age of six,
> One, two,
> Buckle your shoe,
> And save your candle wicks. (p. 72)

Time again has been transcended in an effort to understand our being and to understand Lily Bull-Domingo as symbol of one aspect of being.

Eliade, speaking of the difference between the sacred and the profane in human existence, identifies the sanctified life as "lived on a two-fold plane; it takes its course as human existence and at the same time shares in a transhuman life of the cosmos or the Gods." In that case, the "cosmic symbolism *adds* a new value to an object or action, without affecting their peculiar and immediate values."[44] This is the realm in which Ferril is most successful in his poetic portrayal of the western American experience. The mountains, the region as a whole, become sacred ground to him where experience can become more powerful, embuing human experience with sacred power not readily achieved elsewhere. The past dynamically enters the present in this region; Ferril breathes the fresh air and communes with the past as he reactualizes it in the present.

NOTES

[1] Thomas Hornsby Ferril, *High Passage* (New Haven: Yale University Press, 1926), p. 41.

[2] Edith Hamilton, *Mythology* (New York: New American Library, 1969), p. 17.

[3] Mircea Eliade, *The Sacred and the Profane: The Nature of Religion,* trans. Willard R. Trask (New York: Harcourt Brace, 1959), p. 104.

[4] Thomas Hornsby Ferril, "Writing in the Rockies," rpt. in *Rocky Mountain Reader,* ed. Ray B. West, Jr. (New York: E. P. Dalton & Company, 1946), p. 395.

[5] "Writing in the Rockies," p. 398.

[6] "Writing in the Rockies," p. 396.

[7] Robert G. Olson, *An Introduction to Existentialism* (New York: Dover, 1962), p. 136.

[8] Martin Heidegger, "The Way Back into the Ground of Metaphysics," trans. Walter Kaufman, in *Existentialism from Dostoevsky to Sartre,* ed. Walter Kaufman (New York: Meridian Books, 1956), p. 214.

[9] Olson, p. 135.

[10] Thomas Hornsby Ferril, *New and Selected Poems* (New York: Harper & Bros., 1952), p. 9.

[11] *New and Selected Poems,* p. 9.

[12] Thomas Hornsby Ferril, *High Passage* (New Haven: Yale University Press, 1926), p. 9.

[13] Thomas Hornsby Ferril, *Words for Denver* (New York: William Morrow, 1966), p. 50.

[14] *New and Selected Poems,* pp. 98-107. All references to the poem are to this volume.

[15] *New and Selected Poems,* p. 5.

[16] James Hutton, *Theory of the Earth* (1795; rpt. Weinheim, Germa-

ny: H. R. Engleman, J. Cramer, 1959), II, 200.

[17] Charles Lyell, *Principles of Geology* (1830-1833; rpt. Lehre, Germany: J. Cramer, 1970), I, 63.

[18] Ralph Waldo Emerson, "The Humanity of Science," in *The Early Lectures of Ralph Waldo Emerson*, eds. Stephen E. Whicher and others (Cambridge: Harvard University Press, 1964), p. 32.

[19] Henry Brooks Adams, rev. of *Principles of Geology*, by Charles Lyell, *North American Review*, 221 (October 1868), 465-501.

[20] Ralph Waldo Emerson, "Monadnoc," in *Complete Works of Ralph Waldo Emerson*, ed. Edward Waldo Emerson (Boston: Houghton Mifflin, 1903), IX, 73.

[21] "Writing in the Rockies," p. 399.

[22] *New and Selected Poems*, p. 7. All references to the poem are to this volume.

[23] *New and Selected Poems*, p. 75. All references to the poem are to this volume.

[24] *New and Selected Poems*, p. 43.

[25] *High Passage*, p. 19.

[26] Robert Richards, "The Poetry of Thomas Hornsby Ferril," Diss. Columbia 1961, pp. 119-122.

[27] *New and Selected Poems*, p. 133.

[28] Quoted in Richards, p. 145.

[29] Eliade, p. 68.

[30] *High Passage*, p. 39.

[31] Eliade, p. 34.

[32] "Beyond What Ranges," *Words for Denver*, p. 3.

[33] "Ghost," *Words for Denver*, p. 15.

[34] "The Barn Was Twilight," *Words for Denver*, pp. 19-20.

[35] "There Were Intersections," *Words for Denver*, p. 24.

[36] *New and Selected Poems*, p. 14. All references to the poem are to this volume.

[37] *New and Selected Poems*, p. 68. All references to the poem are to this volume.

[38] Thomas Hornsby Ferril, "Metamorphosis: 1806," *The Colorado Quarterly*, 23, No. 2 (1974), 217. All references to the poem are to this edition.

[39] *Words for Denver*, p. 54. All references to the poem are to this volume.

[40] *High Passage*, p. 50. All references to the poem are to this volume.

[41] *New and Selected Poems*, p. 51. All references to the poem are to this volume.

[42] *New and Selected Poems*, p. 35. All references to the poem are to

this volume.

⁴³*Words for Denver,* p. 67. All references to the poem are to this volume.

⁴⁴Eliade, p. 167.

Alien Myth and Natural Myth in the Poetry of Thomas Hornsby Ferril

Stephen Crane could be called our first writer of anti-Westerns: stories playing upon myth for comic or demythologizing purposes. **Chester L. Wolford** shows how Crane suggests the fall of the Old West in a predominantly comic tale, "The Bride Comes to Yellow Sky," by mock-epic rendering of a western sub-myth, the "Showdown" (or "Walkdown"). Realistic portrayal of actual performance counterpoints heroic expectations which derive from western myth and parallel classical myth. The result is a mock-epic debunking of western myth which dramatizes an era of transition as the plains themselves seem to pour eastward. Wolford also shows how Crane's story gains interpretive significance beyond the comic event through epic-mythic associations by contrasting Crane's tale to a somewhat similar one by O. Henry.

Wolford holds degrees from Georgetown, Maryland, and Pennsylvania State Universities, and is now teaching at the Behrend College of Pennsylvania State University. His essays and poetry have been published in *Prairie Schooner, Appalachian Journal, Pivot,* and *The Louisville Review. The Anger of Stephen Crane: Fiction and the Epic Tradition* has been published by the University of Nebraska Press.

Classical Myth Versus Realism in Crane's
"The Bride Comes to Yellow Sky"*

Chester L. Wolford

"The Bride Comes to Yellow Sky" is partly about the fall of America's Old West as it occurs within the structure of a sub-myth called the "Showdown."[1] An erstwhile outlaw, and relict of the West's heroic days, is drunk and on the rampage. Meanwhile the town marshal is returning home on a train, bringing with him his bride. When the old outlaw, Scratchy Wilson, comes face-to-face with Marshal Jack Potter, Wilson is on the verge of shooting when he discovers the marshal's "new condition." Scratchy backs down, leaving Potter and the bride, law and order, and a new civilization as victors. However, there are other myths in "The Bride" which need to be explored, for through these myths Crane universalizes his story, making the fall of the American West symbolic of all mythical falls from Troy to Yellow Sky.

The outlines of the Potter/Bride story are similar to the myth of Paris and Helen. In both a man returns from a journey bringing a "bride," both avoid confrontations, and both in doing so fail to live up to their positions in the community. In "The Bride" and the *Iliad,* these actions precipitate a fall of the old order of Yellow Sky and the civilization of Troy.

Such similarities could be coincidental, but Crane was "a voracious reader . . . of the classics of Greece and Rome,"[2] and "The Bride" is riddled with significant classical conventions. Two of the characters, for example, are described within the formula of the classical epithet. Jack Potter, besides being

---

*Reprinted from *The Anger of Stephen Crane* by Chester L. Wolford, by permission of University of Nebraska Press. Copyright 1983 by the University of Nebraska Press.

called "the marshal," is Scratchy's "ancient antagonist," and also "the bridegroom." Scratchy himself is variously referred to as "a wonder," "a man in a maroon-colored shirt," "he of the revolver," and "the man." His voice, too, is heroic and reminiscent of Achilles's thundering challenges which leave the Trojans shaking in their armor: his "cries rang . . . in a volume that seemed to have no relation to the ordinary vocal strength of a man."[3] And finally, the classical connection is firmly planted by a Western version of an epic simile. Challenging Potter's house, Scratchy "fumed at it as the winter wind attacks a prairie cabin in the North" (p. 118).

Using classical myth and conventions to extend and deepen meaning is not unusual for Crane,[4] but in "The Bride" classical myth and convention are used for more than merely extending the story's scope. They play a vital part in a mock-epic debunking of the myth of the American West. One of the standard techniques of the mock-epic is to describe realistic, mundane actions in epic language, or to build expectations with epic language in order to deflate the realistic performance which follows. Section II of "The Bride," for instance, provides an epic build-up for Scratchy Wilson who "is drunk and has turned loose with both hands" (p. 114). The reader and the newcomer in the saloon are assured that "there'll be some shootin'—some good shootin'," for Scratchy is "a wonder with a gun" (p. 116). We are told that in his efforts to entice someone into battle, Scratchy will often shoot at a door, a dog, a window, a house, or any other symbol of domesticity. Section III describes Scratchy's more realistic performance; Scratchy fails to live up to the expectations provided by Section II. He misses the dog. He misses the piece of paper nailed to the barroom door. He even commits two cardinal sins among mythic antagonists: he has to reload periodically, and he fumbles and drops his revolver when facing his opponent. A gunfighter may be many dastardly things—mean, cruel, beady-eyed, and unwashed—but he may not be clumsy. And few mythical gunfighters reload their guns. It is all too mundane.

The difference between the expectations of Section II and the performance in Section III is one of the themes of *Troilus and Cressida,* another epic-debunking drama: "that the will is infinite, and the execution confined; that the desire is boundless, and the act a slave to limit" (3.2.89-91).

The realistic description which follows certain classical

conventions also serves to deflate the mythical. Immediately after Scratchy's "cries of ferocious challenge" comes this charming deflation: his boots had red tops with gilded imprints, of the kind beloved of little sledding boys on the hillsides of New England" (p. 117). After hurling more challenges, and after the epic simile describing them, Scratchy, "as necessity bade him, . . . paused for breath or to reload . . . " (p. 118). When Wilson and Potter face each other there is in the language a dignity, an earnestness, even a high epic seriousness: the revolver "was aimed at the bridegroom's chest. There was a silence. . . . The two men faced each other. . . . He of the revolver smiled with a new and quiet ferocity" (pp. 118-119). Puzzled at finding the marshal unarmed, Scratchy then poses some very un-Homeric questions: "If you ain't got a gun, why ain't you got a gun? . . . Been to Sunday-School?" (p. 119).

The difference between expectation and performance is the difference between myth and realism, between what we want and what we have, between what we want to see and what is, and "The Bride" uses this mock-epic technique to debase the showdown, its participants, and the myths of civilizations' falls.

Another way to explore Crane's use of classical myth is to compare "The Bride" with a different story about the fall of the mythical American West, preferably one without significant classical parallels and conventions, and one which does not therefore universalize nor mock the myth of the American West. Closely resembling "The Bride" in setting, plot, characterization, and portrayal of the end of the American West, O. Henry's "The Reformation of Calliope" is such a story.[5]

Set in a small West Texas desert town during the 1880s,[6] "The Reformation of Calliope" describes an aborted showdown between one drunken gunslinger—Calliope Catesby—and three lawmen: Sheriff Buck Patterson and two of his deputies. Catesby shoots his way down the main street of Quicksand, firing at dogs, Mexicans, weathervanes, windows, and chickens (Scratchy shoots at dogs and windows; the Mexicans light out early). Stopped by a barrage of bullets, Catesby fights his way to the railroad station, which provides a fortress from which he can defend himself. Undaunted, Patterson ("Son of P[o]tter"?) charges into the station, is grazed by Catesby's bullet, and is lying unconscious when Calliope's mother, just arrived on the train, walks in to greet her son. Thinking quickly, Calliope manages to pin Patterson's badge on before his mother gets inside. When he regains consciousness, Patterson, too, thinks quickly, for he almost immediately "takes in" the situation, and while "going along" with Catesby's ruse, nevertheless manages to secure the latter's promise to reform. Calliope reforms because he does not want to disappoint his mother. Thus, "The Bride" and "The Reformation" are stories about a showdown which ends without death and without the "winner" winning. Calliope and Scratchy Wilson lose even though they have the "drop" on their opponents. They lose because the game changes; the game changes because a woman intervenes.

The stories' details are also similar. Both Scratchy and Calliope are "terrors," both have unnaturally loud voices (Scratchy's is epical; Calliope's earns him his name), both are inoffensive when sober (Scratchy "wouldn't hurt a fly—nicest fellow in town," p. 116; Calliope is "a quiet, amiable man," p. 302). Since both stories occur in desert towns, their sea imagery is incongruous. One of Scratchy's guns is called his "starboard revolver," and the bride is once described as "drowning" while standing on a dusty street. The "splenetic Calliope," on a similar street, "was steaming down the channel, cannonading on either side, when he suddenly became aware of breakers" (p. 305). A final and very interesting detail concerns the personal "reformations" of Calliope and Scratchy. When he pins on Sheriff Patterson's badge, Calliope symbolically reforms. Scratchy Wilson performs no similar action in "The Bride," but he does say of the feud, "Well, I 'low it's off, Jack" (p. 120). Later, however, in his only other appearance in Crane's fiction, he shows up wearing a badge as Potter's Deputy in "Moonlight on the Snow."[7] With these reformations, the "Old West" has fallen in both Yellow Sky and Quicksand.

The differences between "The Bride" and "The Reformation" are perhaps even more revealing than the similarities, particularly in the use of classical myths and conventions. The significance of the Paris/Helen myth is clear for "The Bride," but the mythic parallels of "The Reformation" all have to do with a divine mother saving her son from disaster. Further, the Paris/Helen myth directly applies to the fall of civilizations, and the classical conventions of epithet and simile are effectively undercut by the detailed and realistic description in "The Bride." The name "Calliope" is, of course, the same one given to the muse of epic poetry, but because there is no other indication of epic parallels in "The Reformation" there is no significant mockery of the myth of the American West.

Further, there is in "The Reformation" no sense of fate, ineluctible, inexorable, classical fate. Whatever potential "The Reformation" has for evoking a sense of fate is sacrificed to O. Henry's "trick ending." "The Bride," on the other hand, has this sense, for all things move toward the showdown.[8] Potter moves toward Yellow Sky in Section I; Yellow Sky's history, especially the clash between Wilson and Potter, is recounted in Section II, setting up the actual clash in Section IV; Section III describes Scratchy Wilson moving toward his destiny in front of the Marshal's home. These movements are paralleled in a larger sense as well, and are epitomized in the description of the collision courses of the train and the river: "To the left, miles down a long purple slope, was a little ribbon of mist where moved the keening Rio Grande. The train was approaching it at an angle, and the apex was Yellow Sky" (p. 111).

Another aspect of the difference between the scopes or relative universalities of the two stories lies in their opening lines. "The Reformation" opens with a description of Calliope, and in spite of the attempt at broadening the scope by mentioning "the earth," the lines have little sense of bigness:

> Calliope Catesby was in his humours again. Ennui was upon him. This goodly promontory, the earth—particularly that portion of it known as Quicksand—was to him no more than a pestilent congregation of vapours. Overtaken by the megrims, the philosopher may seek relief in soliloquy; my lady find solice in tears; the flaccid Easterner scold at the millinery bills of his women folk.... Calliope, especially, was wont to express his ennui according to his lights. (p. 301)

The attempt at largeness here is through a comparison of Calliope to the microcosm of people with regard to their relative reactions to depression. The effect is comic and is intended to be. The effect of "The Bride's" opening paragraph, on the other hand, is macrocosmic; there is a sense of epic sweep and of a movement toward some destiny:

> The great Pullman was whirling onward with such dignity of motion that a glance from the window seemed simply

> to prove that the plains of Texas were pouring eastward. Vast flats of green grass, dull-hued spaces of mesquite and cactus, little groups of frame houses, woods of light and tender trees, all were sweeping into the east, sweeping over the horizon, a precipice. (p. 109)

"The Bride," then, is similar to "The Reformation" in that both recount the fall of the Old West through the myth of the showdown. They differ in that the classical myths and conventions of "The Bride" are used to universalize the fall of the Old West and to mock the myths that tell the story of all such falls.

There is a danger inherent in using classical myth and convention to mock anything in that something epical may rub off on the thing being mocked. That such is the case in "The Bride" accounts for the sense of loss and pity over the end of an age and that age's heroes. One feels it for Hector and Troy, and, to a lesser degree, for Scratchy Wilson and Yellow Sky. One even feels it for the barkeeper's dog, who, though accustomed to being "kicked on occasion," is described in words usually reserved for the horse, the most common and noble of epic animals. When Scratchy shot at him, the dog "walked diagonally," "broke into a gallop," "screamed," "wheel[ed]," and flurried" (p. 117). Certainly, the dog mocks the noble horse, but the dog also gains a little of the horse's dignity from the description. The same is true, especially at the very end, of Scratchy Wilson. In spite of the comedy, there is something Homeric about the description of Scratchy in "The Bride's" last paragraph:

> "Married!" He was not a student of chivalry; it was merely that in the presence of this foreign condition he was a simple child of the earlier plains. He picked up his starboard revolver, and . . . he went away. His feet made funnel-shaped tracks in the heavy sand. (p. 120)

This old and simple warrior of the windy plains of Yellow Sky has been defeated and is sailing home, funnel-shaped maelstroms whirling briefly to port and starboard. Like an old landed sailor, Scratchy is out of his element, his guns as incongruous as oars scratching across the sands of Western Texas.

On the other hand, it is possible that the epic elements need not "rub off" on the story to give it dignity. The mere presence of the epical, standing beside the plot, may illuminate and make explicit the story's implied dignity, high seriousness, even tragedy. For Crane writes in "The Blue Hotel," his other famous western story, that "any room can present a tragic front; any room can be comic."[9] Certainly "The Bride Comes to Yellow Sky" is comic; no doubt it also has its tragic side.

NOTES

[1] Robert Barnes, "Stephen Crane's 'The Bride Comes to Yellow Sky,'" *Explicator,* 16 (1958), Item 39; Scott C. Ferguson, "Crane's 'The Bride Comes to Yellow Sky,'" *Explicator,* 21 (1963), Item 59; Kenneth Bernard, "'The Bride Comes to Yellow Sky': History as Elegy," *English Record,* 17 (April 1967), 17-20.

[2] Cited in Robert W. Stallman, *Stephen Crane: A Biography* (New York: Braziller, 1968), p. 19.

[3] Fredson Bowers, ed., *The University of Viriginia Edition of The Works of Stephen Crane,* Vol. V: *Tales of Adventure* (Charlottesville: University Press of Virginia, 1970), pp. 116-117. All further references to this work appear in the text.

[4] Winifred Lynsky, ed., *Reading Modern Fiction,* 4th ed. (New York: Scribner's, 1968), p. 173; Sister Mary Anthony Weinig, "Heroic Convention in 'The Blue Hotel,' *Stephen Crane Newsletter,* 2 (Spring 1968), 7; Warren D. Anderson, "Homer and Stephen Crane," *Nineteenth-Century Fiction,* 19 (1964), 77-86; Robert Dusenbury, "The Homeric Mood of *The Red Badge of Courage,*" *Pacific Coast Philology,* 23 (1968), 31-37; John E. Hart, *"The Red Badge of Courage* as Myth and Symbol," *University of Kansas City Review,* 19 (1953), 249-256; Chester L. Wolford, "The Eagle and the Crow: High Tragedy and Epic in 'The Blue Hotel,'" *Prairie Schooner,* 51 (1977), 260-274.

[5] O. Henry, *Heart of the West,* Authorized Ed. (New York: Doubleday, Page & Company, 1904), pp. 301-313. References to this work appear in the text.

[6] For dating the events of this story, see Joseph Gallegly, *From Alamo Plaza to Jack Harris's Saloon* (The Hague, Netherlands: Mouton, 1970), pp. 151 ff.

[7] *Works,* V, 179-191.

[8] Ben Merchant Vorpahl, "Murder by the Minute: Old and New in 'The Bride Comes to Yellow Sky,'" *Nineteenth-Century Fiction,* 26 (1971), 196-218.

[9] *Works,* V, 156.

Classical Myth Versus Realism in Crane's "The Bride Comes to Yellow Sky"

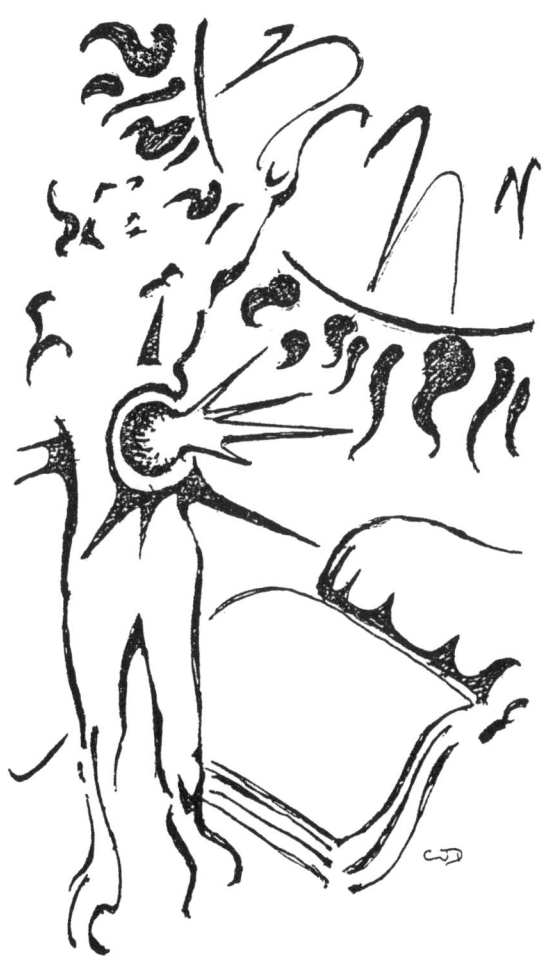

Stephen Crane once referred to himself as a person of the "false East" rather than the "honest West." That "honest" does not mean "realistic" is implicit in **Michael J. Collins'** analysis of three Crane short stories, "The Five White Mice," "The Bride Comes to Yellow Sky," and "The Blue Hotel." Unlike his predecessor Bret Harte, who created a romance world from western motifs, Crane applied elements of the western romance form to realistic content (especially evident in the focus on internal rather than external experience). The result is "ironic myth" (as defined by Northrop Frye) which illuminates the "real" world in which we live: a world more complex, ambiguous, and fraught with a more subtle danger than the world of the Western romance.

Collins graduated from Fordham College and New York University. He is Dean of the School for Summer and Continuing Education and a member of the English Department at Georgetown University.

Realism and Romance in the Western Stories of
Stephen Crane

Michael J. Collins

The world of the Western story is, as many have suggested, a world of romance. While it is clearly not a perfect world (the violence and counter-violence at the heart of these stories make that fact clear), it is, in its simplicity, a pure world, an ideal world. In the typical Western story, the important action is rarely covert or implicit, and the focus is on external rather than internal action; good and evil are clearly defined and sharply distinguished; human problems, relationships, and judgments are generally singular and unambiguous. Like the romance in general, the Western takes us out of the world in which we live and brings us to another world, "not an entire world," but a world which "excludes some reaches of experience in order to concentrate intently upon certain themes until they take fire and seem to be the flame of life itself."[1]

Bret Harte's well-known story, "The Outcasts of Poker Flat," is, in many ways, a fine example of the Western. Except for the simple, binary ironies of honorable gambler and golden-hearted whore (both of whom are familiar figures in the Western), good and evil are clearly distinguished: the heroic charity of John Oakhurst and the two whores contrasts sharply with the treachery of Uncle Billy and the hypocritical, vindictive virtue of the citizens of Poker Flat. The moral question that Oakhurst faces is without ambiguity: he must either stay with his initially messy companions or leave them on the trail. Their own stupidity is apparently not a factor in the decision, and we never learn, for example, what doubts or fears Oakhurst has to face before deciding to stay. The exclusively external focus on Oakhurst, the few words he has to say in the story, and his unshakable calm, even as it becomes ever more apparent that he is playing a losing hand, all combine to suggest another of the characteristics of the Western hero—a sense of style, a recognition of the importance not just of doing what has to be done, but of doing it well. Like the marshal in *High Noon,* like the gunfighter, Chris, in *The Magnificent Seven,* like Shane, John Oakhurst does what he has to do with restraint, with quiet dignity, with control, and, it is important to recognize, with a certain reluctance.

"The romance," says Gillian Beer, "gives repetitive form to the particular desires of a community, and especially to those desires which cannot find controlled expression within a society."[2] Mr. Oakhurst and the countless other solitary, heroic men who appear again and again in Western stories and films find clear-cut moral answers to clear-cut moral questions and live out the implications of those answers with integrity and style, even if it finally means death. In the Eastern world where we all live now, in the atomic world of the twentieth century where, probably out of necessity,

> . . . the dude
> Who lets the girl down before
> The hero arrives, the chap
> Who's yellow and keeps the store,
> Seem far too familiar . . . ,[3]

in this world of ours, these men offer us, as they did our ancestors in the dime novels, the heroes and the heroism that seem too simple and too dangerous for our complex, civilized age.

The world of the Western, of course, his affinities with other fictional worlds. The Western hero is related to such other heroes of romance as Beowulf and the Knights of the Round Table as well as to the familiar hero of Hemingway's fiction and to Raymond Chandler's Phillip Marlowe. He is also finally a man alone, outside society, without wife or family, and his world is, in some ways at least, the territory for which Huck Finn, Natty Bumppo, and Frederick Henry light out. Although ordinarily the Western does not explicitly judge the real world, the hero often stands, as he does in *High Noon, Shane,* and "The Outcasts of Poker Flat," in some contrast to tame and respectable townspeople among whom we all make our homes.

The familiar, repetitive elements of the Western also appear in three short stories by Stephen Crane, "The Five White Mice," "The Bride Comes to Yellow Sky," and "The Blue Hotel." And yet while the familiar elements are there, the stories seem finally to belong not to the world of romance, but to the world that, in Northrop Frye's scheme of things, is the opposite of the world of romance—the world of irony. And Frye's description in his *Anatomy of Criticism* of the central principle of ironic myth helps, I think, to make clear how Crane uses the elements of the Western in these stories. "As structure, the central principle of ironic myth is best approached as a parody of romance: the application of romantic mythical forms to a more realistic content which fits them in unexpected ways."[4] Here essentially is Crane's method in the three stories. In the pages that follow, then, I should like to show how romance and realism combine in each of them, how Crane uses the familiar elements of the Western romance in a realistic setting and thus creates an ironic world that seems a recognizable representation of the one in which we live.

I shall begin by looking at what seems to me the simplest of the three stories, "The Five White Mice." At the beginning the story seems to have little to do with the typical Western. It opens in an American bar in Mexico City: Freddie, the bartender, is mixing a cocktail, not serving straight whiskey to a cowboy in some Western saloon. As the story goes on, the New York kid, who loses at dice, must take his companions to the circus and, as a result, cannot go drinking with two other friends. After the circus, he again meets these two friends, who are now quite drunk, and as he tries to get them home, one of them, Benson, bumps into a Mexican. Benson does not apologize, a man has been insulted, and suddenly six men are facing each other. We are now, for a moment at least, in the world of the Western, waiting for the gunfight that must inevitably come.

But almost at once we are taken out of the Western and back to the real world and to what is actually only an ugly street fight in Mexico City. The Mexican seems perverse rather than heroic in defense of his sense of honor, like the man who murdered another in an argument over a parking space some years ago in Manhattan. The New York kid's sloppy companions are too drunk to be of any help to him, and the kid himself seems immobilized by fear. While we may at any moment witness a gunfight between the two groups of men, the romantic view of things is impossible, because the focus is not on the external drama of the confrontation, but on the complex, internal experience of the New York kid, who seems, as a result, to lack the style, the requisite restraint and control of the Western hero. While he finally does what he has to do to save himself and his friends, he does it like an Easterner (afraid he will fail, unsure of the effect), and thus in what seems a recognizably human way. When the kid draws his gun, he is at first surprised and then angered to find that his adversaries are not the gunfighters of the dime novels, but simply human beings like himself.

The narrator's ironic comment at the end of the story, "nothing had happened,"[5] is the final reminder that it is set not in a simple world of romance, but in a complex, ironic world that seems close to the world in which we live. From the point of view of romance, of course, nothing has happened: our conventional expectations of a gunfight have been frustrated, for when the New York kid draws his revolver, the Mexicans back away. The simple, unambiguous resolution does not, as it must in romance, come about. Rather, fear on both sides (a familiar human emotion) leads to compromise: the Mexicans withdraw, the New York kid ignores their mockery, and the two groups separate with all six men alive. The world of "The Five White Mice" is an ironic, ambiguous, and complex world, a world where a man saves himself by losing at dice, where expectations and estimates are proved false, where a man may recognize several claims and thus decide to get out of town with his bride before the noon train arrives, a world, in short, like the one in which we live.

Elements of the Western romance play a more prominent role in "The Bride Comes to Yellow Sky," one of Crane's best-known stories. It begins with Jack Potter and his bride on the great Pullman, "the environment of their new estate" (p. 110). They seem, in the first part of the story, comic figures, too old and too plain for a bride and groom and ill at ease in the Eastern opulance of the train. Potter is the marshal of Yellow Sky and his recent marriage is significant, not just, as the story suggests, because he is a prominent person in the town, but because it makes him as much of an anomaly in a Western story as he is on the Pullman. Potter is no longer the conventional Western hero, the man alone, like Matt Dillon or Oakhurst or Natty Bumppo before them, but a family man, a man with ties and attachments, a part of the community. By his marriage in San Antonio, Jack Potter, for all his ineptitude on the train, has, as it were, rejected solitude and the West for family, society, and the East.

The second part of the story takes place in the Weary Gentleman saloon, whose zinc and cooper fittings contrast with the brass and silver of the train. The drummer, a denizen of the East, is as out of place in the saloon as Potter and his wife were on the train, for he cannot at first understand why Scratchy Wilson should produce such fear in the town. At this point we are not only, as the story suggests, in the West of an earlier time, but also in the world of romance. Scratchy Wilson, "the last one of the old gang that used to hang out along the river" (p. 116), is shooting up the town, and it soon becomes apparent that a gunfight is taking shape, for the marshal is the only one who can handle him. In Yellow Sky, then, Potter is not a comic figure, but "a man known, liked, and feared" (p. 111).

In the third part of the story Scratchy Wilson, dressed like a little boy in a cowboy suit, appears on the street outside the bar. Although he is drunk and treated somewhat comically, he is, nonetheless, like a figure from romance, quick, agile, competent, and dangerous, a man who can, at will, play with a whole town. Finally, after amusing himself outside the saloon for a while, he begins to make his way to Potter's house, and the gunfight now seems inevitable.

But, like "The Five White Mice," the story frustrates our expectations, although here the frustration has a comic effect. Potter and the bride turn the corner and bump into Scratchy Wilson. In an instant, we are at the climax of a Western romance: the bride, as Crane puts it, is now "a slave to hideous rites" (p. 119). But as Potter and Wilson face each other, the marshal, without his gun, sees "a vision of the Pullman . . . , the environment of their new estate" (p. 119). The marshal will still do what has to be done, but now not simply because he must, but because he wants to insure a settled, ordered, civilized life for himself and his wife. (The knight, as it were, has become a militiaman or a member of the PBA.) The story ends, of course, not like *High Noon,* with a gunfight, but with a comic anticlimax: when Wilson learns that Potter is married, he says it's all off for, as the narrator puts it, "in the presence of this foreign condition he was a simple child of the earlier plains" (p. 120) and, one might add, a displaced figure from the world of romance. Like Potter in the Pullman, like the drummer in a Texas town terrorized by a drunken gunslinger, Scratchy Wilson finds himself in a world he cannot comprehend.

The world that Scratchy Wilson finds incomprehensible is not, of course, the simple self-contained world of romance (from which Wilson himself seems to have stepped), but a world of complex, comic ironies. Yellow Sky and its marshal are changing: society, civilization, the East shape the town, just as they shape the maroon shirt and boots that Scratchy Wilson wears. The East is moving westward: the bride, the train, the drummer all contribute to making the West more civilized and thus more complex. And yet the story suggests that something will also be lost, for Potter, the only man who can keep Scratchy Wilson in line, (and Wilson himself, for that matter) seems in some ways preferable to the smirking porters and passengers on the Pullman (whose manners mask their feelings) and to the drummer cowering behind the bar of the Weary Gentleman. While we are no doubt grateful that Scratchy Wilson will no longer shoot up the town, we are also asked, I believe, to recognize that this new world (the real, settled one in which we all now live) is, like the Pullman train, like Yellow Sky with its married marshal, a complex, ironic, and ambiguous world that can never offer anything so pure and heroic as a gunfight. Jack Potter is no longer simply the man alone, the marshal of Yellow Sky. He has, by his marriage, become a complex human being, a husband as well as a marshal and thus he embodies, as the conventional Western hero never does, the complexities and ironies of life in the real world. And this world, as we all know, is, because of its complexity, never the ideal, and it will remain forever incomprehensible to Scratchy Wilson, a figure as much from the world of romance as from "the earlier plains" (p. 120).

In "The Blue Hotel" Crane makes what seems to me the fullest and most explicit use of the elements of Western romance. Into the Palace Hotel in Fort Romper, Nebraska, comes a Swede from the East who has been a tailor. The other people in the hotel—a cowboy; an Easterner; Pat Scully, the proprietor; and his son, Johnnie—all find the Swede's behavior strange, and it is finally made clear, during the first card game, that the Swede believes he is going to be killed. As the Easterner puts it, "'. . . this man has been reading dime-novels, and he thinks he's right out in the middle of it—the shootin' and stabbin' and all'" (p. 152). The Swede's fears are the greatest during the card game, for in the world of the dime novels, men are often killed over cards.

Like a figure from medieval romance, Pat Scully takes seriously the duties and obligations of a host. He tries to calm the Swede and convince him that Fort Romper is a settled and civilized place, a part of the real world and not the world of romance: "'Why, man, we're goin' to have a line of ilictric street-cars in this town next spring'" (p. 149). The bride has been in Fort Romper for many years now. Scully, like the gambler we meet at the end of the story, is a family man whose oldest son practices law in Lincoln. Finally, in a gesture of hospitality, Scully offers the Swede a drink, and with the whiskey, the Swede's manner changes: he becomes arrogant and bellicose.

In the second card game the Swede's aggressive self-confidence (together, of course, with Johnnie's cheating) ironically creates the very situation the Swede fears during the first game. With "the three terrible words" from countless Western stories and films, "'you are cheatin''" (p. 156), the Swede breaks up the game. As the narrator puts it, "such scenes often prove that there can be little of dramatic import in environment" (p. 156). Suddenly, we are no longer in Fort Romper with "'the four churches and the smashin' big brick school'" (p. 150), but in the familiar world of romance which at times seems more medieval than Western.[6] Johnnie and the Swede are separated, challenges are exchanged, and then, like Anglo-Saxon thanes, Arthurian knights, or Western marshal and outlaw, the two men have their tournament, governed by Pat Scully's strict code of honor, outside the blue hotel. While Crane never lets us forget that the fight is finally only the ugly, senseless brawl of two fools over a game of cards, it is important to recognize how thoroughly the conventions of romance shape it. The fight is a trial by combat, a confrontation of adversaries, the fair fight of so many Westerns, and it is governed by the code of honor to which all Western heroes subscribe. Pat Scully restrains the cowboy when he tries to leap into the fight, and even after the Swede, whom he clearly dislikes, has thoroughly beaten his son, he endures his insults, charges him nothing for his meal, and makes certain that he leaves his house unharmed. We are obviously in a world of romance where honor, fair play, and hospitality are important virtues, where no one asks anyone to pay for his accomodation.[7]

Once the Swede steps out of the blue hotel, however, he is back in the complex, ironic, ambiguous real world.[8] He makes his way through the snowstorm to a saloon and, in a scene reminiscent of countless others in Western fiction and film, attempts to get a gambler to drink with him. But no code of romance governs here. The Swede, clearly a boisterous fool, is, in the presence of a district attorney, stabbed by the gambler, not in a tournament, but in an ugly barroom slaying that could have as easily taken place in New York or Boston as in the modern, respectable, law-abiding town of Fort Romper, Nebraska. But ironically, the gambler who kills the Swede is actually a figure from the world of Western romance, one of the spiritual sons of John Oakhurst, cool, restrained, competent, and, for the most part, honest and honorable. Yet the real world cannot be a world of romance: it is too complex and ambiguous for that. The solitary, honorable gambler of Western fiction is also, simultaneously, a "thieving card-player" (p. 167) and a respected member of the community with "a real wife and two real children in a neat cottage in a suburb" (p. 167). The Swede, an immigrant, a tailor from the East, becomes a character in a dime novel and finally attacks the gambler, a figure out of Western romance who nonetheless lives, unlike the Swede, in the real world: "'What! You won't drink with me, you little dude?'" (p. 168). The ironies here seem limitless, for the truths of the real world (and not the code of the tournament) govern this next to last part of the story. The gambler suddenly stabs the Swede, and his body, "pierced as easily as if it had been a melon" (p. 169), lies alone on the floor of the saloon beneath a cash register whose legend reminds us that in the real world we must pay, in ways we don't always expect, for our accommodation.

In the last section of the story, which some readers find anti-climactic,[9] the world of romance and the real world are seen to intersect. The immigrant Swede, like a hero of romance, acted on principle in the blue hotel: cheating is cheating whether the game is for money or for fun, although the cowboy, a familiar figure in Western romance, has accommodated himself to the way of the world and can not see the point. And then, through the words of the Easterner, Crane makes explicit that while the five men in the blue hotel all played a part in the world of romance, they were also involved in the "murder" of the Swede in the real world of the saloon. Once the Swede left the blue hotel, the code of romance ceased to govern, and Fort Romper became what it always actually was, a law-abiding town in the real world, like New York, Philadelphia, or Washington, where human action and inaction have ambiguous, complex, far-reaching, and unforeseen consequences.

In his "Introduction" to an edition of the prose and poetry, William M. Gibson mentions that "Crane once inscribed a book 'To Hamlin Garland of the great honest West from Stephen

Crane of the false East.'"[10] The contrast of the inscription suggests, I think, the nature of the two worlds we find in Crane's Western stories. While both worlds are clearly present (the stories are set in the West and employ the conventions of Western romance), Crane remains finally, as he recognizes in the inscription, a writer of "the false East," for in his application of "romantic . . . forms to a more realistic content,"[11] his vision is finally the Eastern vision, an ironic rather than a romantic vision. The ironic vision, of course, is the one the modern world, for the most part, finds just, and Crane's Western stories, as a result, reflect what seem to be the truths of our own lives, for they take place finally in a complex, changing, ambiguous, less than ideal world that is very much like the one in which all of us must live.

NOTES

[1] Gillian Beer, *The Romance* (London: Methuen and Company, 1970), p. 3.

[2] Beer, p. 13.

[3] Philip Larkin, "A Study of Reading Habits," in *The Whitsun Weddings* (London: Faber and Faber, 1964), p. 31.

[4] Northrop Frye, *Anatomy of Criticism* (Princeton: Princeton University Press, 1957), p. 223.

[5] Stephen Crane, *Tales of Adventure,* ed. Fredson Bowers (Charlottesville: The University Press of Virginia, 1970), p. 52. All citations of Stephen Crane's stories are from this edition.

[6] In an essay called "The Two Worlds of 'The Blue Hotel'" in *Modern Fiction Studies*, 5 (Autumn 1959), Hugh N. Maclean also proposes that "the story, realistically confined to Romper, takes place imaginatively in two contrasting worlds" (p. 263), the world of the blue hotel and the world of the saloon. His descriptions of these two worlds, however, are finally rather different from mine. "The blue hotel," he says, "is the world of 'what might be,' isolated, mysterious, highly symbolic; it is not an ideal world, but one in which, at least, the actions of men seem to have meaning beyond the immediate environment. The saloon represents the

world of 'what is,' at the heart of society, realistic, all but non-symbolic, and essentially amoral, 'naturalistic'" (p. 263).

[7] In his discussion of ironic myth in the *Anatomy of Criticism*, Northrop Frye recalls that "no one in a romance, Don Quixote protests, ever asks who pays for the hero's accomodation" (p. 223).

[8] In the film version of "The Blue Hotel" (in The American Short Story series) a stranger enters the hotel and kills the Swede there. In an interview with Calvin Skaggs in *The American Short Story*, ed. Calvin Skaggs (New York: Dell Publishing Company, 1977), Jan Kadar, the director, says that since "the stranger in our film, like the gambler in the saloon in Crane's story, is merely a dramatic device designed to serve destiny . . . , it makes no difference whether the stranger comes to the hotel to kill the Swede, or whether the Swede goes to the saloon to get killed" (p. 75). As a result, the film fails to recognize first that the significantly named Palace Hotel lies in the world of romance and then that, in Crane's ironic world, the gambler (as well as the entire scene in the saloon) is not merely a "device . . . to serve destiny," but, as I shall try to explain in a moment, a reminder of similar gamblers and similar scenes in countless Western stories.

[9] R. W. Stallman, for example, says "the grotesque image of the murdered Swede . . . marks the legitimate end of the story. Crane spoiled the whole thing by tacking on a moralizing appendix." *Stephen Crane: An Omnibus*, ed. R. W. Stallman (New York: Alfred A. Knopf, 1952), p. 482. Quoted in "The Two Worlds of 'The Blue Hotel,'" p. 260.

[10] Stephen Crane, *The Red Badge of Courage and Selected Prose and Poetry*, ed. William M. Gibson (New York: Holt, Rinehart and Winston, 1955), p. xii.

[11] *Anatomy of Criticism*, p. 223.

*Realism and Romance in the Western Stories of
Stephen Crane*

Can realism lead to mythmaking? Reaffirming Richard Slotkin's observation that "true myths are generated on a sub-literary level by the historical experiences of a people," **Shelley Armitage** reviews the career of Mary Hallock Foote and shows how her experiences in the West affected her art, promoting a blend of the poetic and the actual which gave her best work a mythic quality. As illustrator and as prose-writer, Foote adapted her eastern art training to western scenes and characters in ways which suggest a sensitive awareness of the tensions, hopes, and fears of western experience. By inverting some of the typical images of nineteenth century romanticism, Foote developed a western myth which contrasts with the more masculine mythic view of Frederick Jackson Turner.

Armitage, whose doctorate is in American Studies (University of New Mexico), has published several articles on the West, as well as essays on photography and cultural studies involving women in sports, American humor, and literary history. A freelance writer, she teaches English and journalism at West Texas State University in Canyon, Texas. She began work on Mary Hallock Foote in a National Endowment for the Humanities seminar. She is co-holder of a Rockefeller grant to study women photographers of the Southwest and is co-editor of *Reading into Photography*, a collection of critical essays on photography.

The Illustrator as Writer: Mary Hallock Foote and the Myth of the West

Shelley Armitage

In *Regeneration Through Violence: The Mythology of the American Frontier, 1600-1860,* Richard Slotkin reasserts the idea that the genesis of myth is essentially "low-brow," that is, it originates in shared, popular experience:

> True myths are generated on a subliterary level by the historical experience of a people and thus constitute part of that inner reality which the work of the artist draws on, illuminates, and explains. In American mythogenesis, the founding fathers were not these eighteenth-century gentlemen who composed a nation in Philadelphia. Rather, they were those who . . . tore violently a nation from the implacable and opulent wilderness—the rogues, traders, missionaries, explorers, and hunters who killed and were killed until they had mastered the wilderness; the settlers who came after, suffering hardships and Indian warfare for the sake of a sacred mission or a simple desire for the land. . . . Their concerns, their hopes, their terrors, their violence, and their justifications of themselves, as expressed in literature, are the foundation stones of the mythology that informs our history.[1]

Slotkin mentions neither mining engineers nor women in his lusty pantheon, and for good reason. Eastern-educated engineers and "protected" women typically suggest those eighteenth-century gentlemen theorizers rather than the grassroots progenitors Slotkin writes of. Yet both these groups played an important, if minor, role in western mythogenesis, for they wrested a living from the land *and* were educated to write about it. Mary Hallock Foote, a Quaker-born and eastern-reared woman who came west with her mining engineer husband in 1876, is a classic example. For over sixty years the Footes lived in the West, Arthur advancing cement, mining, and irrigation schemes, and "Molly" recreating these and other events in woodblock illustrations, short stories, and novels. Mrs. Foote was accomplished in each of these genres, but her original training as an illustrator best accommodated these new environments and people. The techniques required of the illustrator allowed Mrs. Foote to participate in the "subliterary level" of myth-making—that is, to conceptualize the West, not in terms of a sublime eastern style of art or literature, but in reportorial fashion. Certainly she did not live the lives of the rogues, traders, explorers, or hunters, but she etched real life into the block. The result is a vernacular style in her illustrations which, in turn, influenced her attitudes about the West and her consequent writing style.

Before Mrs. Foote went West, her artistic talents flowered in two particularly idealistic settings which conditioned a sensitivity for nature and the social environment. The first was her home in Milton, New York—a farm in the picturesque Hudson River Valley where physical and human surroundings encouraged an optimistic if diligent spirit. The Hallocks were avid readers and thinkers. Their library provided the family English classics along with current periodicals such as the New York *Tribune* and its Congressional Debates which Mr. Hallock delighted in discussing. Intellectual curiosity was a tradition in the family (grandfather Hallock especially loved history), and the Hallocks entertained such astute guests as Susan B. Anthony and other abolitionists. When there was a rift with local "Friends," they became even more resourceful and family-directed, relying on their intellectual interests for entertainment. As a child Mary Hallock showed artistic ability, using walls and furniture for drawing surfaces. Later, as a teenager, the family arranged for her to stay with relatives in New York so that she could attend the Cooper Institute School of Design for Women. This second environment continued to encourage her rosy spirit. Here she studied with such luminaries of woodblock illustration and drawing as Dr. Rimmer and W. J. Linton, and at this time, during the popularity of the Hudson River School painters, she began to illustrate gift books in a romantic style. New York life and art offered her the opportunities of a new, sophisticated, and exciting world, and through her friendship with classmate Helena de Kay, a well-traveled young woman of a prominent New York family, she was ushered into the local high society. Years later, when Mrs. Foote was known as "the dean of women illustrators"[2] and the "best of our designers on the wood,"[3] critic Regina Armstrong detailed the characteristics of the "woman illustrator":

> The personal point of view is peculiarly feminine . . . so it naturally follows that in the interpretation of character, the woman illustrator finds a field especially fitted to her temperamental equipment. The genre attracts her, the conventional is understood by her, and in turn the poetic, the homely, and the picturesque. . . . Owing to her environment and to the customs that surround her, life in its concrete forms lies near to the woman's hand, and in her interpretation of its typical phases she brings a subtle and sympathetic appreciation that goes to the heart of the subject. In matters of caste and circumstance, also, there is no delusion about her classification, although she may display a certain enthusiasm in some lines of portrayal, for she is usually an idealist.[4]

By the time Mrs. Foote completed her training at the Cooper Institute School of Design, these characteristics had emerged from her personal and professional background. Familiar with the personal, the conventional, and the concrete of domestic rural and urban New York, she illustrated for *Hearth and Home* and Longfellow's *Hanging of the Crane* (1874; Plate I) in a style true to genteel subjects.[5]

Thus, when she married and prepared to go West to California, Mrs. Foote outfitted herself according to her cultural baggage and her career. On that first trip West, she took a girl to function as maid and model, woodblocks to be done in illustration of *The Scarlet Letter,* and a philosophy that said "No girl ever wanted less to 'go West' with any man, or paid a man a greater compliment by doing so."[6] Yet the very art form that reinforced her idealistic and genteel personal background also equipped her to observe the subtleties of a new environment; for if, as Regina Armstrong noted, women illustrators naturally observed and recorded "life in its concrete forms" (the interpretation of character, the personal, and the conventional), then such an artist's eye could particularize new people and settings. The resulting picture, moreover, need not idealize the subject, particularly if the new subject were part of the actual environment rather than a formally posed model. Due to the artist's attention to concrete details, the rendering could be realistic instead. Other factors could effect a realistic portrayal as well. For instance, Mrs. Foote, like many illustrators, drew directly onto the woodblock, making immediate the artist's response to the spontaneous subject. Furthermore, the newness of western subjects required other than the genteel style suited to eastern characters and scenes. If the artist had no first-hand observation to draw upon, the work of other artists who had utilized their western experience became a source for the appropriate style. As an example, Mrs. Foote's only illustration of a western subject before she went West was a Catlin-like depiction of Flathead Indians for A. D. Richardson's *Beyond the Mississippi* (1867), done during the same period as her romantic gift-book illustrations. This illustration served its purpose by achieving a fidelity or an affinity for the subject. Unlike the more formal arts, the art of illustration had in its technique and purpose the means for recording new experiences. It had, in its "vocabulary," more flexibility than painting and sculpture. As Joshua C. Taylor notes in *America as Art,* this adaptability made the art of illustration well-suited as a cultural mirror:

> The share that the pictorial arts had in creating the image of America may seem quite subordinate to that borne by literature and the theater, and in a strict sense it was. The style of discourse and the character description were vivid beyond the accustomed scope of most American painters and sculptors. Brought up on a heady idealism of academic theory and taught to draw people by studying casts of antique statuary, they were ill-equipped to catch the flavor of the vernacular style. The visual impact was made less through the elevated arts of painting and sculpture than through illustrations and prints. These formed the real pictorial galleries for most Americans.... The expansion of book illustration and issuance of popularly priced lithographs and engravings coincided with the growth of the self-consciously American image.[7]

Consequently, Mrs. Foote was able to use her skill as an illustrator to capture the essence of the West and thus participate in what Slotkin calls "historical experience" at the subliterary level of myth, creating from this experience an image of the American West which evolves in her letters, reminiscences, and fiction into a mythology expressive of her real experience.

I emphasize the role the West played in leveling Mrs. Foote's personal and professional idealism because her confrontation with hard reality was the first step in her eventual use of art to mediate between the poles of the real and the ideal of what is and what should be. Because of her fascinating accounts of New Almaden, California, in her early letters to friend Helena de Kay Gilder, Richard Gilder as editor of *Scribner's Magazine* (later *Century Magazine*) requested her first written sketch accompanied by illustrations.[8] Done as a young bride, these first illustrations of the West are sublime rather than documentary, but this style disappears in subsequent illustrations. By the time we reach Mrs. Foote's best art work—"Pictures of the Far West" which appeared in *Century Magazine* in 1888-1889— she has achieved an authentic and realistic style. A number of related personal and professional experiences influenced this outcome. Though Arthur Foote tried to shelter her from the rawness of the West, chronologically Mrs. Foote moved from the rather cultivated environment of eastern friends in San Francisco (close to the Foote's first home in New Almaden) to Leadville, Colorado, where she covered the walls of their one-room cabin with geological maps, and finally to the Idaho desert where the couple initially lived in a tent. Psychologically, these subsequent "homes" were increasingly taxing. In New Almaden Arthur quit his job, unable to work for men he did not respect; in Leadville he was faced with the violence of a miners' strike and the problem of absentee eastern investors; in Idaho he attempted to realize the then impossible dream of irrigating up to 600,000 acres of desert. Besides other personal factors, such as Arthur's drinking due to worry over his projects and Mrs. Foote's miscarriage, conditions altered her career. She was forced to give up the gift-book market while in Leadville, noting in her reminiscences that she couldn't get models for her work. Gradually, she adapted her formal training to spontaneous life of the mining camps. Working from actual subjects in New Almaden, she sketched a Mexican water-carrier and the Mexican camp where the miners lived (Plate II). Leadville experiences gave her a host of actual scenes which later appeared in the illustration of her Colorado trilogy, *The Led-Horse Claim* (1882), *John Bodewin's Testimony* (1886), and *The Last Assembly Ball* (1889). When the Footes went by horseback from Morelia, Mexico, to Vera Cruz, she sketched the entire distance—over 200 miles—on horseback. She made other drawings of the villages they passed through. Certainly Idaho, with its "miles and miles of pallid sagebrush," was the ultimate lesson in realism.[9] Neither picturesque nor romantic, it fostered an attention to isolated details— the birds, the rocks, the river. Indeed, each of her western homes challenged in some manner the concept of nature the farm home of her childhood had fostered. Stark scenes, strange ethnic groups and characters, and an absence of the social manners she was accustomed to—all, when recorded on the woodblock, constituted a very different view of life.

A brief review of her treatment of this life in "Pictures of the Far West" will confirm her understanding of it. Included with the serialized essays which she wrote were these pictures: "Looking for Camp," "The Coming of Winter," "The Sheriff's Posse," "The Orchard Wind-Break," "The Choice of Reuben and Gad," "Cinching Up," "The Irrigating Ditch," "The Last Trip In," "Afternoon at a Ranch," "A Pretty Girl in the West," and "The Winter's-Camp—A Day's Ride from the Mail" (Plate III). Robert M. Taft praises these pieces for their excellence and authenticity:

> These illustrations were beautifully engraved woodcuts, for this period marks the golden age of American woodcut illustration; a period which produced magazine illustrations which have never been excelled, and *The Century* was the leader in its field. . . . Mrs. Foote is the only woman who can claim company among the men in the field of the Western picture.[10]

As an example, "The Coming of Winter" shows in detail a typical situation for a homesteader family (Plate IV). The man, gun in hand, stands outside the sod cabin while the wife, holding their baby, looks on. The authenticity of the clothing, the preciseness of the fence, the details of the house—the rubboard, pan, and mop hung on the outside wall—assure the accuracy of the scene. In "Looking for Camp," a lone hunter, his dog and horse, travel down a hill, the moon in the background (Plate V). In particular, the horse (as is characteristic of Mrs. Foote's horses) is masterfully done with careful attention to the mane and saddle trappings. "Cinching Up" depicts a couple out on a ride. The man is adjusting the lady's saddle while she sits on the horse in front of a rugged background. Critical to the fidelity of each of these illustrations in "Pictures of the Far West" is not only the affinity for detail, scene, and character, but a sense of captured motion. Like the photographers of the same period, Mrs. Foote not only documents but implies an intimacy with the scene which allows her to arrest these scenes.

This brings us to another dimension of her illustrations—one that allowed her to suggest in these real scenes an interpretation of her western life. Mrs. Foote was recognized for this quality from the beginning of her career. The first review of her early New York work noted: "It is in the conception as well as the execution of her work that Miss Hallock will delight the appreciative reader. . . . These ideas central to the poem Miss Hallock has realized with a delicacy and perfection worthy of the poem, into which she has entered not only with intelligence but with divination."[11] Regina Armstrong observed this same talent when she discussed Mrs. Foote's work later in her career:

> Mrs. Foote's talent has been more individual [than other women illustrators]; she has occupied a field to herself, perhaps because of the distinct types which interpret her own text, depicting a remote environment. . . . She links the poetic and the actual in a manner which makes them inseparable. This indefinable quality is peculiarly hers, and is admired as much by artists as by laymen.[12]

This quality can best be examined and explained by looking at a series of illustrations that date throughout Mrs. Foote's career. These pictures are of women, probably the earliest subjects Mrs. Foote mastered in a studio setting. All of these illustrations exemplify the "poetic" and the "actual" quality Regina Armstrong notes as inseparable in Mrs. Foote's works. That is, the pictures are convincing in their use of setting and character, but there also is an attitude in the characters which makes the illustrations "speak." Generally, this attitude may be described as "wistful," for the women, whether sad or serene, seem to long for something. Yet there is a marked difference between Mrs. Foote's eastern and western women. For instance, two illustrations of women in eastern settings done during the Footes' tenure in Idaho. "The Hermit-Thrush" (1893), drawn for the *Century's* American Artist series, portrays a lone young woman in the woods, mournfully looking up from the solitary road (Plate VI). In an almost identical pose, "The Mourning

Dove" (1893) carries a similar message: against the backdrop of a lonely road and wood, the woman looks sad and heartbroken (Plate VII). The poetic quality of both is a sentimentality in the tradition of Mrs. Foote's early romantic style. The latter drawing illustrates a poem by Edith M. Thomas which explains this essence:

> It is the wild dove's vanishing note I hear;
> She sits her nest, and darkness and sun, and dew
> Touch her soft throat, but never to utterance clear—
>   "Who, who, who?"
> Only this, but I catch at the slender clew,
> And follow it back till I reach the heart of a wrong—
> "Who, who, who delays thee so long?"[13]

However, in the drawings of women in the West during this same period the poetic quality is not romantic yearning, but a sense of expectation. These women may be posed similarly to the eastern pictures—that is, in an illustration for *The Led-Horse Claim* and for the much later short story, "On a Side Track" (1894), the women look away from the center of the picture—but their expressions suggest strength, patience, and resoluteness. One of the best examples of this attitude is from *The Led-Horse Claim*, a scene in which the young woman, trapped in a dark mining shaft, with only a candle for light, looks expectantly and determinedly into the dark (Plate VIII). One might argue, of course, that this quality is due to the content of the article or fiction the illustration accompanies. Yet an important part of Mrs. Foote's artistic theory was that the illustration should not repeat the "personal situations of the story already described in words," but enlarge upon the subject.[14] Mrs. Foote saw the illustrations as extensions of the text; moreover, because they did "speak," she attempted to use the illustrations to tell a story, or part of a story. In the case of women, clearly these two environments—the East and the West—made very different requirements of them. The story Mrs. Foote was trying to relate in her western illustrations had at its heart a tension between the ideal and the real: the hopeful spirit of her eastern girlhood and the hard realities that she had to cope with in the West. As she says in her reminiscences about life in Idaho:

> I hardly know how to keep a true balance between the two sides of that Cañon existence—the life of dreams it fed in the beauty around us, and the grimy attention it demanded every hour of the day to insistent realities. The children were never really safe without a grown-up eye on them. . . . There were the high places on all their walks; there were rattlesnakes lurking in holes in the rocks; there was the wire bridge, a nightmare to mothers—there was always the river. (p. 290)

Mrs. Foote's illustrations expressed this tension and constituted the subliterary level of myth-making that Slotkin notes in *Regeneration Through Violence.* The West acquainted Mrs. Foote with a new way of seeing; she first articulated this view by reporting it visually for an audience of eastern magazine readers. Working from the direct observation and experience that informed her illustrations, she next moved to the literary arena to fully explain the meaning of these powerful images. Her writing, she said, had "grown from my aborted art, as I found the West and its absorbing material too much for my pencil."[15] The result is a body of writing, including short stories, novels, and reminiscences, in which Mrs. Foote attempts to duplicate the actual poetic quality in her picture in order to dramatize the tension between the ideal and the real. Though her fiction is uneven, no doubt her training on the woodblock with actual subjects enabled her to gradually master particularized settings and carefully drawn characters. Her best works, such as *The Chosen Valley* (1892) and "How the Pump Stopped at the Morning Watch" (1899), are pictorial and imagistic, suggesting the best qualities of her illustrations. Her writings, taken together with the reminiscences, pit tenderfoot against westerner, East against West, the individual against a loose and unpredictable society, and constitute a personal version of the western myth which had its genesis in Mrs. Foote's experiences as a western illustrator.[16]

The most interesting place to trace the elements and development of Mrs. Foote's version of the West is in the reminiscences, *A Victorian Gentlewoman in the Far West.* One obvious mode of development is to juxtapose eastern and western values and experiences, romanticism and realism against one another. Beginning in the early sections of the reminiscences, Mrs. Foote details her Quaker upbringing and life in New Almaden and

Leadville by pitting her early career and its romantic subjects against Arthur's determination to go West. For instance, when she meets Arthur in the Emma Beach home in New York, she says she was working on commissioned sketches for *Hearth and Home* and describes Arthur as having "the blood of farmers and homemakers in him, and the brains of a constructor" (p. 80). When he returns from California in 1876 to marry her and take her West, she says she was illustrating a Longfellow book and remarks on the intrusion of his West into her East: "He unpacked his leathery luggage in . . . grandmother's room, and laid his pipe and pistol on the bureau where her chaste neckerchiefs had been wont to lie" (p. 104). This method of playing the values of the past against new experiences continues in the Leadville section where she translates the difference between the past and present into the difference between romance and realism. For instance, when she and Arthur are traveling to Leadville by buggy over a dangerous pass, a stage almost sideswipes them, forcing Arthur to whip his team up the embankment to avoid disaster. As a result of this strain, one horse dies, and another, hired the next day, dies of lung fever when they finally reach camp. Mrs. Foote writes: "A. paid for both—and how much more the trip cost him I never knew, but that is the price of Romance; to have allowed his wife to come in by stage in company of drunkenness and vice, or anything else that might happen, would have been realism" (p. 172). Regretably, Mrs. Foote was always too modest about her own knowledge of the West and thus would be blind to the irony implicit in her description. She did, after all, travel by buggy exposed to the weather and dangers she describes. Once in Leadville, where her home was the meeting place for men such as Clarence King and James Hague, she learned much about the management, operations, and hazards of the mines. Again, she writes of the tension implicit in the actions of Arthur and his assistants, well-bred and educated men who had to act differently in the West: "This was the absurd side of life in Leadville which made them all seem boys together; that the methods of schoolboys and savages should be the ones these grown men were obliged to use, who were not savages nor excited nor warlike nor angry with anyone" (p. 195).

A second method Mrs. Foote used in the reminscences relies on imagery, metaphor, and motif to reveal her ideas. If we remember the decidely sentimental handling of the pictures, "The Hermit Thrush" and "The Mourning Dove," we can more fully appreciate the meaning of Mrs. Foote's turning images which are conventionally romantic into haunting motifs. When she recounts her first arrival in "darkest Idaho," she writes:

> But what a morning! Meadowlarks were springing up all about us—it was April and we knew there were nests and wild flowers hid in the sage beneath those jets of song.... Their note was a brief song, sad and sweet, that rained down to us from the sky. It haunted us, that song, every spring of all our years in Idaho, as it welcomed up that April morning. The birds and the wind filled the vast, brooding silence—the desert wind that talks, that whispers, that brings messages from the infinite filled with whatever each human soul that listens can put into it.
> (p. 275)

Later, after discussing the "nest-building" she and Arthur attempted in the Cañon, Mrs. Foote remembers, with poignancy, the dove's call:

> And every day and all day the wood doves up the gulch were calling, calling, hid in the willow thickets.... And we knew that Harriet Hawley was dead, and Spencer Foote and his wife were dead, and their little Margaret.... The air was heavenly soft and sweet, wild roses scented every breath of wind from up the gulch and all day the patient, maddening doves kept saying something we could not get out of our heads and could not understand.
> (p. 299)

This last passage, perhaps the most stylistically beautiful in all of Mrs. Foote's writing in its almost Faulknerian imagery and pace, exemplifies how she was able to move from the concrete to the poetic. Moreover, the conventions she uses are not artificial, but expressions of very real conflicts and ironies; yet in using them, Mrs. Foote creates another level of reality symbolically. She is, in fact, the tenderfoot of her own reminiscences and, like her own fictional characters, suffers the tragic consequences. In the following example from the Idaho years, note how she begins the passage with concrete experience and ends with an almost surreal, and certainly nightmarish image. At first, she remembers the particular irony of giving birth to a girl just before joining Arthur in Idaho:

> And a girl baby! Boys for the frontier, but with the arrival of this little downy head next to my heart, that foolish part of me turned back to the East of my own girlhood. This meant farewell music, art, gossip of the workshop, schools that we knew about, new friends just made who would forget us, old friends better loved than ever and harder to part from—all the old backgrounds receding hopelessly and forever. Mexico had not been farther to the imagination that this—and what compensations! You reached it by the gulfs enchanted, by moonlight nights in old Spanish-American cities, by strange, medieval roads. But—darkest Idaho! Thousands of acres of desert empty of history. The Snake River had an evil name—the Boise, the source of our great scheme, emptied into and was lost in it.... I felt adrift, as it were, cast off on a raft with my babies, swept past these wild shores uninhabited for us. My husband steering with a surveyor's rod or some such futile thing. (pp. 265-266)

Such imagery in these selected passages, as well as those that establish the thematic poles of East/West, romantic/realistic, and tenderfoot/westerner, expresses a concept of the West quite antithetical to that recognized by Frederick Jackson Turner and other proponents of the frontier thesis. What Mrs. Foote writes in her fiction and her reminiscences constitutes her version of the western myth which she builds from her conceptions as an illustrator. Turner saw the frontier as a molder of character and as an impetus for individualism, a unifier of the nation that melded various stocks and regions and nurtured democratic forms. For Mrs. Foote, however, excessive individualism resulted in anarchy; unity was impossible because of the diversity of special interests, and democratic forms—especially as manifested in law and order—were often limited because of the newness of the country and a consequent lack of manners governing behavior. Hence, her inverted use of imagery—images typically suggestive of dreams and ideals, such as the bird's call, the nest-building, the surveyor's rod—allows her to construct a myth counter to Turner's thesis. She explains the heart of this myth in this expository passage from *The Chosen Valley*:

> The ideal scheme is ever beckoning from the West; but the scheme with an ideal record is yet to find—the scheme that shall breed no murmurers, and see no recreants; that shall avoid envy, hatred, malice, and all uncharitableness; that shall fulfill its promises and pay its debts, and remember its friends, and keep itself unspotted from the world. Over the graves of the dead, and over the hearts of the living, presses the cruel expansion of our country's material progress; the prophets are confounded, the promise withdrawn, the people imagine a vain thing. Men shall go down, the deed arrives; not impeachable, as the first proud word went forth, but mishandled, shorn, stained with obloquy, and dragged through crushing strains. And those that are with it in its latter days are not those who set out in the beginning. And victory, if it come, shall border hard upon defeat.[17]

This passage clearly relates to Mrs. Foote's repeated references to her husband as a dreamer throughout the reminiscences. As she says of Arthur's stubborn faith in his Idaho irrigation scheme:

> The author of this scheme was thirty-three years old. He had lost two years of his technical training which never could be made up quite to his own satisfaction, though he was always at school, the school of self-training. What he wanted was opportunity, like the days of the early discoverers, or the rise of the American merchant marine, or the Civil War which had taken his older brothers and tested them and wrung them out. And if a man desires to be wrung out to the last dregs and take the risk of failure and years of work with no return, a better job than this could not be found. (p. 270)

Thus, rather than deal with the West in ideal or opportunistic terms, Mrs. Foote's fiction and reminiscences tell a story of constant tension between dreams and reality—a tension which is most often resolved in disappointment. This narrative, as we may call the body of Mrs. Foote's work when we acknowledge the pervasiveness of the repeated tension between the real and the ideal, is a story whose meaning is best explained by Lyman Ward's comment about his grandmother (who is based on Mary

Hallock Foote) in Wallace Stegner's novel, *Angle of Repose:*

> When frontier historians theorize about the uprooted, the lawless, the purseless, and the socially cut-off who settled the West, they are not talking about people like my grandmother. So much that was cherished and loved, women like her had to give up; and the more they gave it up, the more they carried it helplessly with them. It was a process like ionization: what was subtracted from one pole was added to the other. For that sort of pioneer, the West was not a new country being created, but an old one being reproduced; in that sense our pioneer women were always more realistic than our pioneer men.[18]

Despite Mrs. Foote's reputation as a local color writer and, sometimes, a sentimentalist, Stegner's definition of realism fits her well. In both her reminiscences and her letters to editor Richard Gilder, it is evident that she changed both endings and story content to please the editor whose readership preferred a happy ending. The heart of her writings remains, nevertheless, firmly grounded in the perception of the artist's eye. The resulting conception is an effort to dramatize the tension between the poetic and the actual. Mrs. Foote's ability to externalize the subliterary experiences of the West hinged on her sensitivity and technique as an illustrator. The result is an authenticity in her fiction generated by the perception and depiction of a mythical West other than that popularized by mainstream western critics and authors—an inner reality with all its attendant ambiguities.

NOTES

[1] Richard Slotkin, *Regeneration Through Violence: The Mythology of the American Frontier, 1600-1860* (Middletown, Connecticut: Wesleyan University Press, 1973), p. 4.

[2] Regina Armstrong, "Representative American Women Illustrators:

The Character Workers—II," *Critic,* 37 (August 1900), 131.

[3] W. J. Linton quoted in *American Art and American Art Collections,* ed. Walter Montgomery (Boston: E. W. Walker, 1889), I, 1449.

[4] Armstrong, "Representative American Women Illustrators: The Character Workers—I," *Critic,* 36 (July 1900), 43.

[5] The first review of Mrs. Foote's work appeared in *Atlantic Monthly* (December 1874) and praised her work in Longfellow's *The Hanging of the Crane.* Longfellow himself was pleased with her work.

[6] Mary Hallock Foote, *A Victorian Gentlewoman in the Far West: The Reminiscences of Mary Hallock Foote,* ed. Rodman W. Paul (San Marino, California: Huntington Library, 1972), p. 114. Mrs. Foote wrote her reminiscences in the early 1920s. Subsequent page references to this work are included in the text.

[7] Joshua C. Taylor, *America As Art* (New York: Harper and Row, 1976), pp. 93-94.

[8] Mrs. Foote eventually contributed a variety of writing to the *Century* beginning with sketches of life in New Almaden and then short stories and serialized novels.

[9] The Idaho years, 1883-1893, marked the Footes' most difficult period in the West. Arthur not only abandoned the area in which he had trained for the new field of irrigation but, as the reminiscences show, Mrs. Foote finally admitted that the West was to be their home, despite earlier hopes that they would make their "fortune" and return to the East.

[10] Robert M. Taft, *Artists and Illustrators of the Old West* (New York: Charles Scribner's Sons, 1953), p. 174.

[11] "Recent Literature," *Atlantic Monthly,* 34 (December 1874), 745-746.

[12] Armstrong, "Illustrators—II," p. 132.

[13] Edith M. Thomas, "The Mourning Dove," *Century Magazine,* 45 (February 1893), 545.

[14] Letter from Mary Hallock Foote to Richard Gilder, June 1, 1891, The Mesa, Boise, Idaho, the Huntington Collection.

[15] See Armstrong, "Illustrators—II," p. 135.

[16] The full genesis of this myth may be traced through the novels, though I do not discuss them fully here. As an example, *The Led-Horse Claim* (1882) explores the running of mines by uninformed and unrealistic eastern interests; *John Bodewin's Testimony* (1886) dramatizes Arthur's own court testimony against a claim-jumper (a case that paid him the same amount as that earned by the dishwasher for a night at the Clarendon Hotel); *The Last Assembly Ball* (1889) explores the difficulty of "manner" and the social differences between western and eastern society. These novels make use of a "new" hero, the "professional-exile," as Mrs. Foote

called him, who was a tenderfoot easterner—often a mining engineer—who had come West. Though the works are marred by the intrusion of audience-appeal and the requirements of her editors, Mrs. Foote attempted to portray the West's corruptibility, rather than its conventional garden image.

[17] Mary Hollock Foote, *The Chosen Valley* (Boston and New York: Houghton Mifflin, 1892), pp. 313-314.

[18] Wallace Stegner, *Angle of Repose* (Garden City, New York: Doubleday, 1971), p. 277.

Plate I. Illustration by Mary Hallock Foote for "The Hanging of the Crane" (1874), in *The Complete Poetical Works of Henry Wadsworth Longfellow* (Boston: Houghton, Mifflin and Co., 1902), p. 397.

Plate II. "The Water-Carrier of the Mexican Camp," illustration by Mary Hallock Foote for her sketch, "A California Mining Camp," *Scribner's Monthly*, 15 (February 1878), 491.

Plate III. "The Winter's Camp—A Day's Ride from the Mail," from Pictures of the Far West series, *Century*, 39 (November 1889), 57.

Plate IV. "The Coming of Winter,"
from Pictures of the Far West series, *Century*,
37 (December 1888), 162.

Plate V. "Looking for Camp,"
from Pictures of the Far West series, Century,
37 (November 1888), 108.

Plate VI. "The Hermit-Thrush,"
from American Artists of the American Scene series,
Century, 46 (June 1893), 236.

Plate VII. Illustration by Mary Hallock Foote for "The Mourning Dove," *Century*, 45 (February 1893), 545.

Plate VIII. Mary Hallock Foote, *The Led-Horse Claim* (Boston: James R. Osgood and Co., 1882), frontispiece.

Few contemporary American writers have addressed the connections between fact and imagination, realism and myth, more intensely than Wright Morris. As a prober into American culture Morris is unique in combining fictional representations with photographic representations —both drawing upon "facts," both presenting "images" for the reader's or viewer's meditation. In the following essay **Joseph Wydeven** draws upon Morris's fiction, photo-texts, and critical essays to explicate the photographs as mythic statements grounded in Morris's own meditations on the American Dream: history becomes myth through the archetypal dialectic of nature and civilization; Morris's landscape is a metaphysical one.

Joseph Wydeven has published several articles on Wright Morris. His interests include photography and photographic theory in American contexts, and he has recently directed a Humanities grant project on American Indian art and culture. He chairs the English Department of Bellevue College (Nebraska). The present essay was completed prior to the publication of Wright Morris's *Photographs & Words*.

Images and Icons:
The Fiction and Photography of Wright Morris

Joseph J. Wydeven

In thirty-odd books since 1942, Nebraska-born Wright Morris has dealt with peculiarly American materials in an attempt to come to terms with the complex relations between reality and the mythic dream of the West in the American psyche. Primarily a novelist, Morris also put in a long apprenticeship with the camera, establishing a comfortable reputation as a photographer in the two decades after 1933. Much of Morris's concern has been with the ontological status of objects in the environment, particularly with how those objects, viewed first through the viewfinder, afterwards reveal themselves mysteriously in the chemical bath of the darkroom. His first national publication, in 1940, was a photo-text experiment entitled "The Inhabitants," establishing Morris's characteristic method of juxtaposing photograph and prose text deliberately in order to force the viewer to a creative synthesis from the data supplied by the two separate media. In the introduction to that piece he laid down his intentions and his rationale:

> Two separate mediums are employed for two distinct views. Only when refocussed in the mind's eye will the third view result. The burden of *technique* is the reader's alone. His willingness to participate—rather than spectate—will determine his range.[1]

This method—incidentally bringing to mind the emblem tradition which includes Francis Quarles and one of Morris's favorites, William Blake—was employed by Morris in two full-length works of the 1940s, *The Inhabitants* (1946; expanded from "The Inhabitants") and *The Home Place* (1948), and again in the later, retrospective *God's Country and My People* (1968). Photographs and prose had appeared in tandem before, but Morris was the first to function as both writer and photographer, and he made his experiments deliberately exploratory in epistemological terms, exploiting the tension between "factual" photo and "fictional" text. As a result the photo-texts are as important for their theoretical principles as they are for their specific contents.

Morris's reputation has been small and hard-won, and although he has been the recipient of some fine criticism, one has the feeling that he has often been too easily dismissed as a kind of crank, thought on one hand to be too provincial in subject matter, on the other too pretentiously complex to bear the weight of his "regionalism." Until the last few years, only Alan Trachtenberg had looked at Morris's fiction in light of his photography,[2] and it is only recently that the photographic community has taken careful notice of him in critical terms.[3] So far, however, we have developed little of the critical terminology necessary to make sense of Morris's achievement in the combined photo-text mode. If critics of William Blake still complain that the requisite tools for studying the "composite art" of Blake are not yet forged, so much more difficult for critics attempting to make sense of words and *photography*, the latter having a peculiarly difficult ontological status by reason of its complex poise *between* fact and fiction, history and image, the "real" and the imagined. Alan Trachtenberg, for instance, discussing the differences between painting and photography, notes that painting "cannot be a direct, physical *impression* of the actual light bouncing off the surfaces of [an] event. [But] An honest, straight photograph cannot help but put us in touch with history in a manner unique to itself."[4] Morris's photography, of course, is "straight" to the nth degree, and should be studied with Trachtenberg's comment in mind.

The point is that because Morris was a serious photographer as well as a writer of prose fiction, his work—especially in its juxtaposed form—has been considerably self-reflective. This paper is an attempt to link this reflexivity to Morris's metaphysics as a whole; Morris's photographs, often enough, are "archetypal" in character, and in order to explain this it is necessary to begin with some primary definitions. The word "myth" applies in two quite different, but necessarily related ways. First—and this is particularly the concern of his novels, such as *The Field of Vision* (1956) and its "sequel" *Ceremony in Lone Tree* (1960), which have strong social components—Morris uses "myth" in its traditional sense as a cultural tale involving heroes, obstacles and overcomings, quest and triumph over excruciating odds. In his article "Made in U.S.A." Morris notes that Americans have made of the cowboy stereotype the "hero with a thousand faces cut down to our size," thus indicating a possible indebtedness to Joseph Campbell's meditations on myth as well as to Campbell's concern that the present contains not the stuff from which traditional heroes are made.[5]

The second sense of "myth" in Morris is a great deal more complex because, by way of compensation for the absence of cultural heroics, this form of myth returns to nature for its strengths. Morris takes over the organicism of the Romantics and uses it to his advantage: cultural objects (that is, those made by human hands for human use) have correspondences in nature—or else they are imbued by Morris with organic life. Many of Morris's photographs are concerned with the relationships between cultural and organic life: things *built* are similar in scope or function to things which *grow* in a natural environment. More important is Morris's insistence that objects, for him, become icons;[6] and as he views the objects in his lens as icons, the resultant photographs themselves become hierophantic, involved in ritual; the end result is that for him photographs as ritual foundations for meditation—in the Heideggerian sense—and for interaction between viewer and viewer, as well as between viewer and object.[7] But it is necessary to put the photographs aside for the time being, and to look at the evidence from Morris's novels and critical works.

Morris's central concern—indeed it may be his most absorbing theme—is the myth of America in its manifestations as the dream of the West as Paradise-Nirvana. About the dream Morris strikes an attitude of ironic ambivalence, simultaneously revulsed and attracted by the mid-century version of it in American culture. In *The World in the Attic* (1949) Morris first relates *nostalgia* for the mythic past to *nausea*, with nausea being a kind of cumulative nostalgia at last aware of its selective sentimentality. In *The World in the Attic*, Muncy's sense of nausea comes from his realization that he has returned too often to his memories of the past for sustenance. At one point he tries to put his thoughts into order, and he reflects:

> After all is said and done, or dead and buried, or hashed up and warmed over, the land is the potter and where it shows its hand men are the same. On other frontiers,

right now, were the young men who entered Nebraska, with the same dream, just eighty years ago. That dream was young. Was ours growing old? Had we found replacements for these parts of our life? Or had we been victimized by the fact that abstinence, frugality, independence were not the seeds of heroes, but the roots of the great soft life. Out of frugality—in this rich land—what could come but abundance, and out of abundance different notions of a brave new world. For every man—as we now say—a full dinner pail.[8]

The dream is an updated version of the Protestant ethic bequeathed by the Puritans, now sufficiently distanced to have atrophied into myth. The problem with the myth in its twentieth century manifestations is that its organic relations to the land have been severed. The difference between the past and the present in Muncy's version is that the necessity for labor in a cultural psychology of "abstinence, frugality, independence" has given way to an abundance which must destroy the very "virtues" which gave significance to the quest for land in the first place. The result is a breakdown of connections between the land and the people who live on it. It is precisely the problem of broken connections which Morris explores in *The World in the Attic*.[9]

By the time of *The Field of Vision* (1956), Morris's criticism of the atrophied dream is a great deal more pronounced. Like Byron's narrator in *Don Juan*, Morris wants "a hero: an uncommon want"—and it is the uncommonness of the want in American culture which Morris makes his theme. Modern conditions, the book argues through its "hero" Gordon Boyd, have depleted the concept of heroism and made it meaningless. Boyd is aware of his own impotence, thinking at one point: "Profession? Hero. Situation? Unemployed."[10] Nevertheless, Boyd knows that heroes are made by putting ordinary mortals through heroic *experiences,* so that the experiences themselves convey the meaning. And thus it is through Boyd's efforts that Gordon McKee, Boyd's young namesake, enters the Mexican bullfight ring to retrieve his Davy Crockett coonskin hat—a hat now invested with meaning because the boy must risk something to regain it: the boy "becomes" Davy Crockett through a ritual experience; not for nothing is Boyd led to think of "the rites of spring" (*FV*, p. 235). No doubt this is a small victory for Boyd, aware as he is that "each transformation called for another, or the hero remained like . . . Boyd . . . Snug in his flannel winding sheet" (*FV*, pp. 109-110), but its apparent triviality is a mark of the depth of his—and the author's—despair of the modern situation.

The necessity of Boyd's transformative efforts should not, however, be underestimated, as critics are wont to do. When young Gordon returns from the bullfight ring he is saved—always tentatively, temporarily, tenuously in Morris's world—from the other two options held out to him throughout the book: on one hand the world of his grandfather Walter McKee, who is a paragon of security and middle-class affability but who is without powers of perception; on the other hand the myopic world of his great-grandfather Scanlon. Throughout the book Scanlon tries to persuade young Gordon to have his being in the world of the past; he enthralls the boy with tales of the pioneer past which are full of terrors and heroics. Moreover, he tells these stories in the first person, although the truth is that these are events which happened to his father. Scanlon has told these tales so often that he has assimilated them to his own need for heroics, thus transforming *himself* into a hero. Scanlon, that is, has made himself into a mythic figure in order to live at all in the modern world. We are told that "Tom Scanlon lived—if that was the word—only in the past. When the century turned and faced the east, he stood his ground. He faced the west. He made an interesting case, as Boyd had once observed, being a man who found more to live for, in looking backward, than those who died all around him, looking ahead" (*FV*, pp. 43-44). Of course young Gordon finds Scanlon's version of the past heroic—it is the reality behind the coonskin hat the boy wears—and Boyd knows that he must keep Gordon from being trapped in Scanlon's mythic world. He acts on the boy's behalf because he knows that Scanlon's version of the past is dead, having already been used up by those heroes who actually lived it. Scanlon's myth is sterile—for anyone else.

The large theme, then, of *The Field of Vision* is that when heroics are intentionally stifled by the collective culture (which sells coonskin hats but refuses to invest them with meaning), the sole recourse for the individual is to provide meaning through rituals and ceremonies which originate in vital imagination—and it is to make *this* case that Morris provides the parallel story of Dr. Leopold Lehmann and his patient Paul(a) Kahler. Lehmann is a psychiatrist of sorts, having "pronounced Neanderthal connections" to the past, a man who "knew nothing of the body, little of the mind, but [who] had an arrangement of sorts with the soul" (*FV,* pp. 65-66). Having sought connective meaning all of his life, Lehmann finds fulfillment in solving the case of Paula Kahler, who, it turns out, is really Paul Kahler, a man who has transformed himself psychologically into a woman in order to free himself from male aggressiveness (the word "transvestite" is far too clinical a term to suit Kahler's case). Morris makes a great deal of the fact that Kahler has effected a transformation, even if it is a dysfunctional change, because she is living proof— and thus is shown to Boyd—that holistic change is indeed a possibility in the modern world. Morris thus links the Lehmann-Kahler arguments for transformation to the Boyd-Scanlon-McKee story in order to assert a case for Bergsonian vitalism: a willed creative evolution in human potential which creates the possibility for transformative imagination.[11]

It is obvious, then, that Morris was interested in two phenomena in putting together *The Field of Vision*: on one hand he speaks out against the collective culture which through its institutions stifles the imagination and forces renegade minds to the creation of destructive myths; on the other hand, he is interested in *how* myths get made and in the needs they serve— and most important, he is interested in the ways in which the imagination can be brought into effective play to serve both personal and social needs. The critical book *The Territory Ahead,* published the year after *The Field of Vision,* may be considered Morris's handbook—spelling out the problem, as he sees it, and suggesting conceivable antidotes—on the American imagination.

It is the thesis of *The Territory Ahead* that Americans in general, and American novelists in particular, have been entrapped in myth, subject to the belief that in order to capture the essence of the American experience it was merely necessary to *record* nature: America was so vast, in both expanse and idea, that it defied explanation. Morris distinguishes between "raw material" (the *givens* of experience) and "process" (the means by which the raw material is mined), and argues that American culture at large has made the former its fetish, neglecting the "fiction" through which the imagination functions as it processes the "facts" of experience. For Americans only the "facts" have significance, an attitude which Morris calls a faith in "the mythic past," and he links it to our present nostalgia: "Nostalgia, perhaps the most inexhaustible of human sentiments, found in this green world of the imagination its permanent refuge, out of time, out of reach, but not out of mind."[12] In Morris's view the American imagination likes to think itself a kind of conduit through which Nature pours its secrets.

In opposition to such passivity—an attitude to which in other contexts he is himself prone—Morris urges upon us the example of Henry James. Against Norman Rockwell—Morris's favorite enemy, the "technician" in charge of mythic regression—Morris insists upon James as an example of *consciousness:* "the most fully conscious mind and talent of the century, speaking for a nation primarily *non*-conscious, and proud of it" (*TA,* p. 189). In addition there is the social efficacy of D. H. Lawrence, the man who specialized in twentieth century "becoming." Lawrence's influence may be seen in the paragraph with which Morris concludes the main body of his text:

> The artist might well ask how, in such a spinning world as ours, he is to know that he stands in the *present.* There are no pat answers, but there are clues. Since he must live and have his being in a world of clichés, he will know this new world by their absence. He will know it by the fact that he has not been there before. The true territory ahead is what he must imagine for himself. He will recognize it by its strangeness, the lonely pilgrimage through which he attained it, and through the window of his fiction he will breathe the air of his brave new world. Strange, indeed, will be the gods found to inhabit it.
>
> (*TA,* p. 231)

The myth of "Nature, NATURE writ large" (*TA,* p. 45), the critique of which Morris borrows from Lawrence, is only one of the clichés which surround us, and the means by which we may be released from it is the vital possession of the imagination.

Now, on the imagination Morris is something of a throwback to the Romantics, no matter how critical he may be of their passivity. To use the imagination is to utilize a tool provided by nature. In recent statements Morris has reaffirmed his conviction that imagination is primary in defining the human species, but he has gone even further, echoing Keats and Coleridge on the imagination and its organic foundation. In a letter to John

Taylor, Keats spoke of poetry in organic terms, saying "That if poetry comes not as naturally as the Leaves to a tree it had better not come at all."[13] Morris is a strange modern echo when he says that "the imaginative activity is organic . . . the mind thinks just as a plant gives off buds."[14] The relevance of these statements to Morris's photography will be clear shortly, but one more Romantic may be relevant at this point, this time Coleridge, who specialized in differentiating the organic from the mechanical: "The organic form . . . is innate; it shapes as it develops itself from within, and the fulness of its development is one and the same with the perfection of its outward form."[15]

Morris has used this organic metaphor again and again in his fiction and his photo-text works—where indeed that metaphor speaks to the myth-making propensity itself: for Morris, humans make myths because they are themselves continually involved in the archetypal patterns of the diurnal and seasonal cycles. In *The Inhabitants* (1946), Morris's first book-length photo-text, he takes the title from Thoreau and makes the entire work a kind of running response to an epigraph chosen from Thoreau. Thoreau's point is that architectural beauty comes not so much from the materials of the structure as from the "necessities and character of the indweller" who lives *in* the structure which reveals in this manner a corresponding "unconscious beauty of life." Morris expands upon Thoreau: the inhabitants of the structures are inhabit*ed* by the materials in a reciprocal fashion. "An Inhabitant," Morris writes in the first photo-text entry, "is what you can't take away from a house," and it can't be taken away because it is etched into the house itself—or rather, it has become an organic part of the house.

Organicism, then, for Morris, appears to be a kind of reciprocal relationship between neutral nature and the cultural human. If for Coleridge the organic form is "innate," shaping itself from within, for Morris the organic is applied to cultural structures and artifacts which partake in the human by reason of being created as "mirrors" of the human soul which "inhabits" them. And this is essentially what many of Morris's photographs lead us to conclude: what Morris wants to show is not only the dichotomy between the natural and the cultural but the ways in which the two blend into one another. In *The Home Place,* for instance, there is a photograph of a wooden board, carefully planed and cut for human use, which is now half-buried in the earth: the earth, that is, appears to be reclaiming it precisely *as* organic matter.[16]

The reader may find any number of other examples in the photographs—the dust jacket of *God's Country and My People* comes immediately to mind—of Morris's interest in things cultural returning to their natural fundaments through the processes of time and weather. It is as if in Morris's photography, as in his fiction, there is a law of nature which seeks expression: nature recalls; culture resists but capitulates. The archetypal dialectic of nature and culture is history as myth. To borrow a term from photographic history, Morris's photographs are often "equivalents" of this "law" of nature, with Morris emphasizing the ways in which the "inhabitants" haunt—and are haunted by— their structures and artifacts. This is, of course, the reason why Morris so rarely includes humans—and never human faces— in his photographs: the intrusion of a *particular* human would obscure the archetypal message. By its nature a teller of historical truths, photography strives towards myth only by *de*-particularizing and seeking the truth through essential generalization.

Nothing is more useful for getting at Morris's intentions in photography than his use of a passage from Henry James's *The American Scene* quoted at length twice in *The Territory Ahead*, but making its initial appearance in Morris's work as epigraph to his photo-text novel, *The Home Place* (1948):

> To be at all critically, or as we have been fond of calling it, analytically, minded—over and beyond an inherent love of the general many-colored picture of things—is to be subject to the superstition that objects and places, coherently grouped, disposed for human use and addressed to it, must have a sense of their own, a mystic meaning proper to themselves to give out: to give out, that is, to the participant at once so interested and so detached as to be moved to a report of the matter.

What James calls a "superstition"—that objects and places have meanings apart from socially referential ones—appears to be, in fact, something of a conviction held by American photographers —who have not, on the whole, been embarrassed to speak in such "mystical" terms of the relations between vision and what Blake called "corporeal sight." Stieglitz coined the term "equivalent" to speak of the metaphoric relations between emotions and objects seen through the viewfinder; and according to a recent commentator, for Edward Weston "The same movements and rhythms that were recognized in tree bark or sand dunes were also found in heart beats, peristalsis, or music."[17] In short, things in the world can be seen, through "superstition," to be like other things of vaster significance: the role of interpretation—perhaps penetration is a better word—is to uncover and reveal these hidden, disguised, "mystic" meanings. But this "superstition" is as odds, in Morris's work, with another term he uses frequently: the thing-itself.

This term "thing itself" is subject to some misunderstanding in its application to photography. Morris may have borrowed the term from Edward Weston (a photographer with whom Morris has other affinities); Weston wrote in his *Day Books*: "To see the *Thing Itself* is essential: the Quintessence revealed direct without the fog of impressionism—the casual noting of a superficial phase, or transitory mood. This then: to photograph a rock, have it look like a rock, but be *more* than a rock.—Significant presentation—not interpretation."[18] In *The Inhabitants* (2nd edition), Morris wrote that "the-thing-itself must be encouraged to speak. In the matter of selection of such objects, I relied entirely on my feelings about them: They spoke to me or they did not speak. Behind my eyes, in the complex of my nature, I had a reliable Geiger counter. When exposed to radiant raw material, it ticked."[19] In another place Morris speaks of his preference for the "direct frontal stance—face to face to the fact—as in the early daguerreotype portraits. No interpretations were necessary: it was sufficient to let the subject speak for itself."[20] The stress on the "thing itself" is an effort to leave the object intact in its setting while penetrating to its essence—in terms Morris uses in another place, the determination to *reveal* the object rather than to *expose* it.[21]

But Morris's metaphysical interests in photography run deeper than merely an attention to the "thing itself"; he wants to show relationships, as I have suggested, between nature and culture—in terms of "equivalents." Morris's stress on the "thing itself" is to this extent misleading, for "equivalent" and "thing itself" are opposing terms in much the same sense that "metaphor" and "essence" are opposing. In an article written to clarify the distinction between documentary and pictorial photography, Morris introduces the terms *image* and *photograph* (sometimes *picture*): a photographic *image* is one in which the aesthetic elements outweigh the evidential ones. "If we feel shame, embarrassment, or disgust," Morris writes, "we have the assurance that the image has not obliterated the photograph."[22] We might say, then, that Morris wants to make essential metaphysical statements demanding viewer cooperation in reading the evidence from things-in-themselves. These are "images" rather than "pictures," and they function through archetypal, rather than historical, interests: they are, in effect, mythic.

The mythic dimension of Morris's photography may be approached through a term which Morris has used to describe the relations between reality and the imagination viewing that reality: "metaphysical landscape," a term introduced by Morris in *Ceremony in Lone Tree,* perhaps the most intriguing of all of his defenses of the myth-making imagination. In the opening pages of *Ceremony in Lone Tree* old man Scanlon—carried over from *The Field of Vision* and aged a few months more—sits at his window in the Lone Tree Hotel and faces west, peering into "the scenic props of his own mind."[23] Morris tells us that the window through which Scanlon peers has a flaw in it, and it is deliberately through the flaw that the old man looks: it is not reality he sees (reality is something he has shucked off since the turn of the century) but those scenes which have resulted from a "ceaseless, commonplace, bewildering commingling of memory, emotion, and imagination" (as Morris puts the process in another source).[24] We are told that for Scanlon "The emptiness of the plain generates illusions that require little moisture, and grow better, like tall stories, where the mind is dry. The tall corn may flower or burn in the wind, but the plain is a metaphysical landscape and the bumper crop is the one Scanlon sees through the flaw in the glass" (*CLT,* p. 5).

Reduced to its essentials, *Ceremony in Lone Tree* is a novel about the American Dream; much more interesting, it is also about the dreaming of the American Dream. Boyd's question—is it better to be asleep or awake in this modern world?—is one which Morris answers by appealing to the powers of the imagination to enhance life. Moonlight—emblem and atmosphere—floods through the novel: *Ceremony in Lone Tree* is a midsummer night's dream. And the flaw in Scanlon's window—about which we are early told so much—is an equivalent of the imaginative processes as Scanlon seeks to escape reality by replacing it with something better, the "bumper crop" of his imagination. The chair in which Scanlon sits might well be the subject of the photograph reproduced in Plate I, part of a photo-text from

God's Country and My People which also makes reference to a "metaphysical landscape."

The photograph shows a rocking chair flooded with light from the window beside it, the light endowing the chair with an eerie kind of presence which all the more sharply emphasizes the absence of the human being whose chair it is. In Morris's words, the chair is an artifact which "indelibly reveal[s] the hand of man"; referring to the absence of human beings from most of his photographs, Morris writes: "Only in their absence will the reader intuit, in full measure, their presence in the object."[25] There is a metaphysical presence here which is obviously archetypal, and it is clearly part of what Morris wanted this image to convey.

But there is a great deal more. The accompanying prose text concludes with the following (the "it" refers to the land outside the window): "The men called it God's country—but the women asked, who else wants it? That's how it happened, the origin of a species, the corn bowls, the cotton bowls and the dust bowls. The tall corn flowers and burns in the wind but the plain remains a metaphysical landscape, the bumper crop a harvest of weather, fiction and romance."[26] The photograph thus seems to be a statement about the hierophantic imagination, a testament to the imagination which views the "metaphysical landscape." The photo and text combine to testify to the imagination, the photograph showing visually the project of positioning one's body in space and time (the chair is beside the window for another purpose than merely to accept the light) in order to pose the question of what there may be outside the window to be seen, interpreted, transformed.

But the photograph is even more complex, for knowing that Morris has a serious interest in mirrors,[27] we have a right to be puzzled by the shape of the window in this photograph. At first glance to many viewers, the window appears to be a mirror, reflecting light from *inside* the room rather than allowing it in from the outside. Seen in these terms, the question now becomes: does the light come from inside or outside? Does it come from the "presence" in the chair—the human imagination—or from the reality outside the window? The ambiguity may be easily cleared up, of course, by noting that the bar across the window cannot be a reflection of the chair arm—but by the time the viewer has grasped this he has already come to terms with the essential ambiguity which Morris appears to be counting on here.

No matter how the photograph is interpreted, the ambiguity of the light, the chair, and the "presence" in the chair is resolved into an archetypal question: from whence comes the "metaphysical landscape," from "reality" or from the imagination?

Does this interpretation assume too much? Not if we return to *Ceremony in Lone Tree,* in which Scanlon sits at the window with the flaw. Morris compares the flaw to an "eye," and he continues: "An eye to that eye, a scud seems to blow on a sea of grass. . . . Is it a flaw in the eye, or in the window, that transforms a dry place into a wet one?" (*CLT,* p. 3)—that is, which transforms the "real" landscape into a "metaphysical" one? Surely it is the same metaphysical stance on Morris's part which gives us Scanlon at his flawed window and the photograph of the chair near the mirror-window. That metaphysical stance is extraordinarily similar to one assumed by the phenomenological critic Gaston Bachelard, who in his inquiry into *The Poetics of Space* concerns himself with the communication of images from the poet's mind to the reader's. At one point he reminds us a great deal of Morris's Scanlon at his window:

> Like countless others, our poet is sitting dreaming at the window. But he discovers in the glass itself a slight deformation, which spreads deformation throughout the universe. . . . But what happens to the outside world, when it is seen through this little glazed lune, this pupil of a cat's eye? . . . Here the poet makes images surge up on all sides, he presents us with an atom universe in the process of multiplication. Under his guidance, the dreamer can renew his own world, merely by moving his face. From the miniature of the glass cyst, he can call forth an entire world and oblige it to make "the most unwonted contortions."[28]

The imagination of Bachelard's poet is obviously more developed than Scanlon's, but the point remains, for we must imagine Morris himself at his metaphysical window, pondering the significance of what lies outside—through the flaw in the glass, an equivalent for the imagination and its human functions.

The concept of "metaphysical landscape" is useful in a slightly different way in looking at Plate II, one of a number which may be termed Morris's "map" photographs. This particular photograph shows a detail of a log with various patterns etched into it by the weather. The cracks in the wood give the appearance of rivers and tributaries—precisely what one might see in an aerial view of a sun-bleached geographical region. In this case Morris himself provides the key, in the accompanying prose selection from *God's Country and My People*:

> Some time before this landscape became a state, it was a state of mind. The land itself was tipped so the waters flowed eastward, and where it flowed underground they called it Nebraska. There were few records. There was no history. Time was reckoned according to the plagues and blizzards. The territory itself was not yet part of the Union and only the hand of God had shaped it.... Many things would come to pass, but the nature of the place would remain a matter of opinion—a log drying in the sun or the dry bed of a river seen from space.
>
> (*GCMP*, n.p.; 3rd photo-text)

Rarely is Morris so explicit in his linkages between photo and text, but his text helps to support an assumption that Morris shot the photograph in the first place because of the similarity he saw between nature writ large and nature writ small—a metaphysical correspondence which his practiced eye must have been quick to grasp. (For similar kinds of correspondences the reader is directed to Theodore Schwenk's *Sensitive Chaos*, in which the author juxtaposes photographs of air and water currents with others showing similar visual patterns in the structures of tree trunks—and, even more interestingly, in the structures of Greek and Roman art and architecture.)[29]

A photograph similar to the log-image is used, again much to Morris's purpose, to conclude *God's Country and My People*. In another source Morris entitles it "Cracked Earth"[30] and it is another "metaphysical landscape," "map" photograph—a view of the ground apparently from directly above, showing the earth rutted into arteries and capillaries, looking a good deal like a map, or an aerial view of an inhabited region divided off into highways and other thoroughfares. ("Cracked Earth" is the frontispiece of this volume.) To this Morris juxtaposes the following text:

> In the century since the Grandfather crossed the Missouri the landscape has not perceptibly changed. To the north

> the smell of rain, to the south the smoke of dust, to the east rivers of earth still define God's country. On the daily commute we go into orbit, on the hour we take off. Is there more to come out of a higher standard of living than a predictably lower standard of feeling? Are we more moved by what little we know of the past than by what we dream about the future? Our talent is still for dreaming, and our recurrent dream is flight: a few hours away the luminous fueling stop of the moon. House or ark, sea or plain, shimmering mirages or figures of earth, God's country is still a fiction inhabited by people with a love for the facts.
>
> (*GCMP* n.p.; final photo-text)

And so Morris leaves off, having again suggested that the imagination is essential to the fulfillment of dreams and a higher "standard of feeling." The relation between photo and text is here less explicit, making it all the more possible for viewers to exercise the very imagination which Morris calls for in the text. Being open-ended, the photograph and text relationship creates a life-enhancing ambiguity which can only be resolved by archetypal thinking.

These "map" photographs have relevance to Plates III and IV, even as these latter two have a more explicit "historical" focus as pictures from an immediately recognizable world. Plate III, entitled (in *Structures and Artifacts*) "Faulkner Country, near Oxford, Mississippi," is fairly typical of Morris's photographs in its method of conveying a metaphysical meaning. In the photograph the house stands as an emblem of the vulnerability of the human and cultural amidst the natural elements. The photographer has deliberately chosen a vantage point slightly below ground level, so that the house is shown as if sinking into the ground—or rather, as if it is being seized and drawn downward. From the sky as well the house is being threatened, by the black cloud which hovers directly overhead. This photograph is an equivalent of the organic process as the soil virtually devours the house; the drama is in the house's ability to resist.

Plate IV is an even more dramatic instance of this struggle between the forces of culture and the forces of nature. In this photograph the lone house is replaced by the city neighborhood, the tentacled soil by the eroding concrete foundation—a foundation, the photographer's vantage point suggests, which supports the civilization above the ground. The city, that is, is being undermined by the forces in nature which are eating away at the concrete. The sentiment could have been borrowed from Robert Frost in "Mending Wall": "Something there is that doesn't love a wall, / That sends the frozen-ground-swell under it," but Morris's photograph has the impact of the visual to reinforce the sense of human helplessness.

The photographer's vantage point is again very deliberate, and the photograph makes little sense if we are unable to account for the deliberate division into upper and lower portions. Photographic parallels come immediately to mind in relation to purely formal elements of the image. Steiglitz's "The Steerage," for instance, is divided quite as deliberately, the picture split into upper and lower by means of the slightly diagonal gangway which formally separates the curious onlookers above from the "huddled masses" below. Again, there is W. Eugene Smith's famous photograph of the dead warrior's white-clad body being shunted into the sea: this image is divided diagonally from top-left to bottom-right, the upper half showing the ship and the survivors, the lower half showing only the water below—and the body's whitish blur as it prepares to enter the water-world, the world of the spirit.[31] In Morris's photograph, the division is also into upper and lower, and like Smith's image, it is intended to be a metaphysical rather than a social statement. The suggestion in this image is that the culture must be on guard against the casual interests of nature to reclaim the materials which humans have merely borrowed.

Plate V, "Western Kansas, Stores with False Fronts," is somewhat more subtle, and apparently without the pre-meditation of the photographs of threatened civilization just discussed; these structures might almost be taken for the "things-themselves," taken from an uncomplicated frontal stance. This image, too, is "typical" of Morris's work, for many of his photographs are of such structures, stripped to their "essentials"—as the language of Morris's novel *Love Among the Cannibals* (1957) would put the matter. There two structures are indicative of the lives of those who live within them: weary and worn-out, exhausted of effort, no longer capable of pretenses nor interested in the social graces. The building on the left is only half-interested in suppressing its advertising; the one on the right presents an expressionless "face" with hollow eyes: the building sags slightly to the right. One of the inhabitants appears to be described in

God's Country and My People: Doc Toomey, who "lies on a horsehair sofa. He is huge. The door will have to come off when they carry him out. Toomey pulls teeth and sets bones in his office, where the less heard and seen the better.... The giant is soft. He feeds the mice who nest in his unwashed socks" (*GCMP*, n.p.; 16th photo-text).

This photograph of the weary and worn structures may be an equivalent of prose passages taken from far afield in Morris's work. In *The Man Who Was There* (1945), Morris's second novel—and the one which first dealt with the problem of nostalgia for the lost and mythic past—Morris attempts to describe an emotion through an image:

> To the east Lone Tree had lengthened like a shadow, but to the west it ended abruptly on the sky. It not merely ended but the sky swept in to invade it, the flood of light and space washing in upon it like a tide. Washing it away, for the square had receded from the blurred fringe of grass and the slats of a fence like fragments of a battered pier. Whatever remained on this edge of town did so at a risk, and a bad one, for only a huddle of old buildings had survived. They faced to the west—a row of old men who had walked to where the sidewalk ended and stood there thinking their thoughts, ignoring this firing squad of light.[32]

The final image recurs in *The World in the Attic,* where there is "a row of stores facing the burned ditch grass—and nothing else. Like a row of old men with blinded eyes lined up to be shot" (p. 24). The "firing squad," the old men lined up to be shot, suggest the underlying despair and frustration in all those western towns which have seen their ambitions come to nothing. Nothing remains but the need to put in the time—as Will Brady in *The Works of Love* (1951) might put it. This photograph clearly shows something of the emotional costs in such defeat—and in a fashion which mobilizes both the senses and the intellect: we feel the sun beat down on our heads too, as we partake in "small-town nausea."

With "Tombstone, Arizona, Ruined Storefronts" (Plate VI) we move a step or two further in the historical cycle—beyond the ennui of civilization declining through lack of interest or ambition to the virtual abandonment of civilization. In "Ruined

Storefronts" we are given a photograph of civilization defeated: what once was, the photograph tells us, is now no longer, for these ruins no longer shelter life by providing shells for "inhabitants."

But again, we are given here more than a piece of history—as if we need visual proof for the rise and fall of civilization; the photograph is also an image and an equivalent. There are two dimensions to the "depth" of this photograph: in the foreground there are the ruined storefronts, in the background the mountains and the sky. As a photographer, Morris seems to have deliberately shot *through* the structures to what is beyond—again there is the juxtaposition of the cultural and the natural: how long will it be before the grains of wood and the bits of glass are reclaimed by the sand? Is it meant to be ironic that the mountains and the clouded sky are seen through structures in process of decay? Are the "windows" through which we view the natural scene beyond meant, like Scanlon's flaw in the glass, to be a kind of "eye" through which the *culture* views the scene? In light of the great number of Morris's photographs which peer *into* structures—sometimes like a voyeur through curtained windows into mysterious parlors and kitchens—what is one to make of this photograph in which the interior is lacking, replaced by mountains and sky?

The answer, I think, is that the camera-eye in "Ruined Storefronts" is the cultural counterpart to Scanlon's flaw—with this difference: whereas Scanlon has willed his imaginative withdrawal, American culture as a collective has used up the land, grasping it *for* the sake of civilization, and now views the land beyond through the jaded lens of the cultural eye. That the photograph is self-reflective is evident from the long shadow which reaches from the base of the ruins at right-center to the photographer's position in space beyond the frame, just there in front of us.

Or so, at least, goes one interpretation. However one reads this image, it is essential to take into consideration the values which the photographer puts before us in terms of blacks, whites, greys, the illusion of depth, the metaphysics of space. This image gives us a real world: Morris recorded it: there it is before us as it was in the past. The image and the picture meet and press upon us the need for imagination.

Interpretation is first of all meditation, a thinking upon myths and archetypes and phenomenological essences concealed within events, structures and artifacts. As a photographer Morris is unique, for no other photographer has given us entry to his metaphysics as he has, through volumes of words which together with the photographs tell us much that is new about American images and the foundations of American myths in the hunger of the imagination.

NOTES

[1] Wright Morris, "The Inhabitants," in *New Directions in Prose and Poetry 1940,* ed. James Laughlin (Norfolk, Connecticut: New Directions, 1940), p. 147.

[2] See Alan Trachtenberg, "The Craft of Vision," *Critique,* 4 (Winter 1961-1962), 41-55.

[3] See, for instance, Peter C. Bunnell, "The Photography of Wright Morris: A Portfolio," and "Photography and Reality: A Conversation Between Peter C. Bunnell and Wright Morris," in *Conversations with Wright Morris,* ed. Robert Knoll (Lincoln: University of Nebraska Press, 1977), pp. 121-152. See also James Alinder, "Wright Morris: You Can Go Home Again," *Modern Photography,* March 1978, pp. 116-125, 193; A. D. Coleman, "Novel Pictures: The Photofiction of Wright Morris," *Light Readings* (New York: Oxford University Press, 1979), pp. 242-246.

[4] Alan Trachtenberg, "Introduction: Photographs as Symbolic History," *The American Image: Photographs from the National Archives, 1860-1960* (New York: Pantheon, 1979), p. xxviii.

[5] Wright Morris, "Made in U.S.A.," *American Scholar,* 29 (Autumn 1960), 488.

[6] See Morris and Bunnell, "Photography and Reality," p. 148; and Morris, "Preface," *The Inhabitants,* 2nd ed. (New York: Da Capo, 1972).

[7] In *Discourse on Thinking,* trans. John M. Anderson and E. Hans Freund (New York: Harper and Row, 1966), Martin Heidegger develops a phenomenological distinction between "calculative" and "meditative" thought; with some reservations, the terms are applicable to Morris's "fact" and "fiction" respectively.

[8] Wright Morris, *The World in the Attic* (1949; rpt. Lincoln: Univer-

sity of Nebraska Press, 1971), p. 66.

[9] On "connections" in Morris, see also *The Home Place* (1948; rpt. Lincoln: University of Nebraska Press, 1968), pp. 56-61.

[10] Wright Morris, *The Field of Vision* (1956; rpt. Lincoln: University of Nebraska Press, 1974), p. 101. Henceforth abbreviated *FV*.

[11] On Morris's "Bergsonianism" I am indebted to G. B. Crump, *The Novels of Wright Morris: A Critical Interpretation* (Lincoln: University of Nebraska Press, 1978), especially pp. 11-15.

[12] Wright Morris, *The Territory Ahead* (1957; rpt. Lincoln: University of Nebraska Press, 1978), p. 23. Henceforth abbreviated *TA*.

[13] John Keats, quoted in M. H. Abrams, *The Mirror and the Lamp: Romantic Theory and the Critical Tradition* (New York: Oxford University Press, 1953), p. 136.

[14] Morris, in Bunnell and Morris, "Photography and Reality," p. 144; see also Wayne Booth and Morris, "The Writing of Organic Fiction," *Conversations with Wright Morris*, pp. 74-92.

[15] Coleridge, quoted in Abrams, p. 173.

[16] Morris, *The Home Place*, p. 58.

[17] Gary Metz, "The Sense of Place," in *The Great West: Real/Ideal*, ed. Sandy Hume, Ellen Manchester, and Gary Metz (Boulder: University of Colorado Department of Fine Arts, 1977), p. 43.

[18] *Edward Weston: The Flame of Recognition*, ed. Nancy Newhall (New York: Aperture, 1971), p. 41.

[19] Morris, *The Inhabitants*, "Preface."

[20] Wright Morris, in Morris and Jim Alinder, "Interview," *Structures and Artifacts: Photographs 1933-1954* (Lincoln: University of Nebraska Press, 1975), p. 112.

[21] See Wright Morris, "Privacy as a Subject for Photography," *Magazine of Art*, 44 (February 1951), 51-55.

[22] Wright Morris, "Photographs, Images, and Words," *American Scholar*, 48 (Autumn 1979), 462.

[23] Wright Morris, *Ceremony in Lone Tree* (1960; rpt. Lincoln: University of Nebraska Press, 1973), p. 4. Henceforth abbreviated *CLT*.

[24] Morris, "Origins: Reflections on Emotion, Memory, and Imagination," in *Conversations with Wright Morris*, p. 167.

[25] Morris, *The Inhabitants*, "Preface."

[26] Wright Morris, *God's Country and My People* (New York: Harper and Row, 1968), n.p., 2nd photo-text. Henceforth abbreviated *GCMP*.

[27] See, for instance, *Structures and Artifacts*, pp. 55, 71.

[28] Gaston Bachelard, *The Poetics of Space*, trans. Marie Jolas (Boston: Beacon Press, 1964), pp. 156-157.

[29] Theodore Schwenk, *Sensitive Chaos: The Creation of Flowing*

Forms in Water and Air, trans. Olive Whicher and Johanna Wrigley (New York: Schocken Books, 1976); see, e.g., plates 33-34, 35-36, 37-38, and 81-88.

[30] Morris, *Structures and Artifacts,* p. 107.

[31] Stieglitz's "The Steerage" can be found in nearly any book on that photographer's work; Smith's photograph can be seen in *W. Eugene Smith: His Photographs and Notes* (New York: Aperture, 1969), n.p.

[32] Wright Morris, *The Man Who Was There* (1945; rpt. Lincoln: University of Nebraska Press, 1977), pp. 134-135.

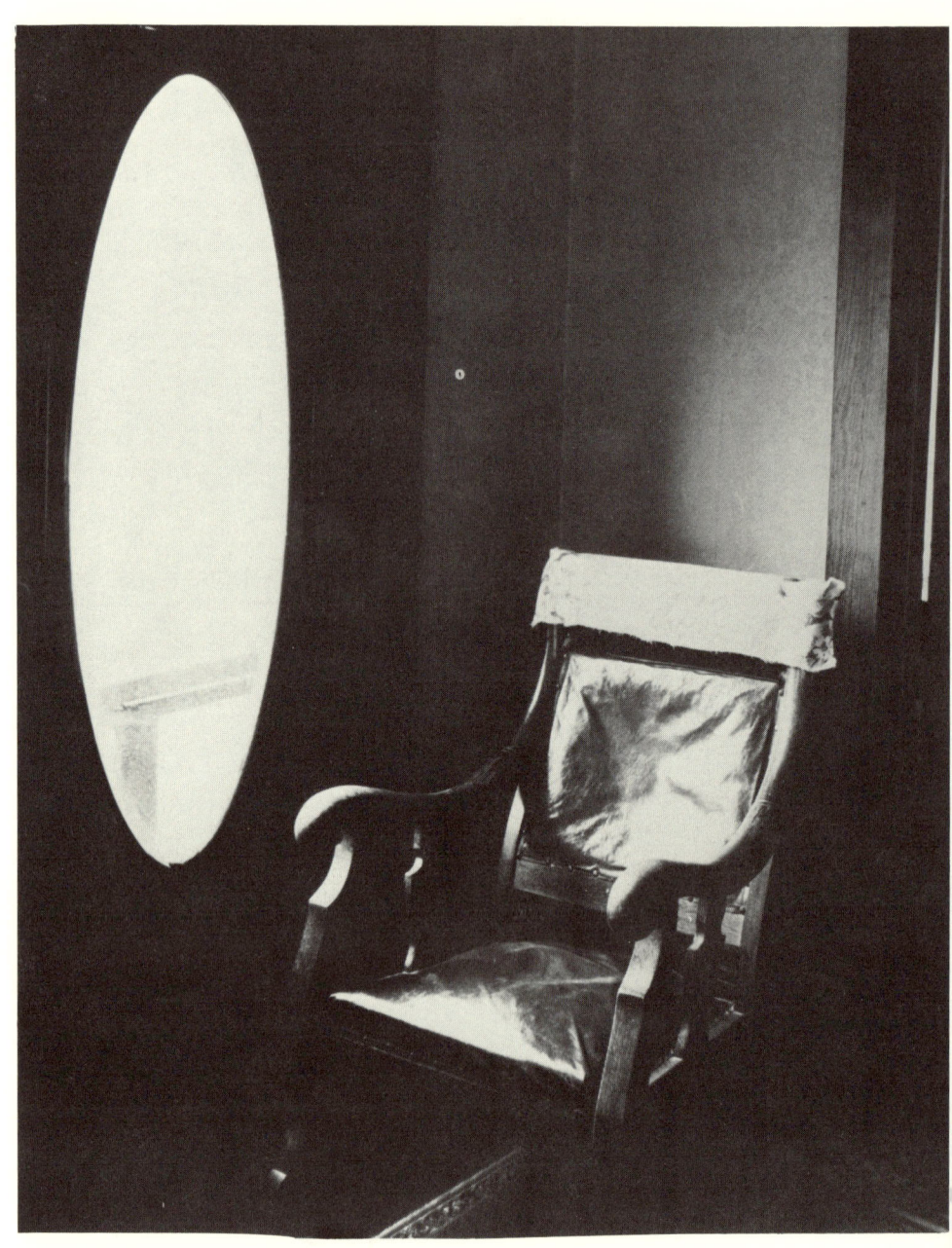

Plate I. "Rocker, Home Place"

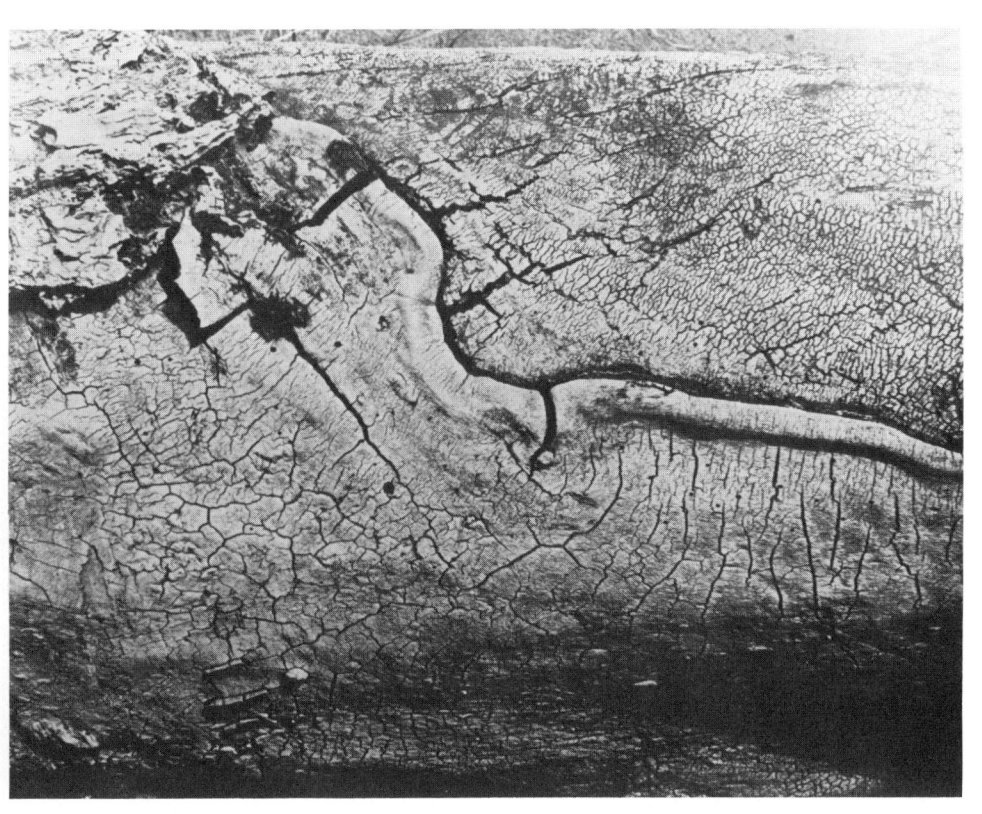

Plate II. ["Metaphysical Landscape"]

Plate III. "Faulkner Country, near Oxford, Mississippi"

Plate IV. ["Cityscape"]

Plate V. "Western Kansas, Stores with False Fronts"

Plate VI. "Tombstone, Arizona"

PART FOUR:
BEYOND MYTH

Is there a viable alternative to celebrating the "myth of the West" or parodying it through anti-Westerns? **Jack Brenner** believes the best western writers have found a way, through what he calls "concerned irony" (serious and committed, not satiric or parodic). Such writers rely upon style for the "authority" of their fiction. Brenner demonstrates his thesis with extended analysis of Welch's *Winter in the Blood.* He concludes that the realism of Welch's portrayal of the contemporary dispossessed Indian's plight is but the beginning point for the author's shaping of a fiction that matters because of the importance of the central character's experience.

The author of essays and a forthcoming book on western American literature, Brenner teaches English at the University of Washington.

Beyond Myth: Welch's *Winter in the Blood*

Jack Brenner

Writers who want to make serious fictional use of the American West are condemned to a struggle with their material. That struggle comes not from the vastness of western landscape, or from the relative paucity of human settlement, but from the fact that the West has been thoroughly mythologized, made into a fiction. The least interesting western fiction, as many have noted, rehearses the ritualistic gestures, celebrates the "truths" of an old story. But for a writer who tries to discern and define the compelling qualities of his own discoveries, the difficulty is to rescue the material from its automatic closure into meaning.

But this struggle to free "subject" from itself does not mean that the writer's only alternative to embracing the myth is to refute it, though some criticis of western fiction seem to imagine only either-or possibilities. "Romantically reconstructing myth or realistically destroying it—these are the two ways of regional literature," Jay Martin announces.[1] Martin seems to be seconded by Leslie Fiedler, who says that for everyone who tries to evoke the West "in fiction by reconstructing its past . . . two kinds of truth come immediately into conflict . . .: the truth of history, which is the truth of reason; and the truth of myth, which is the truth of madness."[2]

Those plump alternatives restrict the possibilities to mythic or anti-mythic fiction. An objection to this limiting need not be based on some custodial, protective attitude toward the significance or meaning of western experience; the real question is whether fiction written from such stark alternatives can be, simply, interesting. Realistic or parodic destructions of the myth are as fully controlled by the myth, though in a negative way, as is incantatory fiction. If western fiction can be viewed as *fiction,* rather than as a reflection or celebration of the myth, then perhaps we can say that the ironies that count are written by ironists who care, who use irony neither to dismiss nor to escape the material, but to make it yield its compelling qualities.

And with that, having touched on large matters that deserve fuller argument elsewhere, I want to turn to James Welch's first novel, *Winter in the Blood*,³ a book remarkably compelled by its own concerns, a story that achieves its power neither by celebrating nor exploding the myth it could so easily exploit. Welch is an American Indian, of mixed Blackfoot and Gros Ventre heritage, and he writes about contemporary reservation life in Montana. Welch's Big Sky country is familiar fictional territory: "the burnt prairie beneath a blazing sun, the pale green of the Milk River valley, the milky waters of the river, the sagebrush and the cottonwoods, the dry, cracked gumbo flats" (p. 2). Not so familiar, except in sociological tracts and a very few novels like Dan Cushman's *Stay Away Joe*, is the Montana of dingy bars and small-town hotel rooms where the sex and drinking is both desultory and desperate. The thirty-two-year-old narrator (who remains nameless throughout the story), unmarried and still living with his mother Teresa and his senile grandmother on a small ranch, is given a flat, dry, restrained voice by Welch, and the control is so marked that some of the fine strangenesses of the book could easily be overlooked. Here, for example, is a description of the Milk River, where the narrator is fishing without success:

> The sugar beet factory up by Chinook had died seven years before. Everybody had thought the factory had caused the river to be milky but the water never cleared. The white men from the fish department came in their green trucks and stocked the river with pike. They were enthusiastic and dumped thousands of pike of all sizes into the river. But the river ignored the fish and the fish ignored the river; they refused even to die there. They simply vanished. The white men made tests; they stuck electric rods into the water; they scraped muck from the bottom; they even collected bugs from the fields next to the river; they dumped other kinds of fish in the river. Nothing worked. The fish disappeared. Then the men from the fish department disappeared, and the Indians put away their new fishing poles. But every now and then, a report would trickle down the valley that someone . . . had seen an ash-colored swirl suck in a muskrat, and out would come the fishing gear. Nobody ever

> caught one of these swirls, but it was always worth a try. (pp. 5-6)

What is so striking there is the cool, even-handed refusal to give explanations. The story the paragraph tells is as "pure" as a fairy tale. Everyone thought the water would clear when the plant shut down, though it didn't. Still, the men planted the fish and the Indians bought new gear, "but the river ignored the fish and the fish ignored the river; they refused even to die there." So the fish vanished. Why? We don't know. Even so, "it was always worth a try." According to Lame Bull, who will soon marry the narrator's mother and who says "I know these fish," the way to catch them is to cook bacon, dump the grease in the river, and "first cast, you'll catch a good one."

Pike fishing in Montana, at least in Welch's report of it, has some of the opaqueness of the Milk River. The prose makes the fish and game men scurry, shows them a bit foolish in their enthusiasm, but the passage doesn't seem really interested in electing them for targets of satire. And the whites don't come off much worse than Lame Bull, who asserts that you can catch fish by greasing up the river, even though the fish seem to have vanished. Is that an inside joke, fairly gentle fun poked at the stereotype of the Indian versed in the ways of animals and fish? Perhaps. But whatever one decides about the "meaning" of the passage, it is sure that "usual" expectations triggered by the words "Indian" and "West" will hardly do to explain that tone of flat acceptance of mystery or incongruity.

A contrast may be instructive. Here is another river, located down at the Cleveland Wrecking Yard and selling for six dollars and fifty cents a foot, the waterfalls more expensive. In Richard Brautigan's version of trout fishing in America, the river comes "stacked in piles of various lengths: ten, fifteen, twenty feet, etc. . . . There was also a box of scraps. These scraps were in odd sizes ranging from six inches to a couple of feet." It is a used trout stream that "must be seen to be appreciated." Birds come extra, at thirty-five cents apiece, "but of course they're used" and so can't be guaranteed. The helpful salesman directs Brautigan through the used plumbing department—stacks of sinks and urinals—and says "I wouldn't want you to think that we would ever sell a murky trout stream here. We always make sure they're running crystal clear before we even think about moving them." Brautigan finds the salesman good to his word: the stacked lengths of trout stream are clear and cold and "I could see some trout in them. I saw one good fish."

Brautigan's river shows up in a book in which Jack the Ripper has become the Mayor of the Twentieth Century and wears "a costume of trout fishing in America. He wore mountains on his elbows and bluejays on the collar of his shirt. Deep water flowed through the lilies that were entwined about his shoelaces.... He wore trout fishing in America as a costume to hide his own appearance ... while he performed his deeds of murder." Now that he's the Mayor, his favorite instruments are a razor and a knife and a ukelele, "pulled like a plow through the intestines." Most of the prose has that stoned-out, off-the-wall quality:

> I remember mistaking an old woman for a trout stream in Vermont, and I had to beg her pardon.
> "Excuse me," I said. "I thought you were a trout stream."
> "I'm not," she said.

Such good-natured japery has led one critic to say that we can't be assertive about Brautigan's work, since he apparently does not care to make sense in the usual ways; and another to hail Brautigan as one of the "post-modern" writers in whose fiction we see a self-conscious rebellion against Jamesian verities of "rendered" fiction. But in spite of the zaniness, the discontinuity or absence of any narrative line, and the fey use of metaphor, Brautigan's river seems to me crystal clear indeed when compared to Welch's. Brautigan's sentiments are as simple as a slogan: in the twentieth century a capitalistic, technological society has defiled, sold, and exploited nature. His tone is less strident and worried, his nostalgia more sleepy and less bitter, than it is in those who express what he says in straighter prose, but where he stands is not difficult to determine.

Welch's prose is more conventional, his river altogether more mysterious. The Milk River does not float us back to a purer, better time, as rivers so often do in American fiction; we can't make of it a symbol of stupid or bullying bureaucratic actions; it is not a great good place, pristine and healing. It is simply there, ignoring the fish. The whole novel has that air of flatly accepting incongruity. As the novel opens, for instance, the narrator is returning to the ranch from a three-day drunk in town:

> The fence hummed in the sun behind my back as I climbed up to the highway. My right eye was swollen up, but I couldn't remember how or why. . . . Coming home was not easy anymore. It was never a cinch, but it had become a torture. . . . Coming home to a mother and an old lady who was my grandmother. And the girl who was thought to be my wife. But she didn't really count. For that matter none of them counted; not one meant anything to me. And for no reason. I felt no hatred, no love, no guilt, no conscience, nothing but a distance that had grown through the years. (p. 2)

As we go on, we find that Welch doesn't fuss the reasons for that distance in the man, doesn't explain. The girl who had come to live with him is now gone, taking with her an electric shaver and a rifle. But that "didn't really count," just as it does not seem to matter about most things. It really *doesn't* matter that the razor has been stolen, since the ranch has no electricity, but the .30-30 belonged to his father, First Raise, an affable, accomplished mechanic who had repaired the whites' hay balers by kicking them—"Twenty dollars to kick a baler awake—one dollar for the kick and nineteen for knowing where to kick"—who froze to death drunk in a ditch. The gun had "once been important to me . . . but I hadn't used it since the day I killed Buster Cutfinger's dog for no reason except that I was drunk and it was moving."

Once he had a father who kicked hay balers awake, once he had a brother with whom he moved some cattle, once there was a girl who came to live with him, once the gun had been important to him. But that "once" does not seem to carry, for this man, the weight of a golden, lost time, does not represent the best days that fled first. Once certain events transpired, certain significance existed, now other things have happened. For no reason. Buster Cutfinger's dead dog and the girl who left are almost equivalent objects. For a good stretch of the story, the man is kept or keeps himself in an ahistorical frame; he is locked into a present tense, apparently beyond hope, perhaps even beyond hopelessness. That present tense is not a particularly sullen one, or desperate, for to be desperate would mean that something counts, or that the past matters, or that a future is possible. The narrator does have memories: one about a pet duck named Amos that he killed through neglect as a child, some that reach into the

Indian past recounted by his grandmother, who is nearly a hundred years old. And the story leads to the surfacing of the memory of his brother Mose's death, a memory he has kept locked away from contemplation, and to the discovery of his real grandfather. But most often the narrator is a man whose right eye is swollen, "but I couldn't remember how or why," or who, waking up in a strange room, can't "figure out how I ended up on the couch with a rubber-back rug over me." For the same reason that the story of the fish and the river can stand as an enigma, the narrator can often view what happens to him with deadly, detached humor: when his mother marries Lame Bull, for example, effectively dispossessing him of the ranch that his father's mechanical skill had bought, he expresses no anger or sorrow, but merely observes that "Lame Bull had taken to grunting now that he was a proprietor" and gives us this portrait:

> Lame Bull had married 360 acres of hay land, all irrigated, leveled, some of the best land in the valley, as well as a 2000-acre grazing lease. And he had married a T-Y brand stamped high on the left ribs of every beef in the place. And, of course, he had married Teresa, my mother. At forty-seven, he was eight years younger than she, and a success. A prosperous cattleman. (p. 13)

Or he can report on the monotony of his own life during an evening spent with the old lady, the grandmother; he turns on the radio, fills her pipe for her, and picks up an old *Sports Afield* magazine:

> I had read all the stories, so I reread the one about three men in Africa who tracked a man-eating lion for four days from the scene of his latest kill—a pregnant black woman. They managed to save the baby, who, they were surprised to learn, would one day be king of the tribe. They tracked the lion's spoor until the fourth day, when they found out that he'd been tracking them all along. They were going in a giant four-day circle. It was very dangerous, said McLeod, a Pepsi dealer from Atlanta, Georgia. (p. 12)

The man's life has that quality of "going in a giant four-day circle," and he reports going to town to get drunk, going to bed with three women (perhaps—he can't remember if he actually did go to bed with one), running into a white tourist who wants to enlist him in some border-running into Canada, being beaten up by the brother of the girl who left, all in that distant, detached, sometimes humorous tone. It wasn't all that dangerous, says Welch.

The disconnected, discrete, one-thing-after-another quality of the man's life has to do with the "distance" he feels. It is announced early in the book:

> I felt no hatred, no love, no guilt, no conscience, nothing but a distance that had grown through the years.
> It could have been the country, the burnt prairie.... The country had created a distance as deep as it was empty, and the people accepted and treated each other with distance.
> But the distance I felt came not from country or people; it came from within me. I was as distant from myself as a hawk from the moon. And that was why I had no particular feelings toward my mother and grandmother. Or the girl who had come to live with me. (p. 2)

"But the distance I felt came not from country or people; it came from within me": the statement accounts for the way that Welch keeps us in the man's disconnected present tense without explaining the causes or reasons. Welch, of course, had ready to his hand a whole battery of racial and sociological reasons for the man's distance, but he chose not to make of this a protest novel. There is no welling of political or racial protest, no attempt to locate for us the causes of the narrator being a passive victim, even though evidence of racial nastiness occasionally surfaces. He had worked in a rehabilitation clinic until "a nurse who hated Indians" told him spitefully that he was being kept on in order for the clinic to get a grant, and there are small incidents with bartenders and waitresses that show him using an exile's cunning to get by. But Welch will not picture the reservation as a ghetto, with "Them" and "Us." There is only him and everybody else. Beaten by other Indians, entangled in the hazy border-running plan, he says "I felt the helplessness of being in a world of stalking white men. But those Indians down at Gables were no bargain either. I was a stranger to both and both had beaten me" (p. 120).

During this drunken three-day trip, the man sees an advertisement for a Western movie starring Randolph Scott which "had probably played in every town in Montana once a year for the past twenty." In a nicely understated but oddly appropriate way, the ad begins to pierce the armor-plate of "it doesn't matter" by reminding him of a childhood conversation with his brother Mose. The man has kept the memory of his brother locked away from contemplation: "Randolph Scott had plugged me dead with a memory I had tried to keep away." What he is keeping away from is the memory of Mose's death, which happened twenty years before, while Mose and the narrator were moving some cattle along a highway. A balky cow had refused to go through a gate, a calf ran out from the herd, and in the chase Mose was run down by a drunk driver. After the memory is triggered, Welch allows the story to emerge slowly, mixing it with the man's desultory drinking, his accidental connection with a woman, the beating. Telling the story this way makes us see that his present detached and aimless activity and the death form a silent commentary; there *was* a "once" that mattered, mattered so much that it could not be faced, and the present is meaningless because he has to keep the distance from himself. But in spite of the whiskey and women, the memory finally emerges whole, leading to a surfacing of his own sense of guilt, breaking the barriers of his self-imposed present tense, releasing him to tears:

> "What use," I whispered, cried for no one in the world to hear . . . for no one but my soul, as though the words would rid it of the final burden of guilt, and I found myself a child again, the years shed as a snake sheds its skin, and I was standing over the awkward tangle of clothes and limbs. "What use, what use, what use . . ." and no one answered, not the body in the road, not the hawk in the sky or the beetle in the earth; no one answered. And the tears in the hot sun, in the wine, the dusk, the chill wind of dusk, the sleet that began to fall as I knelt beside the body, the first sharp pain of my smashed knee, . . . the blood which dripped from his nostrils, his mouth, the man who hurried back from his car, his terrible breath as he tried to wrestle me away from my brother's broken body.   (pp. 146-147)

The past has come into the present, palpable and there; he

is standing in the hot sun, crying into his wine, but the tears are also those he shed in the chill, sleety dusk when Mose was killed. We have not known until now that the man's injured knee, which he refuses to get medical attention for and which is treated like everything else, as though "it doesn't matter," was hurt on the day of the death. It has crippled him since, as his guilt has crippled him in worse ways.

But important as recovering the memory is in helping him to break out of the detached present tense, it is not presented as a miraculous or manipulated cure. As restrained here as elsewhere, Welch lets other events surrounding the dredging-up show what "distance" might mean to such a man. His grandmother dies while he is on his drunken trip to Havre, and he returns to the empty house and glimpses something of the "distance" of the old lady:

> Her rocking chair stood empty and dark . . . the seat where her thin butt had rested was shiny, the bar across the top of the back greasy where her head had lain. The movie magazines piled beside the other chair were gone. . . . For the first time in my life, I was able to look at the room without the feeling that I was invading my grandmother's privacy. But now I saw that almost nothing in the room belonged to her, just the rocker and the cot next to the oil stove . . . [and a] tobacco pouch . . . the arrowhead inside. (pp. 131-132)

He then goes to visit Yellow Calf, an old blind Indian who lives alone three miles from the ranch. He rides Bird, the horse he rode the day Mose was killed, now as comparatively ancient in age as his grandmother; over the wine he has brought, he and Yellow Calf talk about the old woman. He hears again the story of his grandmother's exile from her people: she was the new bride of Standing Bear, a chief, married for only a few months when he was killed on a raid to get meat for his starving band, and the people blamed her for the hard times. The man does not understand: "But why her?" "You must understand the thinking," Yellow Calf answers.

> "In that time the soldiers came, the people had to leave their home up near the mountains, then the starvation and the death of their leader. She had brought them bad medicine."

> "But you—you don't think that."
>
> "It was apparent," he said.
>
> "It was bad luck; the people grew angry because their luck was bad," I said. . . .
>
> "That's true, but it was more than that. When you are starving, you look for signs. Each event becomes big in your mind. His death was the final proof that they were cursed. . . . They looked at your grandmother and realized that she had brought despair and death. And her beauty—it was as if her beauty made a mockery of their situation."
>
> "They can't have believed this. . . ."
>
> "It wasn't a question of belief, it was the way things were," he said. (pp. 154-155)

"It was apparent," the old man says flatly, or "it wasn't a question of belief, it was the way things were." Those things happened, the old man says, and while one "must understand the thinking," explaining them will not explain them away. The old man's distance here is a distance of acceptance, but not of passivity, the same sort of distance that the narrator feels a few moments later when he intuits that Yellow Calf is his real grandfather. He greets the knowledge with laughter that is neither bitter nor humorous, but the "laughter of one who understands a moment in his life." During that cruel winter of need, Yellow Calf had hunted meat for the grandmother and then became her lover. Neither the old lady nor Yellow Calf ever revealed the connection, and the young man has never heard any but the vaguest suggestions that a half-breed named Doagie was not his mother's father. He tries to imagine that hiddenness of his grandmother and Yellow Calf: "So much distance between them, and yet they lived only three miles apart. But what had created this distance? Twenty-five years . . . so solemn and secretive it had not even been rumored?" (pp. 160-161). We have no answer from Welch; he leaves it an enigma. But we do begin to see some of the doubled meaning of the title: the man's present-tense detachment, *that* "winter in the blood," is linked tightly to his blood heritage, and to that winter when Yellow Calf became his grandmother's hunter and the other Indians were herded off to reservations "like cows." (The grandmother was not taken by the soldiers; driven out and alone, she was thought to be of another tribe. Her grandson now understands the "strange triumph" in her voice when she said "like cows.") It is not only his refusal to remember Mose's death that has distanced the man: it is that, yes, but intertwined with Indian history, dispossession by the whites, and the family history of secret and hidden distance—"I never expected much from Teresa and I never got it. But neither did anyone else." All of these strands combine to choke off any possibility of significant connections for the man. That point is made silently by Welch, with a fine, quiet control; I have had to be much more outspoken in arranging the relationships than Welch is in the novel.

Returning from Yellow Calf's on old Bird, thinking on the secrets that have been hidden from him by himself and by history, he finds a cow mired in a slough. Then follows what to my mind is one of the finest passages in the novel. The cow reminds him of the goosey "spinster" cow that bolted on the day that Mose was killed, the indirect cause of his death. She will die if left, but

> I wanted to ignore her. I wanted to go away, to let her drown in her own stupidity, attended only by clouds and the coming rain . . . if I turned away—my hands trembled but did nothing. She had earned this fate by being stupid, and now no one could help her. Who would want to? As she stared at me, I saw beyond the immediate panic that hatred, that crazy hatred that made me aware of a quick hatred in my own heart. . . . I had seen her before, . . . the same hateful eye . . . the wild-eyed spinster leading the cows down the hill into the valley. (p. 166)

But he doesn't ignore her. He gets a rope and hitches it to Bird's saddle horn and begins to pull her out. Hampered by his bad leg, by the rain, by Bird's feebleness, he is nearly defeated and finally, as he has not been throughout the story, he is possessed by anger.

> Goddamn you, Bird, Goddamn you. . . . Lame Bull! It was his cow, he had married the cow, why wasn't he here? Off riding around, playing the role, goddamn big-time operator, can't trust him, can't trust any of these damn idiots, damn Indians. . . . Ah, Teresa, you made a terrible mistake. Your husband, your friends, your son, all worthless, none of them worth a shit. (p. 169)

Sweating, cursing, railing at Lame Bull and himself, he is for once fully caught in a living present tense, and he and Bird get the cow out. Bird dies from the exertion; the man, alone now in the rain, thinks that "Some people . . . will never know how pleasant it is to be distant in a clean rain, the driving rain of a summer storm. It's not like you'd expect, nothing like you'd expect" (p. 172). Welch does not mean that he has crawled back into the deadening distance where there is "no love . . . not anything": it is now a distance of repose, the aftermath of commitment and feeling.

While Welch does not pose pulling the cow from the mud as being analogous to the man pulling himself out of his own slough, being opened to the past and to the present allows a future too. While Lame Bull, in the last scene of the novel, pronounces an impromptu valediction over the grandmother's grave, the narrator thinks about the girl who left. "Next time I'll do it right. Buy her a couple of cremes de menthe, maybe offer to marry her on the spot." The humor is deft, and also pointed: Welch won't let us feel that the man has escaped the ache of distances, or that he will have any kind of successful marriage, or even that he will know how to apply what he's found out about distance to his own. He will still be the man who buys her a couple of cremes de menthe. But this ending is moving nonetheless, and moving because Welch won't claim too much, won't let his river be stacked like cordwood down at the Cleveland Wrecking Yard. The book takes its flat, enigmatic shape because Welch knows that dispossession, when it has been lived through for two generations, is not likely to be dramatically expressed. Perhaps the drama and the meaning of such facts can be shown best in the way that long-standing rage is inherited and smoulders out in self-hatred; the rending truth of dispossession may be that rage turns inward, becomes guilt, and thus makes of the dispossessed a double victim, dispossessed even of himself. That seems to be Welch's truth, and praise is due him for seeing it.

But our praise is empty indeed if the only terms we can use in describing this remarkable novel are those that measure whether Welch romantically reconstructed the myth or realistically destroyed it. *Winter in the Blood* tells, powerfully, its own story, carves its own ironies, merits its own case. Our essential critical task is to locate and describe those energies, not submerge them in some category called "Indian Fiction" or "the West." I have tried to do that by showing how Welch makes his story turn on the word "distance," how he invests it with various dimensions of experience. There are other ways to greet his efforts. But the fiction critics write and call "criticism" should be as alert to and as mindful of the experience it seeks to describe—and that is the reading experience—as the fiction itself is responsible to its concerns, its experience. That this kind of locating and describing is made more difficult when we are dealing with fiction written about the West than it might be in other fictions only sets the task, and does not preclude it.

"I see by your outfit that you are a cowboy" goes the line from the old song, and we can see from Welch's novel that he is an Indian and a Westerner, his book effectively shaped by western experience. Yet his novel is not powerful or moving because the West is his "subject"; it is so because he makes us feel on every page that the tang and ache of his West is its own importance, the shaping of the story into a fiction that matters the crucial task. If all we could say about Welch's novel were the equivalent of "I see you're a cowboy," he would, I hope, politely but firmly ignore us, as the fish ignored the river, the river ignored the fish.

NOTES

[1] Jay Martin, *Harvests of Change* (Englewood Cliffs, New Jersey: Prentice Hall, 1967), p. 106.

[2] Leslie Fiedler, *The Return of the Vanishing American* (New York: Stein and Day, 1968), pp. 164, 175.

[3] Page numbers for quotations are taken from the Harper and Row edition, 1974.

INDEX

Abbey, Edward, *The Monkey Wrench Gang*, 65-66
Adams, Henry Brooks, 112
Adams, Ramon, 47*n*13
Alderson, Nannie T., *A Bride Goes West*, 52, 53, 54
Alexander, Hartley, 96
Alinder, James, 195*n*3
Amazing Rhythm Aces, 77
Anderson, Warren D., 135*n*4
Anthony, Susan B., 152
Aristotle, 31
Armstrong, Regina, 153, 157
Babb, Sonora, *An Owl on Every Post*, 52, 53, 58
Bachelard, Gaston, *The Poetics of Space*, 189
Barnes, Robert, 135*n*1
Beach, Emma, 160
Beer, Gillian, 140
Berger, Thomas, *Little Big Man*, 31, 75, 81, 82, 84-86
Bergon, Frank, 5
Bergson, Henri, 196*n*11
Bernard, Kenneth, 135*n*1
Berry, Don, 23
—*A Majority of Scoundrels*, 32
—*Trask*, 24
Bidney, David, 19*n*1
Bierce, Ambrose, 26
Billington, Ray Allen, 21, 24
Billy the Kid, 34, 35-36
Blake, William, 177, 178, 185
Boone, Daniel, 67
Brautigan, Richard, *Trout Fishing in America*, 209-210, 218
Brenner, Jack, 46*n*4
Bridger, Jim, 67
Brueghel, Pieter, 26
Bunnell, Peter C., 195*n*3,6

Bunyan, Paul, 13
Burns, Walter Noble, *The Saga of Billy the Kid*, 41, 44
California, 27, 35, 38, 153, 155, 160
Campbell, Joseph, 81, 89n13, 179
Carlson, Avis Dungan, *Small World, Long Gone*, 59
Carnegie, Andrew, 22
Carson, Kit, 1, 2
Cather, Willa, *Alexander's Bridge*, 93
 —*A Lost Lady*, 18
 —*My Antonia*, 55, 57
 —*O Pioneers!* 4, 53-54, 55, 57-58, 60, 93-103
Catlin, George, 154
Cawelti, John G., *The Six-Gun Mystique*, 80, 89n12
Chandler, Raymond, 140
Charles, Sister Peter Damian, O.P., 105n13
Chase, Richard, 64
Chesterton, G. K., 34
Clark, Neil. *See* Thorp, Jack
Clark, Walter Van Tilburg, 19, 27
 —*The Ox-Bow Incident*, 3, 79
 —*The Track of the Cat*, 16, 18
Coe, David Allen, 77
Coleman, A. D., 195n3
Coleridge, Samuel Taylor, 102, 108, 183, 184
Collingwood, Robin George, 32
Comstock, Sarah, *The Soddy*, 52, 59
Colorado, 52, 113, 118, 122, 155
Cooper, James Fenimore: Natty Bumppo, 66, 87, 140, 142
Cooper Institute School of Design for Women, 152, 153
Corle, Edwin, *Billy the Kid*, 47n8
 —*Fig Tree John*, 17
country western, 77
cowboy, 11, 18, 75, 82, 84, 86, 144, 145, 179, 219
Coyote Man, 18
Crane, Stephen, 5, 139-147
 Works:
  "The Blue Hotel," 140, 144-146
  "The Bride Comes to Yellow Sky," 86, 129-135, 140, 142-144
  "The Five White Mice," 140, 141-142, 143
Crump, G. B., 196n11
Cunningham, Eugene, *Triggernometry*, 36, 37, 38, 41, 42, 43, 44
Cushman, Dan, *Stay Away Joe*, 208

Custer, George Armstrong, 14
Dakotas, 81
Dana, Richard Henry, 26
Davis, David B., 2
Davis, H. L., 26
de Kay, Helena. *See* Gilder, Helena (de Kay)
Denver, Colorado, 52
De Voto, Bernard, 1, 24, 89*n*10
Dilthey, Wilhelm, 32
Donner party, 32
Doyle, Sir Arthur Conan, *A Study in Scarlet*, 69
Durham, Marilyn, *The Man Who Loved Cat Dancing*, 76
Dusenbury, Robert, 135*n*4
Edwards, Jonathan, 25
Eliade, Mircea, 13, 15, 17, 108, 115, 123
Eliot, T. S., 6, 27
Emerson, Ralph Waldo, 112, 118
Everson, William, *Archetype West*, 23, 25-28
Faulkner, William, 17, 22
Ferguson, Scott C., 135*n*1
Fergusson, Harvey, *Grant of Kingdom*, 14, 18
Ferlinghetti, Lawrence, 25, 27
Ferril, Thomas Hornsby, 2, 4, 107-124
  Works:
    "American Testament," 113
    "The Barn Was Twilight," 116
    "Beyond What Ranges," 116, 117
    "Blue Stemmed Grass," 109
    "Bob Ford in Attica," 114, 120
    "Bride," 119
    "Children Coming Up the Stairs," 118-119
    "From Saturday Evening On," 113-114
    "Ghost," 116
    "High Passage," 110
    "Life After Death," 117-118
    "Magenta," 120-121
    "Metamorphosis: 1806," 118
    "Orientation," 107
    "The Prairie Melts," 116-117
    "Report of My Strange Encounter With Lily Bull-Domingo," 122-123
    "Streets Due West," 115, 120
    "There Were Intersections," 116

Ferril, Thomas Hornsby, (Works continued)
    "These Planks," 110
    "This Foreman," 114
    "Time of Mountains," 111, 112-113
    "Trial by Time," 111
    "Waltz Against the Mountains," 119-120
    "Words for Leadville," 110-111
Fiedler, Leslie, 79, 89n12, 207
Fish, Stanley, 80
Fisher, Vardis, 23, 67
   —*The Mothers*, 32
   —*Mountain Man*, 18, 78
Fitzpatrick, Thomas, 1, 2
Flora, Joseph M., 88n7
Foote, Arthur, 151, 155, 160, 161, 162, 163
Foote, Mary (Hallock), 5, 6, 151-164
   Works:
      The Chosen Valley, 159, 162-163
      "The Hanging of the Crane," 153, 167
      "The Hermit-Thrush," 157, 160, 172
      "How the Pump Stopped at the Morning Watch," 159
      John Bodewin's Testimony, 155, 165n16
      The Last Assembly Ball, 155, 165n16
      The Led-Horse Claim, 155, 158, 165n16, 174
      "The Mourning Dove," 157-158, 160, 173
      "On a Side Track," 158
      "Pictures of the Far West," 155-157, 169-171
      A Victorian Gentlewoman in the Far West, 158-163
      "The Water-Carrier of the Mexican Camp," 155, 168
Fox, William Sherwood, 97
Frazer, James, 104-105n11
Freud, Sigmund, 105n13
frontiersman, 21-24, 26, 27
Frost, Robert, 192
Frye, Northrop, 4, 5, 76, 80, 87, 141, 148n7
Fulton, Maurice G., 48n17
Gallegly, Joseph, 135n6
Garland, Hamlin, 60, 146
Garrett, Pat, and Ash Upson, *The Authentic Life of Billy, the Kid*, 38, 41
Gay, Peter, 31, 46
Gibson, William M., 146
Gilder, Helena (de Kay), 152, 155
Gilder, Richard, 155, 164, 165n14

Ginsberg, Allen, 25
—"Howl," 27
Goldman, William, *Butch Cassidy and the Sundance Kid*, 78
Grant, Damian, 48*n*15
Great Plains, 4, 51-61
Grey, Zane, 75
—*Riders of the Purple Sage*, 69
Gutherie, A. B., Jr., 23
—*The Big Sky*, 18, 78
—*These Thousand Hills*, 78, 79, 86
—*The Way West*, 78
Haggard, H. Rider, 81
Hague, James, 160
Hall, Douglas Kent, *On The Way To The Sky*, 71
Hallock, Nathaniel, 152
Hallock, Mary, 152, 157. See also Foote, Mary (Hallock)
Hamilton, Edith, 124*n*2
Hamlin, William Lee, 47*n*8
Hanna, Marcus A., 22
Harris, Mark, 67
Hart, John E., 135*n*4
Harte, Bret, 26
—"The Outcasts of Poker Flat," 139-140, 142, 146
Hawthorne, Nathaniel, 67
—*The Scarlet Letter*, 26, 153
Heidegger, Martin, 108-109, 179, 195*n*7
Hemingway, Ernest, 140
—"Big Two-Hearted River," 16
Henry, O., "The Reformation of Calliope," 131-134
Henry, Will, 35
Hernardi, Paul, 46*n*2
High Noon, 140, 143
Homer, 5
—*The Iliad*, 40
Hoover, J. Edgar, 14
Horgan, Paul, 31, 32, 40
Hough, Emerson, *North of 36*, 33
Hudson River School, 152
Hunt, Frazier, *The Tragic Days of Billy the Kid*, 41
Hutton, James, 111, 112
Idaho, 156, 157, 158, 161, 162
Indians, 6, 18, 21-24, 75, 83, 86, 116, 151, 208, 209, 213, 218, 219

Irving, Washington, 21
Ise, John, *Sod and Stubble*, 52
James, Henry, 35, 93, 103, 183, 210
   —*The American*, 32
   —*The American Scene*, 85
James, Jessie, 13, 114
Jeffers, Robinson, 26, 27
Jenning, Wylon, 77
Jewett, Sarah Orne, 93
Johnson, Diane, 67
Johnson, Lyndon, 11
Joyce, James, 68
Jung, C. G., 4, 17, 79, 101, 102
Kadar, Jan, 148n8
Kansas, 52, 54
Keats, John, 183-184
Kelcher, William, 47n8
Kerouac, Jack, 25
   —*The Dharma Bums*, 27
Kesey, Ken, *One Flew Over the Cuckoo's Nest*, 75, 81, 82-84, 85
   —*Sometimes a Great Notion*, 27
Kimball, J. Golden, 67
King, Clarence, 160
Laing, R. D., 82
Lambert, Neal, 68
L'Amour, Louis, 75
Larkin, Philip, 140
Lawrence, D. H., 6, 66
Laxness, Halldor, 67
Leadville, Colorado, 155, 160
The Left-Handed Gun (Arthur Penn, director), 47n8
Levine, George, 31, 32
Lewis, Sinclair, 17
Linton, W. J., 152
Little Big Horn, 31
London, Jack, 26, 27
Longfellow, Henry Wadsworth, 153, 165n5
Lucretius, 119
Lyell, Sir Charles, 111-112
Lynn, Loretta, 77
Lynsky, Winifred, 135n4
McClure, Michael, 25

Maclean, Hugh N., 147*n*6
McMurtry, Larry, 75, 88*n*6, 89*n*11
   —*Leaving Cheyenne*, 78
The Magnificent Seven, 140
Manfred, Frederick, *King of Spades*, 5
   —*Lord Grizzly*, 16, 32
   —*The Manly-Hearted Woman*, 5
   —*Riders of Judgment*, 18
Marovitz, Sanford E., 34
Markham, Edwin, 26
Martin, Jay, 207
Massey, Irving, 19*n*2
Melville, Herman, 25, 67
   —*Moby-Dick*, 25-26
   —*White Jacket*, 44
"A Message to Garcia," 14
Metz, Gary, 196*n*17
Meuller, Amelia, *There Have to Be Six*, 52, 58
Mexicans, 131, 141, 142, 155
Mexico, 38, 39, 155, 162
Midwest, 93, 103
Miller, James E., Jr., 104
Miller, Joaquin, 26
Milton, John R., 104*n*6
Montana, 54, 208
More, Sir Thomas, *Utopia*, 65
Morgan, Dale, *Jedediah Smith*, 32
Mormons, 4, 66-71
Morris, Wright, 5, 177-195
   Works:
      Ceremony in Lone Tree, 178, 187, 189
      ["Cityscape"], 191-192, 201
      "Cracked Earth," frontispiece, 190-191
      "Faulkner Country, near Oxford, Mississippi," 191, 200
      The Field of Vision, 178, 180-182, 187
      God's Country and My People, frontispiece, 177, 185, 187-191, 193
      The Home Place, 177, 184-185, 196*n*9
      "The Inhabitants," 177
      The Inhabitants, 177, 184, 186, 188
      Love Among the Cannibals, 192
      "Made in U. S. A.," 179
      The Man Who Was There, 193

Morris, Wright (Works continued)
    ["Metaphysical Landscape"], 189-190, 199
    "Rocker, Home Place," 187-189, 198
    Structures and Artifacts, 190-192, 196n27
    The Territory Ahead, 4, 6-7, 182-183, 185
    "Tombstone, Arizona, Ruined Storefronts," 193-194, 203
    "Western Kansas, Stores with False Fronts," 192-193, 202
    The Works of Love, 193
    The World in the Attic, 179-180, 193
mythology, classical, 4, 5, 14, 94-98, 101, 107, 113, 114, 119, 129-135
mythology, Indian, 4, 11, 14, 17, 24, 94-96
mythology, Judeo-Christian, 14, 25, 28, 107, 113
mythology, western. *See* western myths
Nebraska, 52, 54, 144, 177, 180, 190
Neider, Charles, *The Authentic Death of Henry Jones*, 31, 34, 35-46
Neihardt, John, *The Mountain Men*, 32
Neumann, Erich, 19n2
New Almaden, California, 155, 159
Norris, Frank, *The Octopus*, 26
Oklahoma, 52
Olson, Robert G., 124n7
One-Eyed Jacks (Marlon Brando, director), 47n8
Oppenheimer, J. Robert, 22
Oregon, 81
organicism (Romantic), 179, 183-185
Orpen, Adela, *Memories of the Old Emigrant Days in Kansas 1862-1865*, 54
Orwell, George, *1984*, 84
Ovid, *Metamorphoses*, 114-115
pantheism, 23-25, 28
Parkman, Francis, 21
Picasso, Pablo, 6
Pike, Zebulon, 118
pioneer, 11, 26, 51-61, 181
primitivism, 2, 21-24, 28
Puritanism, Puritans, 22, 180
Putnam, Jackson K., 47n5
Quantrill, William C., 114
Quarles, Francis, 177
realism, realistic, 1-7, 33, 35, 36, 39, 40, 44, 45, 46, 48n15, 65, 69, 93,
    101, 103, 107, 111, 130, 131, 141, 147, 154, 155, 159, 164, 207, 218
Rocky Mountains, 23, 32, 107, 108
Reaver, J. Russell, 105n12

Rexroth, Kenneth, "The Phoenix and the Tortoise," 27
Rhodes, Eugene Manlove, 33
Richards, Robert, 114
Richardson, A. D., 154
Richter, Conrad, *The Sea of Grass*, 14, 18
Rimmer, William, 152
Robbins, Tom, *Even Cowgirls Get the Blues*, 77
Rockefeller, John D., Sr., 22
Rockwell, Norman, 183
Rölvaag, O. E., *Giants in the Earth*, 2, 51, 53, 55-56, 58, 60, 77-78
romance, 65, 77, 80-81, 84, 86-87, 139-147
Sandoz, Mari, *Miss Morissa*, 53-54
  —*Old Jules*, 51, 58-59
Sanford, Mollie Dorsey, *Mollie*, 52
San Francisco, California, 155
Saroyan, William, 26
Scarborough, Dorothy, *The Wind*, 55, 56-57, 60
Schaefer, Jack, *Monte Walsh*, 79, 86
  —*Shane*, 75, 78, 140
Schwenk, Theodore, *Sensitive Chaos*, 190
Scowcroft, Richard, 67
Sellers, R. W., 2
Sergeant, Elizabeth Shepley, 94
Shakespeare, William, 94
  —*Troilus and Cressida*, 130
Skaggs, Calvin, 148n8
Slotkin, Richard, 94, 151, 154, 159
Smith, Henry Nash, 1, 24
Smith, Jedediah, 1, 2
Smith, W. Eugene, 192
Snyder, Gary, 27
Sonnichsen, C. L., 46n4
Sophocles, 45
Sorensen, Virginia, 67, 69-71
  —*The Evening and the Morning*, 70-71
  —*A Little Lower Than the Angels*, 70
  —*On This Star*, 70
Spicer, Jack, 47n8
Stallman, Robert W., 135n2, 148n9
Steckmesser, Kent, 44
Stegner, Wallace, 27, 67
  —*Angle of Repose*, 32, 77-78, 163-164

Steinbeck, John, 26, 27
   —*East of Eden*, 79
Sterling, George, 27
Stieglitz, Alfred, 185, 192
Straight, Michael, *A Very Small Remnant*, 18
"Sweet Betsy of Pike," 52
Taft, Robert M., 156
The Tall Man, 47n8
Tatum, Stephen, 47n8
Taylor, Joshua C., 154
Texas, 52, 55, 131, 134
Thomas, Edith M., 158
Thoreau, Henry David, 45, 102, 184
   —*Walden*, 16
Thorp, Jack, and Neil Clark, *Pardner of the Wind*, 41, 43
Trachtenberg, Alan, 178
Tristan, 78
Trump, Fred, *Uphill in the Sun*, 59
Turner, Frederick Jackson, 21, 22, 23, 24, 162
Twain, Mark, 21, 26, 140
Upson, Ash. *See* Garrett, Pat
Utah, 4, 66, 67, 71
Vidal, Gore, 47n8
Vorpahl, Ben Merchant, 136n8
Walker, Don D., 46n4, 47n5
Walker, Jerry Jeff, 77
Waters, Frank, *People of the Valley*, 16
Wayne, John, 12, 15, 19
Webb, Walter Prescott, 33, 50, 51
Weinig, Sister Mary Anthony, 135n4
Welch, James, *Winter in the Blood*, 7, 208-219
Westbrook, Max, 40, 47n5, 48n15, 101
western history and historians, 2, 21-24, 31-34, 40, 46, 51, 68, 71, 110, 114, 178
western myth(s), 1-7, 11, 15, 18, 22, 26, 28, 65, 76, 77, 80, 87, 94, 107, 113-115, 129-135, 151, 154-155, 159, 162, 164, 179-183, 195, 207-208, 218-219
Western(s), 5, 33, 65, 75-88, 139-147, 214
Weston, Edward, 186
Wheelwright, Philip, 104n5
Whipple, Maurine, 67
White, Stewart Edward, *These Folded Hills*, 78

Whitman, Walt, 26, 102, 108
Williams, Wirt, 35
Wilson, Edmund, 25
Winthrop, John, 25
Wister, Owen, 75
 —*The Virginian*, 78, 84, 85, 86, 87
Wolford, Chester L., 135*n*4
women in western literature, 4, 51-61, 66, 69-71, 75-88
Wylder, D. E., 89*n*12
Wynette, Tammy, 77
Wyoming, 67, 71
Young, Brigham, 70
Younger, Cole, 114